THE DEEPEST WOUND

THE DEEPEST WOUND

HOW A JOURNEY TO EL SALVADOR LED TO HEALING FROM MOTHER-DAUGHTER INCEST

Forward by Dr. James Newton Poling, author of
The Abuse of Power and Deliver Us From Evil

Therapist Afterward

Linda C. Crockett

Writer's Showcase
San Jose New York Lincoln Shanghai

The Deepest Wound
How a Journey to El Salvador Led to Healing from Mother-Daughter Incest

Writer's Showcase
an imprint of iUniverse, Inc.

For information address:
iUniverse, Inc.
5220 S 16th, Ste. 200
Lincoln, NE 68512
www.iuniverse.com

This is a true story. The names of some of the individuals have been changed to protect their identity.

ISBN: 0-595-19922-4

Printed in the United States of America

Dedication

"The Deepest Wound" is dedicated to the children who have endured atrocities usually ascribed to torture chambers within their own homes, inflicted by those who claim to love them.

Those of us who survived are surrounded by the spirits of those who did not, strengthening and encouraging us to speak the truth.

For the victims of child abuse who have been silenced by death, fear, denial or shame....I speak.

Epigraph

"But if anyone causes the downfall of one of these little ones who believe in me, it would be better for him to have a millstone hung round his neck and be drowned in the depths of the sea."

JESUS

Matthew 18: 6

Contents

Foreword

I first met Linda Crockett in May, 1996. A mutual friend introduced us, someone who knew our interests in Central America and domestic violence were similar and we might be able to support and learn from one another. Since that initial meeting, we have corresponded weekly or more often, visited in one another's homes, and worked together planning a conference on accompanying survivors of family abuse. Our own relationship has been one of accompaniment as Linda has supported me through levels of study and understanding about issues of oppression in different forms, and I have accompanied her through a remarkable journey of healing, writing, and thriving.

We have both learned from this journey together. First, we have learned about the resilience of the human spirit in situations of extreme evil. Second, we have learned about the depths of extreme evil perpetuated by humans on other human beings.

In this narrative, Linda tells us about the resilient courage of the human spirit. We read the story of a girl-child who was accompanied by angels when her mother, father, extended family, and society betrayed her. We read the story of resistance and struggle of the poor in El Salvador against an army trained and equipped by the United States government. We read the story of an adult survivor of child abuse who resisted the sexism of her culture and refused to accept silence about the abuse of children and its consequences. And we read the story of a community of advocates who accompanied those who were threatened by violence.

Linda discovered something new in her experience about human courage and healing when she visited El Salvador during a time of civil war. She learned to know and love persons who resisted the violence imposed on them by their own government, persons who knew how to heal those who were tortured for the purposes of terrorizing the population, and persons who believed that God's love accompanied them when they could see no end to their suffering. This vision of the accompanying God became a source of hope and strength for Linda's own healing journey.

Through their care, Linda Crockett remembered her own unjust suffering as a child, and recovered the memories of the lady in white and Peter, angels who accompanied her when no human beings were there for her. In her healing journey she found friends who could support her as she gained the strength to exorcise the demons from her past and build a new life. In the midst of these struggles, Linda found her own inner spiritual resilience that lifted her depression, parted her dissociation, and gave her new hope for herself and others.

For those of us who have accompanied Linda in her journey, this experience has given us new faith in the resilient love of God who does not stop loving and healing us regardless of the human evil we encounter and the injuries it inflicts on us. Jim, her therapist, revised his theories and practices of pastoral counseling in order to accommodate Linda's search for healing. Gary, her friend from journeys to Central America, brought comforting touch that was crucial to Linda's healing. David, her massage therapist, learned to follow the clues from Linda's body rather than rely on his own judgment from his professional training. I, her professor-friend, learned how to trust Linda's inner spirit rather than my own training as a pastor, teacher, and scholar. Together we created a new community of persons dedicated to justice, healing, and witness.

In this narrative, Linda Crockett raises uncomfortable questions about evil in human life. We need courage to hear what she has to say, and to examine our own biases that prevent us from seeing the truth.

Some mothers (and parents) are cruel to their children, seeking to destroy their bodies and spirits. Some governments murder their own citizens for political and economic gain. Some cultures silence adults who have suffered so those in denial will not have to be uncomfortable. Personal and social evil is hard to witness, believe, and accept.

Evil in families is difficult for most people to understand. How can parents and other relatives, who are pledged to love and protect one another, become the agents of violence? The global feminist movement has brought the issue of family violence to the attention of nearly every society in the world, and now it is more difficult to ignore the cries of victims and survivors. However, the naiveté of so many continues to deny the abuse of children by their own mothers. Linda's story helps to make plain how mothers can become enemies of their children, deliberately plotting to destroy their bodies and spirits instead of facing their own demons and seeking healing. Children are the most vulnerable members of every society, and yet they are often the least protected from abuse, war, and poverty. Linda calls for a concerted effort from everyone to listen to the cries of children and provide protection.

Historians and theologians have carefully studied evil between governments in the forms of war and oppression. International law has made progress on understanding issues of human rights within countries, for example, the possibility of genocidal activities like the Holocaust in Germany, slavery in the United States, and sex industries in several countries. However, there continues to be much denial about the fact that citizens are often the most threatened by their own elected governments. We use euphemisms such as "civil war," "social unrest," and "ethnic conflict" to describe kidnapping, torture, murder, bombing, and massacres by militarized governments against their own people. El Salvador in the 1980's and 1990's was such a country, and evil policies of the government were rationalized and funded by the United States. Linda's narrative exposes the corruption of U.S. policies in El Salvador and tells us about the reality for real people on the ground.

We have heard the voices of survivors of child abuse at a national level with results such as new laws, policies, and agencies aimed at prevention of domestic violence, sexual assault, and child abuse. However, changing laws does not change reality. We have witnessed a backlash of political movements designed to silence survivors in their charges against parents, family members, and sexually assaultive men. Groups such as the False Memory Syndrome Foundation, father's rights groups, and others deny the epidemic of violence against children and women and assert the rights of parents and men who have had traditional authority. Linda's narrative exposes the evil of these conspiracies and calls on all of us to hear the cries of survivors who have lived to tell their stories and seek justice.

This is not an easy book to read because it challenges many of the foundational ideas on which our lives are based—that our families, our churches, our schools, and our nation are good, and that these traditional authorities work for the benefit of all. If we let go of these ideas, where will we place our trust? At a deeper level, Linda's narrative invites us to trust in God and human nature in a more profound way than usual. In the midst of overwhelming evil and destruction of bodies and spirits, there are persons who never give up the search for love, community, and hope. The resilient persons who hold on to these values reveal the reality of a God who never gives up on the world. We can believe in the God of love and power when we see the resilience of the human spirit in extreme circumstances. Even when human evil overwhelms us in families, in nations, in terror, in social stigmas that marginalize survivors—even in these circumstances, we can rely on the love and power of God to sustain us and heal us from our wounds. We may not survive the evil that comes into our lives, but God is not overwhelmed. The human spirit will rebound with love and hope in the future, and the victims will not be forgotten in the mind of God. Our families, our churches, and our countries may betray us, but God will never betray us. Love will return again to bring humans together in loving community.

As Linda has said to me in many different ways over the years, "The accompanying God was so strong in El Salvador. It was not just that the people felt God's love, they firmly believed God walked with them. This gave them the hope and courage to continue. It has been the same for me. A God who does not love from afar but who walks by your side. A God who weeps at your suffering, who works hand-in-hand with you for justice, and who does not close God's eyes when you are raped but holds fast so you are not alone. A God who sometimes dances with you in the quiet spaces when the bombs stop falling (or the memories of rape and abuse stop assaulting your consciousness)."

Praise be to God and thanks be to survivors like Linda who reveal God's love for all.

James Newton Poling, Ph.D.
July, 2001

Dr. Poling is an ordained minister in the Presbyterian Church (USA), a pastoral psychotherapist, and Professor of Pastoral Theology, Care and Counseling at Garrett-Evangelical Theological Seminary, Evanston, Illinois. He is the author of many articles and books including *The Abuse of Power: A Theological Problem* (Abingdon Press, 1991) and *Deliver Us From Evil: Resisting Racial and Gender Oppression* (Augsburg Fortress, 1996)

Preface

I am a survivor of severe childhood sexual abuse. I am also a person who has walked with the Salvadoran poor in conflictive zones under the control of armed forces once given the dubious distinction by Amnesty International as one of the world's top violators of human rights. I am well qualified to write about war, torture and rape.

I was forced to live in a secret war zone in a middle-class family in an all-American rural community when I was a child. I voluntarily entered open war zones in El Salvador when I was an adult. The first nearly shattered me. The second was the key to remembering and healing.

Although much has been published on the topic of incest as society has slowly accepted the reality that many children are abused by trusted family members, the issue of mothers as perpetrators remains one topic that is seldom discussed. Culturally, we have come to accept that fathers can abuse their children. But we remain largely in denial of the reality of sexual abuse by mothers. *The Deepest Wound* is an attempt to bridge the silence and denial.

Much of the abuse that I suffered was sadistic. My experiences were unlike those of many other incest survivors in that my perpetrator used ritualized structures that included the interspersing of pain with pleasure in a methodical and deliberate fashion that often carried a connotation of being scripted. Treatment for survivors of political torture is more closely tailored to what I needed to heal than most methods that are used with incest survivors.

From the Salvadoran poor, I learned the importance of safe touch and holding for survivors of torture. This was a real challenge to Jim, my psychotherapist, who approached therapy with the traditional notion that touch should be used sparingly—if at all—within a therapeutic context. This notion became a stumbling block over which our relationship almost shattered.

Because of the lessons imprinted in my soul from my experiences in El Salvador and Jim's willingness to learn from and accompany me, we were able to gradually incorporate safe touch into the healing process. Yet it was always clear that Jim set the boundaries. His was the power of the adult to my child.

Various feminist publications have been critical of the "power over" nature of traditional therapeutic relationships, and development of dependency is often negatively viewed. I do not wish to argue that survivors be content with rigid and hierarchical therapies that do not empower them. Jim's greatest delight was in watching the frightened and traumatized child who first came to him emerge as a strong and competent woman who finally understood her own history and was determined to live well in spite of it.

The course of therapy illustrated in *The Deepest Wound* reflects a healing path that allowed me to develop the kind of fierce dependency a child has for a parent with Jim. It allowed me to acknowledge that he had greater power than I. Paradoxically, it was my ability to move through dependency that created the capacity for autonomy to develop and eventually allowed me to claim my own power.

Accompaniment moves beyond traditional notions of therapy with survivors.

During the most tumultuous years of healing, most of my supportive relationships with others dissolved. Friends who accompanied the poor in Central American war zones could not walk with me as I entered the war zones that exploded within me as I plumbed the depth of remembering childhood horrors. Much popular recovery literature gives the impression that survivors will find the support and nurture they need by reaching out to friends. This is a naive approach, especially for survivors of severe abuse, because it ignores the impact of past abuse on current relationships and sets survivors and supporters up for painful failure.

By detailing the loss of close relationships as I moved deeper into my pain, readers learn of some of the dynamics that occur when the most gentle friend begins to wear the face of her perpetrator to a survivor.

Accompaniment of a survivor of childhood sexual abuse is a challenging journey for all who embark upon it. It leads us into the suffering of the one we accompany. Those who walk with survivors are sometimes forced to confront some of their own deepest wounds. The brave and compassionate souls who persevere often find that the survivor is not the only one healing through the relationship.

The Deepest Wound was written as an essential part of my own healing. Yet I was keenly aware during the writing process that its destiny was not to remain within the private realm of my journals. It is a story that binds the wounds of the tortured in faraway prisons with the wounds of those who have suffered the largely invisible holocaust of sadistic childhood abuse in their own homes. It is a tribute to the human spirit that refuses to be crushed and an invitation to the reader to enter the world of the survivor.

Linda Crockett
May, 2001

Acknowledgments

I am eternally grateful for the accompaniment of Jim, my therapist, who created a safe place for the traumatized child within me to heal. Without his courage, patience, wisdom and love, I would not have survived the remembering and this book would never have been written. Jim kept hope alive for me when I could not. When we worked together, it felt as though we were on sacred ground. Despite his gender, he rose to the challenge and became the only real mother I have ever known.

It was a blessing and gift to include another "Jim" among those who accompanied me in the mid-point of my healing. I was writing this book as part of my own process of recovering from incest when I met Jim Poling. I was drawn to this pastor and theologian who expressed and lived a solidarity with survivors one rarely finds among professionals in the field. He read each raw chapter as it emerged, providing me with invaluable emotional support while affirming my writing skills and encouraging me to seek publication when I was ready.

Part of my healing process has been to chose new "family" that I can trust to sustain, guide, nurture and challenge me as I break free of the chains of the past and reclaim my place in the world. Gary Cozette is my chosen brother. He taught me the importance of safe touch, and affirmed the Child's right to be held. In his arms, I found complete safety, and began to let go of the shame I harbored over what my abusers had done to me. Gary's courage in living openly as a gay person in a committed relationship inspired me to tell my story publicly.

Silence protects no one except those who exploit and violate the vulnerable.

David Haines faithfully negotiated the hidden mine fields of trauma stored intact within my body with gentle massage and Trager movement. David's persistence and willingness to modify his therapeutic approach to meet my needs gradually allowed me to reclaim the body which I had abandoned as a child. That today I live within my own flesh and not apart from it is in large measure due to my experiences in bodywork with David.

Sam Rice has become not only a friend who knows how to accompany but one of my guardian angels, guiding me on some difficult paths at critical times.

The skillful editing of Karen Carnabucci transformed the original book which emerged from the depths of my pain into a much stronger narrative with multiple layers of detail to engage readers. Her background as a former journalist and her years of experience as a therapist greatly aided editorial work on the project.

Karen Lovelace contributed many hours of her time to the tasks of reading and providing critical feedback. Special thanks to Arlene Barnhart for her amazing proofreading skills, as well as her belief in me as a writer and her encouragement to publish.

And finally, I am grateful to my husband and two sons, who allowed me to create the kind of safe and protective family I longed for as a child. The cycle of abuse which spans families across generations has been broken with us.

Prologue

A Child Survives

The small child curled up in the shelter of the huge rock that was her refuge. She instinctively knew that she needed a safe place to heal her wounds when her body had been battered and violated.

The little girl, who quietly watched many things in her life, noticed that other children who were hurt or frightened would be able to run to their mothers and fathers with their bruises and tears. She saw those other parents bringing mending and comfort to their children. But she could not find comfort in her own home. For her, safely was measured in the distance from the hands and face of an abusive parent.

Such was the plight of the little girl. She pressed her back into the coolness of the rock and stared without seeing at the sunlit field and grove of trees through which she had run. She had crept to this place from her house after her mother's rage had been spent upon her small body.

She had come home from school earlier that afternoon, dragging her feet as she approached the door of her house. She knew as soon as she saw her mother's face that today would be one of the days when her mother would hang the green blanket across the window that faced the road.

The child's body ached from the beating as she slowly left the place inside her mind where she fled on the days her mother's face changed. She wrapped her arms around herself and rocked. The place between her legs hurt so much and yet she did not dare touch herself there. The child had no name for this place of pain; she only knew that it was a bad and dirty place. It was the reason that she was punished so much. She knew that when her mother's fingers touched her down there, the bad feeling came into her body and she sometimes peed on her mother's hands. For this, she was severely punished.

Later, her mother would put lotion on the places that hurt and make gentle, soothing sounds. By then, the connection between the wounds and the one who inflicted the pain would be mostly severed.

The child made small whimpering sounds. There was a white roaring sound in her head, and her stomach hurt. With the instinct of a wounded animal, she allowed the memory of what had taken place in her house to be swept away into a corner of her mind where it could not hurt her any more.

The little girl had become adept at the art of self-numbing. She even knew how to leave her body and flee into an imaginary world where no one hurt her, where she was loved.

A familiar face suddenly appeared just outside the shelter of her small cave. It was her friend Peter, and he smiled at her.

"Hi!" he said, holding out his hand. "Do you want to play with me?"

The little girl looked out of the darkness at the boy framed in the golden afternoon sunlight. "I hurt," she said gravely in a small voice.

"I know." Peter looked sad, and his hand brushed her cheek. "But you can't stay under this rock all day. Come and play with me!"

The little girl nodded and stiffly climbed out from the cool hollow of the boulders. Her legs were shaky, and her body didn't seem to work right. Her eyes were dull, and the white noise was still in her ears, muffling even the songs of the birds.

Peter put his arm around her. "Would you like to talk to the trees?" he asked.

She nodded. Peter was her only friend, and he seemed to carry magic with him. When she was with him, she forgot about her mother. She took his hand, and they walked slowly to the shady grove just beyond the rocks.

The trees rustled in welcome as the children approached. Peter held up his hand, and a maple tree bent down its leafy arms and made a cradle. The child climbed into the tree, then felt herself rocked gently by its branches.

Peter perched on a branch just above her and grinned. He carved a stick while the tree continued to rock her. Branches swayed in the breeze, and she fell asleep listening to the music they made.

As she rested in her green cradle, the hurt and pain receded into a far corner of her mind. Peter helped her to carefully store away the memory of what had occurred earlier that afternoon. He talked to her as she slept, and her mind began to weave bandages to cover the wounds.

He was magic, and he always knew what she needed.

He stayed with her as she slept. When she woke up, she saw his face and felt safe. A smile tugged the corners of her mouth.

"It's time to go back," he told her softly.

A nameless fear gripped her, and she clutched her stomach. The smile receded, and her face grew solemn.

The tree whispered, "Don't be afraid. We'll be here whenever you need us." Slowly, the leafy arms bent and set her gently on the ground.

Peter walked with her through the dusk back to her house. As they stood outside the door, she felt the familiar numbness creeping through her body. She held tightly to Peter's hand. She knew without asking that he could not enter the darkness of the house. She did not understand why.

Peter squeezed her hand.

"I'll come back," he promised. And as suddenly as he had appeared, he was gone.

A shudder ran through the little girl's body. She waited for the rest of the numbness to come. When it did, she opened the door to her house and went inside.

Chapter 1

The Heart of War

"At the heart of war is rape."

I was visiting El Salvador in 1989 at the height of the country's brutal civil war that had already claimed the lives of more than 65,000 people when I first heard those words. My friend Bill was assuring me that I was not going crazy as I shared my fears about my ability to work as a volunteer delegate.

Bill and I sat at the kitchen table in a Lutheran church guest house in the capital city of San Salvador where we were staying during this particular trip. It was quiet in the sunny kitchen. The rest of the delegation was occupied in a meeting. Felicita, the Salvadoran woman who cooked, cleaned and nurtured delegations in her role as guest house coordinator, was taking a nap.

Bill was a North American pastor living in El Salvador. He knew a great deal about trauma and its aftereffects on survivors. His work with the Salvadoran poor brought him into daily contact with survivors of rape, torture and other atrocities. The military pursued a strategy of terror against poor communities involved in advocating for economic reform in a country where the vast majority of citizens lacked basic housing, food and medical care. These communities were considered by the government to be in collusion with the armed resistance movement, which they viewed as inspired by communists and subversives.

When his work schedule permitted, Bill led church delegations from the United States that came to work with the poor in El Salvador in their struggle for justice. Sensitive and gentle, his slight frame was often bent under the weight of his guitar and a backpack filled with books. He was a walking encyclopedia of knowledge about El Salvador, and I felt fortunate he had agreed to provide translation and pastoral leadership for our group of volunteers. Delegates under his care learned about the history, politics and culture of this tiny Central American country nestled between the Pacific Ocean and the perimeters of Guatemala, Honduras and Nicaragua.

Most delegates had never been exposed to war or Third World poverty. Despite the delegates' intense educational and emotional preparation process, nothing could prepare most middle-class people from the United States for the horror of war or the extreme poverty they would encounter during a delegation visit. Bill's music at times comforted and sustained overwhelmed volunteers as well as peasant communities struggling to survive in war zones.

By my third year of volunteer work with short-term delegations, I had come to admire and trust this pastor who risked his life for poor peasants the world largely ignored. I had decided to risk sharing my fear that perhaps I was not capable of doing this work any longer. I did not want to pose a danger for other delegates or the refugees who trusted us to be alert and responsive to the constant dangers faced in their communities.

As Bill listened intently, I told him that I had been experiencing nightmares, headaches and insomnia. I was having trouble concentrating. The memory fragments of rape and childhood sexual abuse that had begun to intrude after my first trip to Central America two years before were becoming progressively more vivid. Thoughts about my mother's suicide in 1975, six weeks after my twentieth birthday, came into my mind with increasing frequency. Shortly before she swallowed a deadly dose of prescription medication, my mother scribbled her final words, "Linda, I can't go on hurting you…" on a school excuse card. My sixteen-year-old sister came home from school to find the yellow card, weighted by stones, in the front yard and my mother's body on the kitchen floor.

Frustrated and frightened, I could not understand why thoughts about being hurt by my mother were drifting through cracks in a closet I had considered irrevocably sealed after fourteen years. Nor could I see any connection between my mother and my current task of listening to the stories of survivors of atrocities in El Salvador.

I saw that Bill's face reflected the same compassion that I observed when we talked to Salvadoran women who had been raped by soldiers. I described how I was molested when I was five by a teen-age cousin and his friends and raped by a family acquaintance when I was twelve. At fifteen, I was gang raped.

I had always remembered these incidents but had never attached any emotional meaning to them. I was outraged about abuse and human rights violations when they happened to other people. But I considered myself to be in a different category, outside the pale of humanity. What happened to me did not matter. I never felt that my body was really part of me. I did not share the concern of other female delegates about the possibility of capture and rape by the shadowy para-military forces commonly known as "death squads." I figured one more rape would not make any difference to me.

As I talked with Bill, I felt a familiar numbness slowly creeping up from my toes. When it reached my head, I was in that blessed, wonderful state where I was quite sure even a knife through my gut would not cause me pain. I listened from what seemed like miles away as Bill assured me I was not going crazy and explained that my entry into the strife of El Salvador had triggered memories and emotions from my own traumatic past.

I did not know it then, but this would be the last delegation Bill would lead in El Salvador. A few weeks later, the armed resistance would launch a major offensive against the capital city. In retaliation, the army would bomb the slum neighborhoods and murder community leaders suspected to support the resistance. One of these communities was Bill's home. He and a fellow pastor would hide for two days under a table in their house while bombs destroyed most of the surrounding area. They would manage to survive the bombardment and flee the country for their lives. Marked by the military as subversive, Bill could not go back to El Salvador. When I returned in subsequent years, I always missed him.

✳   ✳   ✳

I was thirty-two years old when I first entered the war zones of Central America in 1987. At the time, I was chairperson of the evangelism committee at my church in Pennsylvania. The pastor routinely stuffed my mailbox with appeals for help from around the world so that my committee could review them. However, he knew that the rural congregation, parochial and conservative, seldom agreed to respond to needs outside of their own families and community.

One day I opened a letter from Salvadoran Lutheran Bishop Medardo Gomez, asking for accompaniment of his people in the midst of a war in which thousands of innocent civilians had already been killed. He wrote that they were walking the way of the cross and that they did not want to walk alone. They wanted to be accompanied and supported in their journey and suffering. The bishop appealed to Christians to emulate Simon of Cyrene, who helped Jesus carry the cross as he walked to his execution at the "place of the skulls" on Golgotha. The letter had been sent to churches in various parts of the United States.

I could not have found El Salvador on a map. But that letter found its way into my heart. Although I did not recognize her then, the child within me who had never been protected understood the urgency of the cry of the Salvadoran poor. I felt compelled to respond without comprehending why. Understanding would come only after I plumbed the depths of my own pain, remembering abuse I had forgotten in order to survive.

I immersed myself in learning about in El Salvador. I began to teach myself Spanish, using books and cassette tapes. I read reports from human rights organizations describing the routine use of torture by the armed forces to terrorize poor communities. I was horrified to read of children surviving the destruction of their homes only to die from mal-nutrition, common colds and diarrhea for lack of food, shelter and medicine.

For generations, a wealthy minority exploited the economy for their own benefit. Most people lived in abject poverty. A largely Catholic country, peasants accepted the traditional church teaching that their suffering was to be borne without complaint and their reward would be in heaven. By the 1960s, however, a number of priests and nuns working in poor communities began to question the wisdom of insisting on submission to the injustice inherent in the economic and social systems of the country. The proclamation during Vatican II in 1962, in which the Catholic Church asserted that God had a "preferential option for the poor," opened the door for increased attention to social justice issues.

Encouraged by priests and nuns, base Christian communities formed as peasants gathered to study the Bible and view their reality through the lens of the Gospel. They began to believe that God was on the side of those who suffered injustice at the hands of the powerful. This belief was a radical departure from long-held tradition that the power held by governments and other authorities was given by God, not to be rebelled against. A growing conviction that it was not the will of God that their children die from poor nutrition in a country so rich in resources led the poor to organize themselves to demand economic justice.

The Salvadoran military was supported largely by the wealthy oligarchy, which controlled the majority of land and resources. The peaceful protests and political organizing by the poor were met with harsh military repression by the 1970s. Death squads captured community leaders; their mutilated bodies were later dumped in the streets of their neighborhoods as a warning to others to remain silent. Although the death squads operated in heavily militarized areas, using army jeeps and weapons, the government disclaimed any involvement with them. Peasants and college students in various parts of the country began to take up arms to defend their communities and stop the repression. A national coalition of these scattered groups formed in 1980 as The Farabundo Marti Liberation Front, popularly known as the "FMLN." Men and women took to the mountains on horses to train in clandestine camps with homemade weapons and rusty guns. Eventually, money and support from other parts of the world, including the Eastern bloc, would help to support their struggle for justice. Civil war began.

By the early 1980s, the United States had aligned itself with the Salvadoran government. In the context of the Cold War, the struggles of the poor in Central America were viewed as communist-inspired. Funds flowed to the military, despite the rape and murder of four U.S. church women by the National Guard on December 2, 1980 as they traveled the road from the airport to the capital city one night in a church van. The sisters, like the Catholic archbishop who was murdered earlier that year, were portrayed as supporters of the FMLN by Salvadoran politicians. High-level U.S. officials suggested that the women had run a roadblock on the road that night, provoking the guardsmen to drastic action.

Oscar Romero was an extremely conservative cleric and a friend to the wealthy when he was appointed to the office of Catholic archbishop in 1977. When priests who were working with the poor in rural communities began to be harassed and murdered by paramilitary death squads, Romero began to visit the countryside to assess the situation. He was horrified by the poverty and outraged by the repression routinely levied against the poor by the government. A timid man by nature, he gradually became an outspoken advocate for the people, drawing the wrath of the oligarchy and military.

At a packed service in the cathedral in San Salvador in March 1980, he appealed directly to the young soldiers to put down their arms. Invoking the name of God, he thunderously commanded them to stop killing their brothers and sisters. He was murdered a short time later as he celebrated communion. Senior military officials were implicated in his assassination. In his death, he became a martyr that inspired the escalating struggle for economic and social justice.

Almost ten years later, an elite battalion of Salvadoran soldiers who had been trained at the now-notorious School of the Americas in Fort Benning, Georgia, would storm the gates of the University of Central America, murdering six priests, their housekeeper and her young daughter. Like archbishop Romero, the Jesuits were outspoken advocates for the poor. But unlike the killing of Romero, the four U.S. church women and tens of thousands of Salvadorans, the murder of these particular priests who were frequent visitors to the halls of the U.S. Congress had a major political impact. The incident led to peace negotiations brokered by the United Nations, and the days of military aid were clearly numbered. Protests mounted in the United States about the role of the School of the Americas when major newspapers began to report that its graduates, Panama's Manuel Noriega among them, had been responsible for some of the worst human rights abuses in Latin America.

Between the murder of Oscar Romero in 1980 and the slaughter of the six priests in 1989, stretched a trail of blood and tears, etched by the suffering of the poor. My journey into my internal war zones would begin on this trail with the Salvadorans. Inspired by their hope and courage, I would learn to struggle for my own liberation and healing. In the process, I would learn about my own history.

*   *   *

My pastor was alarmed when he realized I would not be dissuaded from involvement in El Salvador. He counseled that the congregation, founded before I was born by conservative members, was not mature enough to make a commitment to this kind of work. He seemed upset that I wanted to walk "the way of the cross" he preached about from the pulpit.

Fortunately, Marianne, a woman from my church and about fifteen others of various church affiliations in the region felt called to respond. We spent months in prayer, discussion and reflection. We invited people from Washington, D.C., and Baltimore who were leading delegations of accompaniment to speak. The premise of accompaniment was that the presence of North Americans—many of us church volunteers, ordained ministers and others—would deflect hostile actions by the military directed toward the peasants, providing them with some level of protection by our presence.

The war in El Salvador was a dirty little secret. The fact that the United States was pouring more than a half-million dollars a day into the conflict was not widely known by the taxpayers who funded it. However, in the wake of the murder of the four church women, another high-profile death or injury to a U.S. citizen could call unwanted public attention to human rights abuses in El Salvador and jeopardize the military aid. The kind of solidarity demanded by accompaniment required us to place our bodies on the line in order to protect the poor.

Politically, I was outraged that the United States, founded on principles of democracy and freedom of speech, was supporting a corrupt and violent foreign government. I felt compelled to risk my life to protect these suffering people. Despite the fact that I had two young children and a husband who was opposed to the venture out of concern for my safety, I was one of the first to say I would go. Ultimately, five of us formed what would be the first delegation of many in the interfaith grass-roots organization in central Pennsylvania that would coalesce after our initial visit.

Marianne and I asked for a service of commissioning from our congregation. This turned out to be too controversial, as it would have given official sanction to the mission. Several men opposed women going to a war zone. Others insisted we were being duped by communist propaganda. When it was clear we were going with or without their support, the leadership finally allowed a service of blessing with the understanding that this was *not* the ministry of the congregation. It was a personal calling.

*   *   *

Our delegation was due to arrive in El Salvador in October 1987—about the time that five thousand refugees promised to return to the country despite fierce opposition from the government.

The refugees had survived the military "scorched earth" operations during the early 1980s when the country's air force bombed dozens of rural communities under the pretext that they provided support and shelter to the FMLN. The military's strategy was simple: the armed resistance fighters were the fish. The people were the ocean. Drain the ocean and the fish would die. Houses and fields were burned to the ground, crops were destroyed, and livestock was slaughtered. Survivors were forced to flee with ground troops in pursuit.

Many eventually arrived at a huge and bleak United Nations camp called Mesa Grande just across the northern border in Honduras. By 1987, many of the displaced people had spent years in the camp and were longing to return home. They announced that they were going to cross the border into El Salvador in October. If the United Nations would not provide buses, they would walk. They intended to come en masse, and they planned to return to their original lands to rebuild communities destroyed by the army.

Most refugees were farmers, deeply linked to the land. When a Salvadoran man sifts rich soil through his fingers when he is planting seeds or a woman pats out a thick tortilla with corn grown and harvested with her own hands, there is spiritual meaning as well as practical action taking place. The land is holy. The corn is sacred. When people are separated from their land, their spirits wither and die. They asked for international accompaniment to return to their land.

Two days before we were scheduled to leave the United States, a powerful explosion destroyed part of the building that housed the Lutheran Church of the Resurrection in San Salvador. Bishop Gomez, who himself had been captured and tortured a year before, sent word that conditions in the country were extremely dangerous due to the pending return of the refugees. Church leaders were receiving death threats. He wanted to know if we were still willing to come. We were.

*   *   *

We did not sleep our first night in El Salvador. The congregation asked us to accompany them in an all-night prayer vigil since it was not safe for the people to gather on their own. As darkness fell on the sprawling city of more than a million people, soldiers with machine guns silently took up positions on the street and surrounded the sanctuary. The Salvadorans were fearful, but they refused to cancel the vigil.

We pulled our chairs into a circle to symbolize our equality as we prayed, talked and sang through the night. People told of family members murdered and tortured because of their work for the church. They understood the oppression and poverty in which they lived to be similar to the conditions under which Jesus ministered.

Jesus was persecuted because he fed the poor. He denounced the powerful for their abuse of the vulnerable. He healed despite prohibitions in the law. He taught the outcasts they had value in the eyes of God.

Despite the 100-degree heat, I felt chills as I heard people speak. The Gospel was alive in the hope, struggle and resistance of the poor gathered in the church that night. There was no separation between what was preached and the commitment required of those who did the work of God. For the first time, I was with people who were continuing to write the Bible as they lived it. They became my teachers. And eventually, they opened me to my own pain so I could heal.

*   *   *

One week after the prayer vigil, our delegation was huddled in the living room of the church guest house in San Salvador. The house was located near the First Infantry Brigade. Tales of torture taking place inside the Brigade were common, adding to the atmosphere of fear that permeated our gathering. Earlier that evening, the street was filled with soldiers marching out of the great iron gate of the fortress-like structure. It was unusual for them to leave at night. Their high black boots stomped in unison as they marched in silence, and it seemed as if that ominous sound lingered in every corner of the house.

Due to the possible violent reception that awaited the refugees returning from Mesa Grande, the exact time that groups would begin to cross the border back into El Salvador had remained a secret. We had spent most of the day at the Church of the Resurrection, packing emergency aid kits for the refugees. Calls of concern from all parts of the world were coming to the church where Bishop Gomez had announced at a press conference that the church would support and accompany the refugees. The government had shut down the airport, making it impossible for more internationals to enter the country. Those of us already inside had to maximize our effectiveness.

Finally, we received word that the refugees would begin crossing the border into El Salvador that night. Anxious and unable to eat much of the dinner Felicita had prepared for us, we adjourned to the living room to determine what we would do next. Our delegation leaders became embroiled in a heated argument over whether or not we should attempt to get to the Honduran border without military permission to travel. Traveling without a military safe conduct pass would be dangerous. We could not risk our usual manner of travel in a small church van with a Salvadoran driver. The van would never make it through the road-blocks. Bishop Gomez did not want us to be picked up by the military and expelled from the country. Some U.S. and European delegations had devised plans to split up in pairs and head for the border by public bus, hay wagon and other less conspicuous means of transportation.

Mike and Mary, two Lutheran pastors in our small delegation, were heatedly arguing with Margaret, a Catholic nun from Washington D.C., who had joined us in El Salvador. Margaret, who had worked in El Salvador for several years, favored heading for the Honduran border. Mary, a pastor with a strong feminist social justice perspective, had been to El Salvador once before. She was determined to protect the refugees and was leaning in this same direction. Mike, the only male delegate, was angrily predicting all manner of negative outcomes and did not want us to risk travel.

None of them bothered to ask the others in the delegation, comprised of Joyce, Marianne and me, how we felt about going. We were, after all, only lay people, with no official church position. The three of us sat quietly, listening to their arguments of the pros and cons. Not being included in such an important decision added to our sense of helplessness and vulnerability. It was as though we were children, anxiously listening to all-powerful parents arguing about what we would do. I felt myself growing small. The furniture in the room seemed curiously large. I was reverting to what I would later recognize and name as child-space.

As the argument in the room grew heated, a smatter of gunfire suddenly erupted in the street just outside our screened window. Everyone jumped, and the room was silent for a moment. The gun battle moved down the street, and the pastors returned to bickering.

Marianne, who like me had faced family opposition to her involvement in the delegation, was finally overcome by her fear. Giving in to the palpable tension in the room, she began to cry softly. The leaders were oblivious to her pain, too engrossed now in a fight about whether to take a break and pray for guidance, as Margaret suggested. Mike asserted that prayer was a typical Catholic response in the face of the need for action. A theological argument ensued that had nothing to do with our current situation.

Marianne's sobs grew louder. Joyce, a soft-spoken plump woman in her fifties, quietly reached out and put her arm around the younger Marianne, pulling her into a close embrace to comfort her.

I had no fear in El Salvador until that moment. And I never knew fear in all my subsequent visits there, including time spent in war zones where the military was bombing and strafing, to rival the deep terror that ripped through my body when I saw one woman hold another. Clutching my stomach in pain, I quickly left the room, unable to breathe, wanting to run into the street—even if guns were firing there. In the panic, my mind was flooded with one certainty: I would never show any weakness in this place because I never wanted to risk being held by a woman.

Long after the others were asleep that night, I wrote in my journal by the dim glow of my flashlight, too agitated to sleep. As I described the incident of one woman holding another and my terror in response to that embrace, I wrote: *"No woman will ever hold me like that. I would rather die. Better a bullet in the street than to be held by a mother."*

*   *   *

Following our safe return from the initial trip to El Salvador, delegates and supporters quickly formed an organization called Project *Via Crucis*, which translated from Spanish is "The Way of the Cross." Our purpose was to prepare and send delegations to El Salvador, to educate congregations and our communities about what was taking place there, and to lobby Congress to end U.S. military aid.

As one of the founding leaders of the organization, I made presentations to community groups and churches, sometimes driving several hours to get to a particular location where I was asked to speak. I wrote letters to senators and congressional representatives about the human rights violations by the armed forces, protesting the war against civilians being waged with our tax dollars. I helped to organize group visits to Washington, D.C., for constituents to meet with their representatives. I learned the importance of developing good relationships with key congressional aides. I trained delegations and continued to study Spanish, using a combination of tutoring, short-term college courses and self-directed learning.

I was also holding down a demanding full-time job in the corporate sector. My husband and I were raising two young teen-age sons. Neither of us made much money. Despite two incomes, we barely had enough money to get by from week to week. We were absorbing not only significant travel expenses to El Salvador, but also many of the costs of the project, as it had no funding to reimburse coordinators for phone bills, gas and other costs incurred as we struggled to educate communities about our work.

My nightmares had begun a few months after the first trip to El Salvador. Horrific images of tortured bodies and death squads stalking people in the night were intermingled with even more disturbing images of myself as a small child, laying naked on a bed, being sexually fondled by my mother while my father slept nearby, oblivious to the travesty taking place beside him.

I would wake during the night, shaking and nauseated by the dreams. I could tolerate the images of the death squads, but I could not bear the images of my mother's face, looking at me with her eyes burning with a strange light while she touched my small body. Because I became afraid to sleep, I began to stay awake at night. As soon as I would start to relax, the state of vulnerability would trigger my terror—and I would be wide awake, sitting up with my heart pounding and trembling from head to toe.

In the beginning, I would miss one full night's sleep. Exhausted and lethargic, I began to have trouble in my corporate job, as it was fairly complex and required a clear mind. I would get through the day by telling myself that surely I would sleep that night. After all, human beings need sleep to survive.

But nobody told my body that. Soon I was not sleeping for stretches as long as three nights. I suffered from extreme anxiety; bits and pieces of my childhood kept streaming into my consciousness every waking moment. The control I so greatly prized in my life was disintegrating. I immersed myself in the work of Project *Via Crucis,* trying to run from the increasing fragmentation and pain I felt. I tried my best to be attentive to my sons. I forced myself to function at work, knowing that our family needed my earning power to survive economically.

But inside I felt like I was falling apart. I began writing in my journals about being small and hurt, about blood and broken bodies, about my imaginary friend, Peter, who was my constant companion until I was ten years old. I felt indescribably sad, but I could not name the source of my grief.

And I did not even have the means to relieve my pain with tears. I would later remember that I lost the ability to cry years ago, when my mother threatened me with even greater harm if I dared to show any emotion when she hurt me. But at this moment, I only knew that it seemed someone had stolen my tears. I felt afraid when I saw other people cry. I also felt a sense of sadness, as my inability to cry was one more way in which I was set apart from the rest of the world.

In desperation, I sought the advice of our family doctor for my insomnia. He said I had become exhausted, which was understandable given that I had a high- pressure job, two small children and was involved in travel into Central American war zones. He reassured me that I simply needed to get back into the habit of sound sleep. He prescribed what was to be a short-term solution—a minor tranquilizer that he recommended that I take each night. He was sure a 30-day supply was more than adequate.

Although the pills did not stop the onslaught of memory fragments of childhood, they did bring welcome, dreamless sleep. I clung to them like a lifeline, as they restored my now fragile sense of control. When my doctor balked at refilling my prescription for an extended period of time, I changed doctors. I was terrified of my dreams and determined to keep them at bay. Rather than taking a look at all that I was attempting to do—holding down a full-time job, raising a family and organizing Project *Via Crucis*—I was angry with myself for allowing childhood memories to seep into my life and distract me from important things. I wanted to direct my energy to the Salvadoran struggle—not focus on my own pain.

Although I did not yet comprehend this turn of events, my entry into accompaniment of the Salvadoran poor in the context of war had triggered an activation of the interior conflictive zone that is the inheritance of every untreated survivor of childhood sexual and physical abuse. A child who is sexually abused learns to survive in a war zone. Unprotected, she is subject to psychological, physical and spiritual destruction—particularly when the abuse occurs within the context of her family.

Much of my childhood was like a blank page; I simply had no memories for long stretches of time. There were fragments of some school experiences, but I could not name most of my teachers. I remembered pieces of Christmas Day in 1959 when my sister was born and I was not allowed to open my presents because my parents had to rush to the hospital. I was extremely uncomfortable when friends reminisced about childhood birthday parties or told simple tales about growing up. I felt myself to be socially deficient in that I could never contribute anything to the conversation, short of describing the summer of molestation at five years old and being raped at twelve years old. These were not the sort of experiences others talked about, so I learned to be silent about my past. I was unaware that other more profoundly painful memories of sexual abuse at the hands of my mother lay deeply buried behind the walls I built as a child in order to survive.

I did know that something deep inside of me was badly broken. It seemed as though if I just concentrated on the work in El Salvador, somehow I could keep from facing the pain that kept surfacing in so many ways. I wrote in my journal each night, reflecting on what it means to see God through the eyes of the poor. Then suddenly, as though my mind had disconnected from my hand, I would begin writing about being badly hurt as a child with no one to help or comfort me. I wrote about wishing that I could be invisible and wrapping myself in an imaginary world to escape from the reality in which our family lived. I would be disturbed and ashamed when I found myself writing about these things in my journal. I believed they had no place there. What happened to me was of no importance. What happened to the Salvadorans mattered.

*   *   *

Unspeakable massacres occurred in El Salvador, such as the one at El Mozote, a remote village in the eastern part of the country. The Atlacatl Battalion, an elite Army unit trained by the U.S. government, murdered almost 1,000 civilians on December 13, 1981. Rufina Amaya was the sole survivor. Most of those killed were children. Four of the children belonged to Rufina.

When the army stormed into El Mozote early one morning, the soldiers first separated the men from the women and children. They locked up screaming babies and frightened mothers in several houses. They executed the men first, shooting them and then slitting the throats of those who still lived. In the afternoon, they came for the women, leaving the abandoned children crying for their mothers who were marched off to suffer the same fate as their husbands.

Rufina, who had been led out with the first group of twenty women, managed to slip behind a small bush just behind the line of fire. When the women fell, Rufina hid under bleeding bodies and the bush. She watched as subsequent groups were brought out, lined up and shot. The soldiers were joking and laughing as they killed the women, who they said were FMLN guerrillas. When the women were dead, they brought out the children.

The soldiers then burned the bodies, destroying evidence of the massacre. After spending a week alone in the mountains, covered with blood and in shock, Rufina made her way to a small village where people were amazed to find that even one person had survived the massacre at El Mozote.

Rufina believes that God allowed her to survive so she could bear witness to what happened to her community. Salvadoran military leaders would claim that the inhabitants of El Mozote were subversives, killed in battle. The excavation of mass graves revealing tiny skeletons and evidence of execution-style killings more than a decade later would finally officially validate Rufina's story.

Rufina and I met in 1994 at a conference in New York where we were making presentations on healing from severe trauma. She survived the trauma of seeing her whole community and family massacred and then being told by the government that it never happened. I survived the trauma of being repeatedly sexually, physically and emotionally abused by my own mother when I was a child. The denial within my family and in the wider culture was every bit as solid as the denial of the Salvadoran government about what happened at El Mozote.

Until 1992, when the report of the Truth Commission sponsored by the United Nations verified atrocities that took place during the war, survivors like Rufina were ridiculed in the major Salvadoran newspapers. Peasants who told of massacres by the military were called liars, and people who survived torture by the state security forces were accused of exaggeration and hysteria. International workers who documented human rights violations were branded as communists. Church leaders who advocated justice for the poor were labeled as hopelessly naïve.

In a similar vein, U.S. culture has grown increasingly hostile to survivors who speak out about their abuse. Survivors subjected to sadistic abuse face open hostility and constant challenges to their credibility not only in the media but also in courts in which they seek legal redress.

Well-funded organizations of primarily affluent people claiming to be falsely accused by their adult children of sexual abuse sprang up in the early 1990s. One backlash group coined the term "false memory syndrome" and fed it to the media, where it was largely picked up as though it were a medically accepted diagnosis rather than a political phrase. A headline in The San Jose Mercury News on October 11, 1992 warned "Repressed Memories, Ruined Lives." The New York Times Book Review on January 3, 1993 carried an a article titled "Beware the Incest Survivor Machine." In national magazines, photos appeared of well-dressed professionals with gray hair who claimed their children's memories of abuse were "implanted" by conniving therapists. Women were depicted as passive objects easily convinced by a stranger that someone they love molested them.

The False Memory Syndrome Foundation was founded by a couple who claimed their daughter, a respected college professor, falsely accused her father of sexual abuse. Prominent foundation members, doctors and lawyers among them, offered themselves as "expert" witnesses at trials of accused perpetrators, discrediting the memories of victims. Clinical researchers who document the affects of childhood abuse and survivor advocates are said to be on "witch hunts." One backlash organizer is fond of asking, "Do we look like child abusers?" The appeal to class worked well, creating a public climate of suspicion toward adults who spoke of being abused as children.

Rufina understood this dynamic perfectly. It mirrored her experience in El Salvador in the years following the massacre. When we talked about how trauma had shaped our lives, one aspect became starkly clear: the psychological damage I suffered growing up in a secret war zone in a middle-class home in the United States was similar to the experience of Rufina who lived in an open war zone in the Third World where battles were waged with bombs and bullets. We shared post-traumatic stress symptoms such as insomnia, extreme startle responses at certain unexpected sounds, constant watchfulness for danger, nightmares, depression and anxiety.

Yet in other ways, our responses to the atrocities we endured were quite different. People traumatized in adulthood bring a range of coping mechanisms to their recovery and healing. But a child repeatedly abused in her home does not have the chance to develop those skills. In addition to remembering and working through the trauma, I also faced the formidable challenge of moving through lost stages of childhood development and acquiring the skills for basic human relationships, including trust, initiative and autonomy. A child who is beaten or raped by a parent learns to focus her energies to dissociate from the pain; she instead develops the necessarily protective and useful skills such as self-numbing, escape from her body, and the creation of an imaginary world where she is safe and loved.

A key factor in Rufina's healing was that she was able to receive validation and support from the Salvadoran people who needed no official confirmation of the military's actions. The thriving community of El Mozote had ceased to exist. The atrocities of the armed forces were well known by the poor among whom Rufina found compassion and sustenance after the loss of her children, husband and home.

My wounds were more private, nearly invisible. There was no one willing to hear my pain, to listen to my story of the perversions that took place within the walls of our small, isolated house when I got home from school in the afternoon.

*   *   *

Even today, the abuse of little girls by their mothers is discounted, disbelieved and denied. When I tell my story to others, I am often met with incredulity. People have a difficult time comprehending that mothers can sexually abuse children, particularly their daughters. Many people have no words of comfort to offer me. I have become accustomed to the shocked silence that typically follows this revelation. Unlike Rufina, who found meaning in her survivorship and told her story again and again, eventually releasing some of the pain after years of struggle, I was repeatedly forced to bury my trauma, pushing it to the furthermost regions of my mind in order to survive.

*   *   *

I began to experience blinding headaches, which recalled memories of the migraines I developed when I was about ten years old after my mother threw me across the room during a fight with my father and cracked my head against the wall. I developed chronic pelvic pain and bladder inflections. The doctors could not offer any explanation about why they occurred so often. I was diagnosed with a benign uterine tumor and an ovarian cyst. The cyst was surgically removed, but I continued to feel almost-constant discomfort in my pelvic area and anxiety.

When I was thirty-three and about to make my second trip to El Salvador, a doctor finally recommended a complete hysterectomy in response to my repeated complaints that I could not tolerate the pain "down there." I would not have minded the surgery. But I refused to take time off from my work in Project *Via Crucis*.

At a friend's insistence, I sought a second opinion. This new gynecologist asked careful questions about my stress levels and life history. When the interview concluded, I was shaking and feeling as though I had somehow left the room and only the shell of myself sat in the chair to answer the doctor's questions. I do not remember what he asked me, but I suspect it had something to do with whether or not I had ever been sexually abused. I do not remember how I responded.

He gently told me that he believed it would be best to delay surgery at this time and that he strongly believed I should talk to a psychotherapist. He said that although my pelvic pain was undoubtedly real, he believed there was a good possibility that it had deep psychological roots. He encouraged me to see a therapist as soon as possible and gave me a few names. As the visit ended, he stressed that he would be willing to coordinate medical treatment with any psychotherapist I chose. I almost ran from the office. I was not ready to face whatever was inside of me. I never went back.

Prior to this time, I functioned in most areas of my life by virtue of my ability to numb myself to my experiences. I did not feel the stress or pain of daily life that other people seemed to routinely encounter. People saw me as competent, strong and able to cope with anything.

They did not know I felt detached from the reality in which they lived. It was as though I existed in some far away place where no one could touch me. I not only had few memories of my childhood, I also had trouble remembering important events in my adult life such as my wedding and the birth of my children. I was a ghost, drifting through a realm I could never be a part of. Periodically, I felt like I entered a deep fog where death beckoned and I longed to follow.

In reality, it was the land of my childhood and I had never left it. Although I had walled off my childhood experiences inside of me, I had lost the ability to access the origins of that place of pain and isolation. My work in El Salvador began to turn the key.

*   *   *

As Project *Via Crucis* expanded and the war in El Salvador heated up, getting delegations into the country became a major challenge. The Salvadoran government, mindful of the need to maintain a low profile in the U.S. press, did not welcome international visitors determined to visit war zones as witnesses and advocates for the peasants. It preferred that attacks on civilians not be observed by international volunteers who had access to media and the ears of U.S. senators and Congressional representatives, some of whom were clearly becoming uneasy with reports of atrocities by the military.

Visas became very difficult to obtain. However, our visas were grudgingly granted because we presented letters of recommendation from legislators who supported our work and letters from business leaders written on company letterhead, urging that visas be issued. Because many of the delegates were professionals, including doctors, accountants, engineers and ministers, the advantage of their social status was used for leverage.

After we were in the country, we had to struggle to secure access to the communities that requested our help. Permission to enter a war zone required a *salvo conducto*, or safe conduct pass, from the military, a harrowing experience. To be issued *salvos*, the entire delegation was required to present themselves at the *Estado Mayor*, or High Command, a massive stone complex in the capital city that was surrounded by barbed wire and armed soldiers. Each delegate would be grilled separately by an officer, except for those who did not speak Spanish who were allowed to have the delegation leader present to translate. Even with safe conduct passes, delegations attempting to visit communities of refugees in conflictive zones were often harassed, arrested, detained and deported.

It was in this context that I traveled to El Salvador numerous times during the course of seven years, participating in delegations of accompaniment usually lasting about two weeks.

Accompaniment is the gift of being present with someone who is suffering. It means being willing to walk with those who are in pain, risking your own life if that is called for. I entered into accompaniment of Salvadoran refugees in 1987 as if we were walking together on holy ground. Five years later, I would find the courage and strength to ask a compassionate and skilled psychotherapist to accompany me as I risked entering my own internal war zones. The stakes were as high for me as they were for Salvadoran refugees: a matter of life and death. No one should have to walk through places of hell on earth alone.

The Bargain

I live inside and I keep the pain
I am the collector of all things bad
my stomach absorbs the blows
my head cradles the pain
my vagina is torn and my mouth is stuffed full.
But it is my job to guard the pain
for the others cannot bear it.

I am sentenced to death within the body of the one
who appears in the world.
Long ago, we made a pact
agreed that there was no other way to survive
that one of us must be the keeper of the pain

and now comes the light through the crack
the possibility of release
they are asking me to cry
        to feel
                to be
but how can I hold up my end of the bargain I made long ago

the pain is mine, but I don't feel anything
I absorb but I don't hurt
if I spill out the terrible wounds
someone might die from this pain and it would be my fault

    because I didn't keep my bargain.

Chapter 2

Beginning to Tell My Story

From my journal...
I took a major step at our community retreat this weekend. I put together what I've remembered, and I told four close friends. I asked for their accompaniment if I decide to take some time away from our solidarity work in El Salvador to heal. They unanimously supported my entry into an intentional healing process and promised to walk with me so I would not be alone.

*   *   *

I felt at the breaking point when I finally took the risk of sharing my internal struggle with Susan, Jenny, Stephen and Emily at a winter retreat of our group.

Project _Via Crucis,_ now in its fifth year, was flourishing. Our grassroots group enjoyed the financial support of several hundred contributors, and we had expanded our work to include small economic aid projects to El Salvador that promised to develop into long-term relationships. We had a governing board of eight directors and continuing plans for new delegation visits.

This gathering at the old church-owned farmhouse in a wooded area in central Pennsylvania had been designed primarily for assessment of the effectiveness of the most recent delegation visit to El Salvador and planning for our work as the core leadership group. Planning to stay for the weekend, we brought bags of food to prepare in the huge country kitchen, our Bibles and briefcases bulging with paperwork about PVC, as the project had come to be called.

Although the project was flourishing, I was nearing exhaustion and collapse. It had been three years since I had received Bill's assurance that I was not going crazy, but nightmares, anxiety, insomnia and intrusive memory fragments continued to make my days miserable. Yet until this point, I had not shared my suffering with those I worked with closely in the project with the exception of Susan, who was a survivor of sexual abuse.

Susan had undergone a lengthy course of psychotherapy ten years before when she was a college student to address molestation by her father and was now matter-of-fact about her past. Like Bill, Susan understood that the childhood molestation and subsequent rapes were traumas that had been aroused by my work in El Salvador. She encouraged me to find a psychotherapist, but I had refused. My priority was the work in El Salvador.

I appeared "normal" to those I worked with by sheer act of will and my ability to separate from my painful reality when I became overwhelmed. A part of me functioned at a high level, performing what I would later understand to be the workload of several people. At the time, I did not realize that by virtue of being human, I needed to balance my work with rest, relaxation and fun. I did not know about these aspects of living. I only knew how to survive, a day at a time.

I had been contemplating suicide on a daily basis. I told myself that it was inevitable that I follow my mother's example. I knew she wanted me to die, and I believed her power reached beyond the grave. My procrastination was seemingly prolonging my agony. Sometimes I would sit for hours with a handful of pills, longing for the death that I knew they would have the power to bring. Death would mean nothingness, an escape from the kaleidoscope of fragmented images and thoughts from my childhood that whirled through my brain.

My mother had often beat me. But until the last few years, memories of the beatings were treated just like the ones of being raped and molested. I knew it happened, but I figured it was not important. Now, my mind was flickering through scenes from my childhood with vestiges of my mother's face, raging, as she stripped off my clothes to beat me. Images of the kitchen in the small house we lived in when I was a child had catapulted from faded obscurity into vivid recollection of details such as the color of the wallpaper and the pattern of the linoleum floor. The kitchen especially terrified me but I did not know why. I had always carried a sliver of memory of being taken to the doctor to get my sliced-up genitals repaired when I was very young. Now, that sliver had taken up permanent lodging in a corner of my brain and refused to be banished. These images filled me with shame. I could not share them even with Susan.

I was also growing concerned with my dependence on sleeping medication, now in its fifth year, and I was noticing that I needed increasingly higher dosages to bring the dreamless sleep I craved. I had been addicted to street drugs when I was a teenager, and the signs of dependency were familiar to me. I counted my pills almost every day and made sure I had my prescription filled long before the old one ran out. Even though I took the sleeping pills only at night, I always kept a few in my purse when I left the house. Not having immediate access to them made me nervous. The doctor did not question my long-term use or need for greater dosage. I suspected he was not a good doctor, but I liked him because he gave me the pills that I wanted.

Two factors always brought me back from the edge of actually killing myself: the need of my young sons for a mother and the commitment to life that I had witnessed embodied in the struggles of countless Salvadorans during my years of volunteer work. It was for these reasons that I had asked for a block of time on the retreat agenda to talk about what I termed as "personal issues."

The five of us had become close during the five years of organizing annual delegations to El Salvador and community education about the civil war in the United States. Emily was a talented musician and gifted with high intelligence. She had a mind that seemed to process data faster than a computer and played the violin with a passion. Jenny and Stephen were committed partners in life and professors at a regional college. Stephen brought a philosophical bent to our discussions and often helped us to reflect on the deeper meaning of what we were doing beyond what was apparent. Jenny, who taught women's studies courses, contributed a feminist perspective rooted in an abiding faith and with Susan created wonderful ritual space for worship. They arranged smooth stones from a lake, colorful leaves from the surrounding woods and rich scoops of Pennsylvania soil with Salvadoran hand-carved wooden crosses to grace the altar in the room set aside in the retreat house for worship. We shared strong commitments to social justice and peacemaking; among us we had supported civil rights in the 1960s to feminist consciousness raising and protesting the Vietnam War in the '70s to environmental justice in the '80s.

In El Salvador, we walked in war zones, knowing we risked capture, injury or even death. We prayed with each other and reflected on Biblical passages that inspired our work. The words spoken by Bishop Oscar Romero one week before he was murdered were written in our hearts: *"This bloodshed, these deaths, are beyond all politics. They touch the very heart of God."*

However, we generally shared very little information on personal levels, particularly around emotions, and knew virtually nothing of the deeply wounded places that festered, unhealed, in some of us. When we got together, the intensity of the needs in El Salvador consumed our energy. It is difficult to talk about your bad week at work when an emergency call has come in to report that a community you work with has just been bombed or a Salvadoran friend has been captured by one of the death squads.

Like many activists, we were focused on need to change unjust structures. We rarely stopped to reflect on our own hopes, dreams, fears and pain with each other. This was not the model of community we saw demonstrated among the poor people in El Salvador. In Christian-based communities, every aspect of life was shared. Faith, food, scant material goods and emotional succor for the small and large crises of daily life were central organizing principles. Yet there seemed to be invisible walls, both cultural and personal, that kept our group members from any sort of real emotional connection about our own lives. As my relationships with Salvadorans deepened, and I absorbed lessons from their lives in communities, I found myself drawn to attempt to live as they did. I began to question how we could say we were in solidarity with the poor and yet not really know each other.

Late on Saturday afternoon, the sun slipped below the gently rolling mountains, and a chill hung over the living room. Stephen and Jenny started a fire in the huge stone fireplace. We had reached the place on our retreat agenda marked for my time. As the five of us sat in a circle on the rug in front of the dancing flames, I began to tell my story.

Although there had always been huge chunks of my childhood years that were totally blank, such as those from the time I was six to nine which I called the "lost years," there was also much that I did remember. And what I had always remembered and began to articulate on that winter afternoon was clearly upsetting to my friends. That much was evident in their faces, which mirrored a growing horror as I calmly told my story.

*   *   *

My mother, Doris, came from an extremely poor family that lived in one of the small ramshackle towns that dotted the Eastern Shore of Virginia. She often talked bitterly about the cruelty of her father, an alcoholic who beat his family when he was drinking. Ironically, he loved animals and was kind to various pets in the family, never hurting them and making sure they were well fed, even when his children were hungry. My mother talked about going to bed with her mouth watering for a Ritz cracker, a special and infrequent treat, after having eaten nothing for dinner on days they ran short of food.

My father, who was reared in a rural Pennsylvania Dutch community, met my mother's mother when he was a young man serving his stint in the U.S. Navy and stationed in Virginia. After enduring years of her husband's abuse, my grandmother Frances managed to borrow enough money from friends to buy a bar and fishing tackle shop at the water's edge when the marriage finally dissolved. The pattern of heavy drinking had finally caught up with my grandfather. He was no longer able to rule by terror as his health and strength deteriorated.

Doris had been sent to live with an older sister to escape her father's brutality. In a casual conversation, Frances told my father about her daughter and a meeting was arranged.

My mother moved in with Frances in the little apartment behind the bar, and started dating my father. At eighteen years old, she was a beauty—tall and slim, with long dark hair and blue eyes. She was the delight of the sailors who regularly visited the bar on their leaves from the nearby base, much to my father's dismay. He viewed this attractive woman as his prize and was not about to share her.

My mother became pregnant with me within a year, and they were married. Whether or not either of them regretted the early marriage—or would have been married if there had not been a pregnancy—I don't know. But I do know that my mother hated my father for bringing her to the rural Pennsylvania community to live in 1954 shortly after their marriage. As my mother remembered it, he promised that the living situation would be temporary and when they had accumulated enough money, they would move anywhere she liked. In the meantime, they would live on land his father had given to him.

For the first year, my parents lived with my grandparents while my father built a small brick house on a plot of land just a few hundred yards away. It had a tiny kitchen, parlor and one bedroom. It was heated by a huge black iron stove that stood in one corner, there was no indoor plumbing. Drinking water was carried in buckets from my aunt's well next door. A small wooden outhouse tucked into the trees at the edge of the woods in the backyard served as bathroom. Large potato chip cans provided most of the seating in the parlor. Sheet curtains rather than wooden doors divided the three rooms.

Surrounded by meadows and bordered by woods, the nearby houses were occupied by my father's siblings. Raised to be deeply suspicious of strangers, most chose mates from the same county and built homes within the matrix extending out from their birthplace.

My father's relatives looked askance at his bride. They had never seen anything like her short skirts, halter tops and flashy jewelry. She smoked cigarettes, which was considered to be strictly within the province of men. On the rare occasion a stranger happened to walk down the road, my aunts and grandmother quickly locked the doors, drew the shades and hid. Anyone outside the family was not to be trusted.

The abrupt transition to the conservative community, where the Old Testament was often quoted, was a culture shock for my mother. She despised her new home, its neat farms so different from the casual party atmosphere of the towns on the Eastern shore that catered to off-duty sailors looking for a good time. She felt isolated and completely out of her social environment with no support other than my father. She had no friends, education, job skills or money.

The neat brick house was about two miles from the nearest town by dirt road. We were surrounded by my father's extended family, which she considered every bit as strange as they viewed her. My grandmother practiced "pow-wow" medicine, and at times concocted packets of herbs, insects and other odd things to be worn around one's throat to ward off evil spirits. When "Gram" made a packet for my baby carriage, my mother threw it away, cursing her as a witch. She generally did not allow my father's relatives into our house. She swore she would rather be alone than associate with "those people."

My father was a carpenter by occupation. A taciturn man, he had little to say when he came home from work, which infuriated my mother who was usually spoiling for a fight about moving away from the area. When my father talked about the "Good Book," he worked himself into a frenzy, shouting about the judgment awaiting anyone who violated even one of its rules. My father's God ruled by fear and the infliction of harsh punishments.

When I was five, my sister Diane arrived to expand our small family. My mother was frantic in trying to care for my baby sister, who had been born on Christmas Day with a chronic heart condition. An ill and consequently irritable infant, Diane's arrival served to accelerate the see-saw of constant arguments followed by icy silences that had become the environmental climate in our small house.

I preferred to spend most of my time outdoors. My younger sister and I did not play together, and I had no playmates my own age. I entertained myself with my imaginary friend, Peter, who played in the fields and woods with me. He knew I did not like to be inside my house and was always waiting for me just outside the door. Peter could not enter the house. In my child-mind, I understood this was because he was good and the house was bad.

When my teen-aged cousin Tommy arrived at our door one summer morning and asked my mother's permission to take me on a picnic in the nearby forest, she readily agreed. My father had also built the house where Tommy lived with his parents. It was just across the street from ours, and it had indoor plumbing.

Thrilled to be chosen by my grown-up cousin for a rare outing, I skipped along happily through the woods, holding his hand. When I asked him where our picnic basket was, he told me it would be there for us when we got to the special place. After we had walked some distance, we were joined by two of his friends, who had been waiting for us in a thick grove of trees.

Tommy explained that boys had Popsicles inside of their pants, and he wanted me to taste them. Surrounding me in a close circle, the three boys unzipped their pants and pulled out their penises. I had never seen a penis before and was a little frightened by these strange appendages which seemed to be growing as the boys played with them. Every way I turned, I was eye level with a strange-looking "Popsicle." Then Tommy produced a small jar of honey and dripped the thick liquid over the tip of his erect penis before forcing it into my mouth, telling me to suck until the honey was all gone. In turn, each one of the boys did the same. I gagged and told Tommy I didn't like these Popsicles. He assured me I would learn to like them.

Afterward, Tommy impressed upon me how important it was that I should not tell my parents about what happened—that the Popsicles and the special place in the grove of trees was our secret. And if I were good, he would bring me back there every day and we would play together.

Desperately lonely, I kept the secret, and Tommy kept his promise. Each day that summer when it was not raining, he would appear at our door. My mother, distracted with caring for my sister and immersed in her own unhappiness, never questioned the propriety of a little girl spending hours in the woods each afternoon with a teen-age male.

Gradually Tommy and his friends told me of their plans for the rest of the summer. They were building a small shelter in the grove of trees, into which they would bring a table. When the table was in place, they would put me on it and "fuck" me. In response to my questions about what "fuck" meant, they promised me it was a wonderful game and I would like it. To prepare me for this grand event, they took turns wiggling their fingers into my small vagina to "get me ready."

Their rough fingers hurt me, and I grew increasingly reluctant to walk to the woods with Tommy. But I had been trained to never question the authority of an adult. Tommy was a teen-ager, practically a grown-up, and I thought I had to do what he said. If I did not immediately do exactly what my mother told me, I knew I would be hit. I didn't want Tommy to hit me.

The summer months passed, and the games continued. Sometimes, the boys put me in the center of their circle and urinated on me. If I didn't cup my hands and catch the hot streams quickly enough, they would squirt my head and face, always making sure to wash me off in the water of a nearby stream before Tommy took me home.

Finally, one day close to the end of summer, my mother asked me what we did in the woods every day. I told her it was a secret and that I had promised not to tell. She began to shake me, demanding that I answer.

Terrified, I blurted out the story about the construction of the shelter, the table and the mysterious and impending "fuck" which was to take place. She became hysterical, shaking me so hard my teeth rattled and screaming that I was going to be sorry for letting "that bastard" touch me. My mother called my father and demanded that he come home from work, an unprecedented event.

As soon he walked in the door, my mother flew at him in a rage. Hurling expletives at him, she blamed him for what happened to me in this "God-forsaken place." My father set down his lunch bucket and listened to her without saying a word. He remained standing just beside the door, his arms folded over his chest.

I huddled in a ball in the corner, forgotten by my parents. I had become just one more piece of ammunition that my mother could use in her ongoing argument with my father. The world was falling apart, and I felt I was to blame. After she had finished her tirade, my mother demanded to know what my father was going to do. She wanted to call the police. My father adamantly refused. He glanced at me, then quickly averted his eyes.

"Tommy is my sister's boy," he said quietly. Tightening his tool belt, he walked out the door and went back to work.

We never spoke of the incident again. Yet it was always there, the air itself tainted with what I had done. My aunts talked about it in hushed tones in shorthand sentences they surely assumed I could not understand. But I did. I heard them say that it was a shame, and that Tommy was really a good boy. He was a little "slow" but worked hard in his special education class. I assumed I was the bad one, since he was good. He smirked at me whenever I saw him, which happened rather frequently at one or another relative's house.

My father, who had been my only source of physical affection, stopped holding or touching me. In fact, for a long time, he refused to speak to or even look at me. I knew I had become defiled, unclean in his eyes. I began to believe I was invisible, and I increasingly retreated into a world of my own making, playing for hours with my imaginary friend Peter. Peter was all the things I was not. He was brave, clever and strong. Nobody hurt him. He knew tons of tricks and games. And sometimes, he held me when the pain became too much for a little girl to absorb. There was no one else.

*   *   *

My mother controlled virtually all aspects of my life, limiting my access to the outside world to every extent possible. I went to elementary school on the bus but never visited any schoolmates and never dreamed of asking anyone to our house. She made me believe that she could even see inside my mind; she often delivered a stunning and swift slap to my face if she was convinced that I was thinking of rebelling against her or even distancing myself from contact with her.

"I know what you're thinking!" she would hiss, thrusting her face within an inch of mine while my eyes were watering from the blow.

"You just get that thought out of your mind, and wipe that look from your face."

I became adept at the art of revealing nothing in my face and eyes, a practice that earned me the reputation in my adult career life as a rarity—a completely unemotional woman—and would serve me well in work settings dominated by corporate culture. And as my face learned to become blank, so did my mind.

The span from ages five to nine encompasses what I used to call the "lost" years with only sparse and fleeting memories of school and church events. I remembered, for example, standing on the hill under a tree outside the elementary school I attended in third grade and watching the other children play out in the grassy field. I was alone, as usual. By the tender age of eight, I already felt set apart from the world. I could not fathom being able to run, play, and scream with happy abandon. I knew that my emotions and actions had to be carefully controlled. It was not safe for me to play in the boisterous way of children. I felt safe close to trees and by myself. But try as I might, I could remember virtually nothing that took place inside our house during those years.

I do recall two events when I was ten. One was the birth of my brother, Jack, which prompted the family's move from the Little House to a larger and more comfortable residence that my father had built on an adjoining lot. The new house, which we named the Big House, was an imposing two-story structure with four bedrooms, a huge kitchen, living room with fireplace and fully equipped bathroom. It felt like a mansion compared to the earlier cramped quarters which was converted to a workshop and garage. Despite my mother's outspoken hatred of her life in Pennsylvania, it appeared that my father was continuing to refuse to leave the land of his birth and broke his promise to relocate.

A second incident that I never forgot took place just after we had moved into the Big House. I always thought of it as the day my music died.

My mother resented the fact that her poverty-stricken family was never able to afford piano lessons for her when she was a child. To compensate for her own deprivation, she bought a monstrous black piano and made me start piano lessons in first grade, sending me to the house of a piano teacher in a nearby town for weekly instruction. My teacher was a fat gray-haired woman with glasses and a mole on her chin. She took up most of the piano bench, leaving me only a small corner to sit. She was fond of slapping my hands when I played the wrong note too many times and tramped hard on my feet when I did not use the pedals properly.

I disliked the piano as much as my teacher, but the lessons were one of many ways in which my mother imposed her own will and desires on me, never taking into account my needs, interests or dreams. One afternoon when I was ten, I left my daily practice unfinished and crept down the road for a clandestine visit to my grandmother's house. I was seldom allowed to visit her due to my mother's hatred of my father's relatives. But that day, for some reason, I felt brave enough to sneak away from the oppressive atmosphere of our house to risk a visit. It was Thursday, and I knew Gram would be baking bread.

Gram was a tiny hunch-backed woman with a strong Pennsylvania Dutch accent. She wore long flower-print dresses and thick hose, and I never saw her without an apron. She was born, grew up, raised a family of her own and grew old in the same log-frame house. Tommy's mother spent most of her days at Gram's house, helping her to clean and bake. She was there this particular day.

I was sitting at the oilcloth-covered kitchen table enjoying a slice of freshly baked bread with butter, listening to my aunt and Gram talk in the Pennsylvania Dutch dialect when my mother burst through the door. Her eyes were wild with fury, and she could hardly speak. The bread stuck in my throat, and my stomach twisted in knots.

"Get out of this house, you little bitch!" she hissed at me. The cords of her neck were throbbing with anger, and her hands were clenched into fists. My grandmother and aunt tried to intervene by attempting to talk to my mother, but their pleas that she not hurt me had no effect. My grandmother stood frozen in place, helplessly twisting her apron. My aunt was slowly backing up as though she was ready to bolt through the back screen door.

I slipped by my mother and ran for the front porch, but she caught up to me in a moment. She grabbed my hair with one hand and began to flail at my back and buttocks with the other then kicked me and ordered me to walk, still holding fast to my hair. Twisting around, I saw the horrified faces of my grandmother and aunt looking out the kitchen window. My mother rained blows on me with her hands and fists, beating me all the way down the road back to our house, normally a five-minute walk, screaming obscenities.

When we returned to our home, she threw me face down on my bed. Still screaming like a wild woman, she ripped the clothes from my lower body and began to beat me, her hands smashing down on me with strength driven of rage. She threatened to cut a switch if I cried so I stuffed sheets into my mouth to ensure no sounds inadvertently escaped my lips and willed my body into numbness that eventually—and mercifully—eased the pain.

The room was silent except for the sound of my flesh being beaten. She finally stopped hitting me when I ceased to move or struggle but laid placidly and accepted my punishment, obediently following her instructions to spread my legs wide open and not tense my muscles in any way. I had gone to a place inside of me where she could not hurt me any more. It was a small victory.

She ordered me to the piano that stood in the corner of the room. Dazed, I sat on the hard bench and stared at the ivory and black keys in front of me in confusion. She stood with her arms crossed and ordered me to play for her. My fingers refused to work, and I felt as though I had never seen a piano before in my life. But then a strange thing happened: I felt my mind split.

To this day, I cannot adequately explain what I experienced. I just know that I suddenly saw my hands take up their familiar position on the keys and begin to play. I heard the music as though it was coming from a great distance. I was somewhere across the room, not connected to my hands or the music. My mind seemed to have separated itself from the whole process. Those piano-playing fingers were working on their own. I was not afraid. My battered body did not hurt. My mother stood impassively beside me and listened. I played faultlessly, without error.

Nodding approvingly, she opened her book of hymns and commanded that I play "How Great Thou Art" and her other favorites. I played for a long time, completely detached from what I was doing. Inside, I felt amazed—someone else was playing the piano with my hands. I didn't have to worry about making mistakes or how the hymns sounded at all! With a feeling of utter freedom, I gave my music over to her. She could have whatever she wanted. The music was no longer mine, it was hers.

I would take piano lessons for nine years, becoming an accomplished pianist. The last two years of lessons would be spent with a teacher of renown, for whom I had to audition in order to be accepted as a student. He took only the best and most gifted. My secret was I had no emotions whatsoever connected to the music. It functioned in some walled-off part of me. Since this teacher seemed to believe that music had to be played with great expression, I studied the passion of others and copied it for my own. I played whatever was asked of me, and I seldom made mistakes.

One day when I was 20, shortly after my mother committed suicide, I sat at the piano and discovered to my consternation that I could not remember even the basic chords. Feeling something close to panic, I pulled out a music book. The scores were completely incomprehensible, much like trying to read a foreign language I never studied.

My music was gone. When my mother died, she took it with her. In reality, it had not been mine since the day she beat me for visiting my grandmother when I was ten.

*   *   *

Between the ages of ten and twelve, I started to suffer from migraine headaches, and I fainted frequently. Occasionally, I let out short screams, the sound involuntarily rising out of me before I could stop it.

I began to encounter a beautiful Lady in White, who held out her hand to me when the pain was unbearable and I wanted to die. When I felt myself slipping away into the emptiness of unconsciousness, the Lady would appear in the darkness, holding out her hand to me and smiling. She wore a long white dress, and her blonde hair was adorned with a garland of flowers. She never spoke to me, but I could feel love and protection radiating from her presence. It was as though she gave me energy to live. Unlike my imaginary friend Peter, who came into my world and played with me in the fields and woods surrounding our home, the mysterious Lady drew me into her world. It was a place of beauty, where there was no pain.

We always walked across a bridge into a meadow filled with flowers, trees and bubbling brooks. She would hold me on her lap, tenderly stroke my hair and will me back to life. One day, I began to faint in the kitchen. As I fell into the swirling darkness, I saw the Lady materialize. She was coming for me, and I longed to go with her. But suddenly I was back under the harsh glare of the bright kitchen light, gasping and choking on the cold floor. My mother had thrown cold water in my face and was shaking me roughly. I protested that I wanted to go with the beautiful Lady. My mother was angry and seemed frightened. She told me in no uncertain terms that I was hallucinating again, and there was no Lady. Always careful not to provoke her, I kept my silence. But sometimes, when I was coming out of a fainting spell, I would begin talking about the Lady before I realized what I was saying.

I missed a lot of school because of the headaches and fainting spells. In February 1967, my mother had kept me home for most of the week. After several days of being at home with my mother, it felt as though a scream was building up inside of me that was going to erupt and destroy the world. By February 14 —Valentine's Day—I had reached my limit. I sat like a frightened and silent rabbit on a chair in the empty living room, listening to my mother bustling in the kitchen as she prepared dinner. I watched the clock on the mantle above the fireplace, counting the minutes until my father would arrive home from work. I knew I could not let the screams out when I was alone with my mother. And I was terrified that I would not be able to hold it inside until my father arrived.

Finally, just a few minutes before his usual time of arrival, I completely lost control. When the screams finally burst free, I did not realize they were mine. It was not until my mother began slapping my face in a frantic effort to quiet me that I grasped that the sounds were ripping from my gut and through my throat.

I remember my father hovering in the background while my mother slapped me repeatedly across the face. When the slaps did not quell the screams, my father finally picked me up and carried me out to the car. We drove to the office of our family doctor. Although I had suffered the fainting spells and headaches for two years, I had never been taken to the doctor to find the reason for them.

The doctor gave me an injection to calm me. When he asked my parents if they knew what caused me to scream or the origins of the headaches and fainting spells, my father looked at the floor and remained silent. My mother blamed a head injury that I had incurred about a year before, saying I had bumped my head while playing beneath the kitchen's breakfast bar. It was true that I had suffered a blow to my head serious enough to cause unconsciousness, but not while playing in the kitchen. What my parents neglected to say was that my head had been hurt when my mother threw me against the wall one day during a fight with my father. On her way to diving at his throat in a rage, I was merely an obstacle in her path. She picked me up like a rag doll and threw me out of the way. I remember dimly sliding to the floor after I hit the wall, hearing my parents shout at each other.

The doctor recommended a complete neurological examination, and he arranged for an emergency admission at the local hospital. After more than a week of extensive tests, including a painful spinal tap, the doctors were convinced my problems were not neurological in nature. My case was turned over to Dr. Weiss, the hospital's chief of psychiatry. I do not recall much about his physical appearance, and I did not particularly like him. He was cloaked in the kind of professional veneer that allowed no emotional connection with his patients. But I remember his voice and the little contraption with a swinging ball on his desk. He would tell me to watch the ball and relax. As I did, I would feel myself slipping into the dreamy trance-like state to which I was well accustomed. I did not need to be hypnotized to enter this realm. I had perfected the art of doing so years ago.

I have little memory of the weeks I spent in the hospital. I know that I was asked many questions by Dr. Weiss and others to which I tried to respond. But communication about the world in which I lived with my mother was exceedingly difficult.

The abuse that I was enduring was too bizarre to be coherently described by a child. Most of the time I lived in what felt like a dream broken only by pain. I did not know that other people did not live as we did. My mother was like God to me: she made the rules, and created the world, my world. The fact that she was the perpetrator and that the abuse was often incorporated into accepted child-rearing practices of the day such as corporal punishment compounded the difficulty. My father had repeatedly warned me never to speak of anything that went on inside of our house to others. My relatives taught me to be afraid of strangers. Nevertheless, the doctors began to suspect that something very out of the ordinary was happening which involved my mother.

I was given batteries of psychological tests. During this period, my mother visited daily, often bringing a bottle of cod liver oil and making me swallow a huge spoonful. She said that just because I was in the hospital didn't mean I could not be "cleaned out" as she called it. For a long time she had been obsessed with what she said was my "inside dirtiness" and tried to control the most intimate and minute of my body functions. About two years before, she initiated the practice of giving me enemas every day when I returned home from school.

The ritual was predictably the same every day. She would make me lie down on the bathroom rug while she filled the red enema bag. She always greased her finger with petroleum jelly before inserting it into my rectum, telling me that the enema tube would not hurt as much. She would fill me with water and then point me to lay on a cot covered with a plastic pad in a nearby bedroom. I was instructed to hold the water until she told me I could relieve myself. Sometimes, she disappeared into another part of the house, and I would call out frantically after a long time went by, begging her to let me get to the toilet. When she finally allowed me to void myself, there were days I could not make it to the bathroom in time. After I finished cleaning up my mess as she watched, she would spank me for not having better control of my bodily functions.

For as long as I can remember, my father points to my hospitalization at twelve years as the beginning of the time when my mother was "not right in the head." When he says this, there is always the intimation that I am to blame. If it had not been for me, my mother would have been just fine, according to his logic.

In reality, she was ill long before I was taken to the hospital. It just became so glaringly evident during this event that he could no longer completely deny there was a problem. After my first few days away from home, he claims she virtually stopped sleeping and eating. She paced the floor all night, reading medical books and writing long letters to the doctors. She begged my father to get me out of the hospital before the doctors killed me. I believe she was frightened that I would tell the doctors of the bizarre things that went on in our comfortable middle-class home. She also may have seen me as an extension of herself and may have feared a part of her was being found out. For the first time, I was not totally isolated and within her realm of control. The reins of power she held with me were slipping.

After several weeks, the psychiatrist called my father to his office for a private meeting. He indicated that he strongly suspected abuse, and he believed my mother was involved. He told my father that it was clear that something was happening in my house that was driving me to the edge of sanity. He believed the headaches, fainting spells, dizziness and screams were somatic conversion symptoms.

He urged my father to consider long-term residential treatment for me, warning that a return home could have the gravest consequences. He pleaded with my father to seek treatment for my mother.

My father's response was to call the doctor a bastard and threaten to sue. When he told my mother of the accusations, they quickly rallied to confront what they considered a challenge to their authority. With the help of a relative who was a physician, my parents removed me from the hospital that same day. Dr. Weiss wrote letters to the family doctor, my parents and the principal of my school, making it clear that my therapy had been terminated without his consent.

In a letter to our family doctor, Dr. Weiss wrote: "I told Mr. Kline that his daughter was ill but his wife was far more ill, and that he should seek treatment for her before it is too late. This is a family that has struggled up from nothing and has made a good life . . . but it is a sick family and they need help." Another letter noted the many "disturbing factors" present in my case and the agreement of the two leading neurologists who examined me that I required psychiatric treatment. In a letter to my parents, he posed the question: "If Linda had a head injury why did you delay for a whole year in receiving therapy from a recognized neurologist, especially since you thought it was getting worse?"

But his questions and comments fell on deaf ears. I was taken to a doctor in another city who was an acquaintance of our pastor. Despite the assessment of the doctors at the hospital that I was in danger in my home and increasing signs of my mother's instability, the pastor staunchly supported my parents. After all, they went to church each Sunday, worked hard, paid their taxes and owned a nice home. They could not possibly be involved in something as sordid as child abuse; that simply did not happen among families in his congregation.

The new doctor immediately diagnosed my "problem" as related to my sinuses. Within a week, I had surgery to remove a spur from a sinus cavity.

My parents were vindicated. I had needed bona-fide surgery, disproving the claim of the doctors who treated me in the hospital that my symptoms were the result of abuse. An unknown doctor wrote an excuse to cover my long absence from school, attributing it to "sinus headaches."

For years afterwards, my father obsessively told anyone who would listen how "those bastard doctors tried to take our daughter away." Indignantly, he would pound his fists on the table shouting, "And they said her mom abused her! The best mom in the world! I should have sued those bastards and that hospital for all they were worth!" For more than a decade, he told this story to friends, relatives and strangers alike. Anyone who talked to him for more than ten minutes was treated to the hospital story.

*   *   *

Following the surgery, my mother would not allow my paternal relatives to enter our home. Although my cousin Nancy, four years older, repeatedly asked to come for a short visit, my mother adamantly refused, citing need for my rest.

I was once again completely isolated and spent long hours alone. I began to wander the house at night in my sleep, often ending up in the back yard. I was shocked awake when my mother, hearing the door open, came searching for me. She was angry that I kept going outside at night. Perhaps I was unconsciously searching for a way to once again escape the confines of my home.

But my life was about to take a dramatic and unexpected turn. When I returned to school that spring, my mother's behavior abruptly changed. Although she continued her practice of suddenly slapping my face and occasionally flew into fits of rage over small things, like a carelessly washed platter, she largely ignored me. She stopped giving me enemas when I came home from school and seemed to lose all interest in controlling my thoughts, actions and activities. She seemed not to care if I stayed in town after school and did not come home until evening.

She was beginning to live in a strange interior world that only she inhabited. She would pace for hours, muttering to herself about things that made no sense at all to me. When she was not pacing, she would sit silently at the kitchen table, as still as a statue. Sometimes, I would come home from school to find her still dressed in her nightgown, staring out a window with her arms folded across her chest and rocking herself.

Then there would be the times when she was filled with energy so charged it was frightening. With the radio turned up full blast, she would dance with abandon, sweat streaming down her face. Her arms would flail wildly, and she would flirt, argue and sometimes scream at her invisible dance partners until she finally collapsed in exhaustion. She began to chain smoke and lost so much weight that she became unusually thin. She became paranoid, convinced the phone was tapped and she was being constantly watched, a victim of an evil government conspiracy.

Part of me feared my mother was crazy. Yet I could not admit it even to myself. Although her iron fist of control over me had slipped since my hospitalization, I still believed she had tremendous power. I trusted her perception of reality more than I trusted mine.

*   *   *

After school ended for the year, my sixteen-year-old cousin Nancy acquired a handsome new boyfriend. Rick was seventeen and was tall and muscular with thick blond hair that fell carelessly over his eyes. He was extremely popular at school, and girls fell all over themselves to attract his attention.

Rick spent several weeks in August helping us paint my grandmother's porch. Seeking ways to make a good impression on Nancy, he was exceedingly attentive to me, teaching me how to paint properly and occasionally engaging me in a boisterous game of tag. I had never played with anyone like this before. He called me "kid"—which I understood as an affectionate way of speaking and interpreted as a sign he liked me. Eager for attention, I quickly became attached to Rick and imagined that he was like the protective older brother that I had always longed for.

One September evening I attended a dance at the local recreation center. I missed my ride home with a friend's parents. I was standing in line, waiting to use the phone to call my mother to pick me up. Suddenly, I felt a hand on my shoulder.

"You need a ride, kid?" It was Rick. Happily, I accepted since his offer would mean that I didn't have to spend the few minutes with my mother.

In a few more minutes, however, it was apparent that we were not heading to my house. He turned down a dark country road. Popping a beer can out of a six-pack, he handed it to me. "Drink up, kid," he said. "I want to show you this really cool place." I had no experience with alcohol and did not like the bitter-tasting beer. But since Rick gave it to me, I drank up so I would not hurt his feelings.

We drove further out into the countryside, eventually stopping at a small dark cemetery high on a hill. Rick pulled the car into the gravel driveway beside the deserted church that stood like a lonely sentinel guarding the tombstones in the pale moonlight. He turned off the engine. "Isn't this a great view?" he said as he helped himself to another beer.

He draped his arm around my shoulders, and I felt a fog of confusion descend upon my mind. My brain could not comprehend what was happening as he pushed a lever, and the front seat of the Rambler lowered to form a flat bed. It happened so fast that I felt stunned.

"Rick, I think I need to go," I heard myself say. My voice sounded unreal and far away. What happened next was rape.

*   *   *

Rape through the eyes of a 12-year-old girl…

My seat is gone. He turned it into a bed. He is pulling me back so that my head is close to the rear window. (But he is RICK, Nancy's boyfriend, and he wouldn't do anything to hurt me.)

He is touching my breasts now. He's rough with his hands. He has changed. This is not the Rick I know. I push at him, but I can't move him at all. He is unzipping my jeans, pulling them down. He says, "COME ON! HELP ME WITH THIS!"

No, no, I don't want to. I feel scared, and nothing is real. I am going away in my mind…the jeans are stuck and he gives them a great jerk and they are off. He pulls off my panties, and I am so ashamed to be without clothes. (But he is RICK, Nancy's boyfriend, and he wouldn't do anything to hurt me.)

I watch him unzip his jeans and pull them down along with his shorts. He doesn't take his jeans all the way off, though. I am naked, and he still has his jeans on part way…he climbs on top of me. I am saying over and over, "No, please no, don't" but he doesn't listen…PAIN suddenly! I am moved to a whole other level—I can't believe how much this hurts. His face is angry.

"HELP ME!" he demands. "PUT YOUR LEGS UP AROUND MY WAIST. IF YOU ARE A GOOD GIRL AND HELP ME, IT WON'T HURT SO MUCH." It hurts too much so I decide to help him. Still, he is very big and can't get it inside of me. "PUT YOUR FEET UP ON THE ROOF. SPREAD YOUR LEGS WIDE. IT'LL BE OVER SOON IF YOU'RE A GOOD GIRL."

Trained by my mother to assist in my own punishments to avoid infliction of greater pain, I comply as best I can. Finally, it is finished. I can't find my panties. I don't feel anything.

Driving home, he says not to tell anybody, especially Nancy. We pull into my driveway. He tells me we can still be friends.

I go into the house and lock myself in the bathroom. I wipe the blood from my legs. I go away in my mind. I never tell anybody.

*   *   *

There was a silence in the room at the retreat center when I finished speaking. As a group, we had listened to the testimonies of dozens of Salvadorans who were raped, tortured or beaten by the military. Although sickened by the unremitting tales of human brutality, at least one of us always found some words of comfort, however inadequate, to offer to the survivors. But words seemed to have fled my four companions. Each seemed unable to speak, lost in reflection on the implications of what I had shared with them.

As the silence grew, I felt myself floating away. I was sure they would all hate me now, and I was preparing to not feel that particular hurt. Voices inside my head were clamoring, shouting that I was stupid for thinking any of this mattered. I should not have told them. Finally, Susan broke the silence.

"We'll be with you," she whispered, her eyes glistening with tears. "You won't be alone with this." Susan, more than the others, knew the hard road I was facing. Her candid disclosure of her own traumatic experiences and her faith in the process of healing helped to give me the courage to share my story with the group.

The others nodded in assent. They began to talk, but I have no memory of what they said. Their words were bouncing off of my mind like pebbles too tiny to cause a ripple in still water. My ears felt as though they were stuffed with cotton as my self-protective survival mechanisms kicked in.

I went into the kitchen to get a drink of water. Jenny followed me. "Can I ask you a question?" she said softly. I nodded. "How did it feel for you to tell us all of that?"

Time seemed to stop. The glass of water that I held instantly froze in my hand on its way to my mouth. I looked at Jenny, and I noticed there were tears in her eyes. I took a deep breath. "I didn't feel much of anything. Mostly, I just feel kind of numb."

She bowed her head for a moment, then looked into my eyes. "I thought so," she whispered. "And that was the most frightening thing of all to me. You told us about these horrible things that happened to you with absolutely no emotion."

We returned to the others in the living room. Susan reached out to take my hand, and I let her hold my cold fingers. Although extensive therapy almost a decade earlier had alleviated many of the worst symptoms she suffered as a result of her abuse, the terror of life in El Salvador had unleashed flashbacks of her childhood molestation. Still, she believed she had done enough work on her own recovery to maintain her balance in a country at war. But she would discover, as I did, that the similarities between the abuse she suffered as a child and the violations committed by the authorities on Salvadoran peasants were far too similar to allow for any psychological distance.

The personal and the political are intimately linked when we speak of torture.

Chapter 3

A Commitment to Heal

I careened wildly on an emotional roller coaster during the weeks following the retreat. Exhilaration at the relief of finally being able to articulate some of the pain trapped inside of me alternated with swift plunges into depression as I despaired that I had revealed too much to my friends. In between those two emotional extremes was the feeling of dread as when the roller coaster is perched precariously at the tip of the biggest hill and you briefly wonder if you will be thrown out of the car and dashed to pieces on the way down. Afraid of being seen as weak, I feared that my friends would now view me with a mixture of horror and pity rather than regarding me as the strong, competent person they knew as a leader.

Exhaustion alternated with periods of hyperactivity. I mopped floors at 2 a.m. and cleaned out closets in which the deepest recesses had not seen the light of day in years. I could not sit still long enough to eat a full meal and couldn't eat even if I could sit still since I had little appetite.

Images of past painful experiences, like short clips from an old movie, continued to flash though my brain, and I felt emotions that I could not begin to name. My body ached, and my head hurt.

In a desperate attempt to stop the uncontrollable images, I began a process of deliberately numbing myself to survive. As the turmoil within became muffled, I imagined that I heard steel doors slamming shut.

Although I did not understand how the numbing process worked, I had always known that I contained a complex system of compartments, doors and locks so that I could put bad things into closets, shut away where they could not hurt me. I felt a cool, detached sense of triumph at being able to shove the pain back into the box inside of me where it belonged. I slid into the welcome darkness of depression.

Drawing on her own process of healing and years of therapy, Susan encouraged me to search for my "inner child," who she said held not only the pain of the abuse but also the keys to healing. According to Susan, this child part also embodied my ability to act in spontaneous and playful ways.

In truth, looking for a part of myself who could be hurt as easily as a child was not a comfort to me. The vulnerability of children had always terrified me, and I doubted that I ever had an ability to act in spontaneous and playful ways. The reality was I had never possessed spontaneity as a child, having learned to live in a constant state of watchfulness. As an adult, I was also afraid of play and simple body movement. Once, when our North American delegation joined with Salvadorans for an impromptu game of soccer, I sat on a rock at the edge of the field, paralyzed with fear by the exuberant flow of the game and the raucous laughter and uninhibited body movement exhibited by the players, some of them in their sixties with limited agility. I watched the game with an unnamed sadness, remembering that in elementary school I was never able to join other children at play for reasons I could not understand.

But I still did not believe I had an inner child—at least not the kind that Susan was talking about. For all of my adult life, there had been periods of time when I clearly heard a child crying. Sometimes the sound would wake me from a deep sleep, and I would jump from my bed, desperate to locate the source of the weeping. I would check the rooms of my children and find them sleeping peacefully. Creeping back to bed, I puzzled over this strange phenomenon that seemed far too real to be merely a dream. It never occurred to me that the child who wept inconsolably was a part of myself.

I wrote in my journal extensively during this period as a means of preserving my sanity. As was my custom for years, I also wrote so that I would remember who I was and where I had been. Time seemed to evaporate into mist; I could not construct a whole life history as I heard other people do. During the darkest periods of my life, I wrote so that I would leave trails in the fog that seemed to surround me. Perhaps some day I would be brave enough to find the source of my pain. For the most part, I just tried to put down markers.

*   *   *

From my journal…
I went searching for the inner child. The old ones told me she is dead.
"She died a long time ago. There is nothing to resurrect." They spoke with
cold assurance. "We are old," the pain whispered. "More ancient than you
know. If you cast us out, there is nothing left. The child is dead. We
remain." Torture is familiar. Tenderness is not. Which, then, is more to be
feared?

*   *   *

I was home alone one evening. As was my habit now, I held my bottle of tranquilizers in my hand while I paced, reassuring myself with the knowledge that if the pain got too bad, I could end it all by taking the pills. Each prescription refill contained a three-month supply; I knew this amount was more than adequate to do the job. Sometimes I fell asleep clutching the small bottle like a security blanket. I was constantly exhausted yet felt unable to sleep and only aware of feelings of anxiety and stress. Despite my lack of energy, I decided to do some exercises to see if I could relieve tension.

I was lying on my back doing leg lifts when suddenly I felt pinned to the floor by what seemed a great weight crushing my entire body. Darkness enveloped me, and it was as if I could taste death at my own hand. There was a strong sense of being commanded to follow my mother into the darkness of death, and I felt myself moving toward the same path she had chosen—to the place where I would be hers forever. My arms were somehow pinned above my head, and although I struggled furiously I could not move them. I fought to keep my legs together, but I felt them being slowly spread apart. I felt as if I was about to be raped by someone I could not see.

I had knowledge on two distinct levels: The first was that no living person was in the room with me. The second was that somehow my mother's spirit had entered the room. I could feel the weight of her body holding me down. I could smell her stale cigarette breath and the greasy moisturizing lotion she slathered on her face until it was shiny. It was as though I was being raped by a destructive and powerful energy that would not be thwarted, even by death. I don't know how long this sensation lasted—probably no more than a minute, but it seemed like an eternity. Gagging and gasping for air, I gathered all my strength and shoved at the unseen energetic force, uttering one word that was more wail than shout: "NO!"

I would NOT follow her into death. And I would NOT be raped again.

As inexplicably as the mysterious invisible weight had come upon my body, it suddenly lifted and disappeared. I was so stunned by the physical force of what I had just experienced that I huddled on the floor, unable to move. Finally, I managed to crawl to the phone in the kitchen. I was shaking so hard that my teeth were chattering. The whole house seemed huge, as though I had entered a giant's domain. I felt distinctly child-like as I studied the wall phone from the perspective of the floor. I was not sure I could reach it. After some maneuvering, I was able to dial the right numbers with hands that seemed unfamiliar, small and awkward.

When Susan answered, my voice sounded as though I had just traveled in time back to the age of five. The inner child that she spoke of had indeed finally surfaced. But she was not at all the magic and playful sort of entity so blithely written about in much of the popular recovery literature. This child was as real as I was when I was five, frightened and holding more pain and suffering in her few years than most people experience in a lifetime.

I have no recollection of what Susan said to me on the telephone that night. But I do know that her calm voice was a lifeline for the frightened and hurt child who had literally crawled into the kitchen to call her.

I was profoundly disturbed by the experience of feeling attacked by a destructive force that felt like my mother's spirit. At times I feared I was beginning to slide into a realm of insanity from which there would be no return. I told no one, other than Susan, what happened. For weeks, I tried to rationalize that the experience may have happened because I was so preoccupied with suicide. This might explain the encounter with a vision of death by my own hand, although given my lifelong aversion to emulating my mother in any way, the idea of killing myself was fraught with conflict. I did not want to imitate her in life—or in death.

However, comparing my thoughts of hurting myself to her suicidal choice still could not explain the sense of being raped by her spirit. I tried to convince myself that I had flashed back to being raped by Rick when I was twelve, but I intuitively knew that the conviction was weak. The energetic force trying to penetrate me had been the spirit of my mother, powerful even from beyond the grave. And the thought of her entering my body brought waves of nausea flooding through me. Inside, I heard the newly awakened child part begin to cry in terror. And no one could console her.

*   *   *

I knew almost nothing about psychotherapy. But I understood that I was in a process of what felt like labor and that I needed the assistance of a midwife to survive. Yet I deeply distrusted the practice of traditional institutionalized medicine. I had never met a medical doctor I trusted. They all seemed autocratic and remote, dictating treatment without explanation. They listened to my accounts of pain with expressionless faces, cutting me off to ask sharp questions which confused and frightened me. They prodded, poked, cut and medicated without ever making what felt like a human connection with me. I did not want a therapist that would function in a similar distant and authoritarian mode.

My political and spiritual consciousness had been forming during the years of solidarity work with the Salvadoran people. Slowly, I had begun to conceptualize my own process of healing as a long journey to liberation. Just as the Salvadorans struggled to know and understand their history, I would have to do the same. And just as they faced incredible opposition in their demand for justice and peace, I would also face a culture hostile to hearing stories of child sexual abuse taking place in middle-class America in a traditional family setting.

I knew that I could not effectively work with a therapist who had no knowledge of the liberation struggles of Third World peoples. I needed someone who would honor the connection of the personal and the political at the deepest level. I wanted a therapist who had at least a basic understanding of liberation theology, which is the practice of reading and understanding the Bible from the perspective of the poor. And I knew, in my deepest places, that I could not work with a woman.

Initially, I despaired of finding a suitable therapist in the conservative area where I lived. Then a friend told me of a local pastoral counselor who stood in the cold rain one night at a sparsely attended local memorial service for Oscar Romero, the Salvadoran archbishop murdered by the military for his outspoken condemnation of the repression of the poor. The counselor's name was Jim. His wife was active in a Central

American solidarity group in a local Presbyterian church, and he had traveled to Nicaragua with her with a delegation. Nicaragua, like El Salvador, was embroiled in a civil war in which one side was funded by the United States and innocent civilians were being killed.

Jim had left his position as a pastor at a large progressive church and founded a local interfaith counseling center with a group of other helping professionals. I instinctively knew that anyone who would stand in the rain to honor a Salvadoran martyr who most people in my town didn't know was someone I might trust. In April 1992, I wrote Jim a two-page letter that explained the pain and memories that had begun to surface in El Salvador and my need to heal in an environment with a psychotherapist skilled in working with abuse issues who would also honor the importance of my connection to the Salvadoran people.

One week later, Jim called. He said he was deeply moved by my letter, and he hoped he could help. He had a warm voice and an easy laugh. I felt strangely comfortable talking with him. We agreed to meet in a few days. The relationship in which I would eventually come to feel safe enough to allow the violated child to surface and heal was born during that brief telephone conversation. But I had no way of knowing that then; I only knew I wanted to be "fixed" in a few months. I needed to get back to El Salvador. I had wasted enough time on my own pain.

*　　　　　　*　　　　　　*

From my journal…
Dear Susan,
I don't want to distract you or others from the work of solidarity with our Salvadoran sisters and brothers. But I am falling apart, and have no words to tell you how frightened I am. Sometimes a darkness seems to engulf me, and I struggle to remember I serve a God of life and hope. But I'm afraid that if the darkness stays too long, I won't be able to find my way back. The things I need most—community, touch, tears—are the things I

run from. I have to present this strong competent image to the world. It keeps the vulnerability and fear at bay. I am terrified of connecting with any vestige of my childhood. I don't know if I can survive it again. Linda

            *   *   *

The non-profit counseling center was an old renovated farmhouse a 30-minute drive from my home. On its staff were psychologists, licensed therapists from a variety of disciplines and a psychiatrist. A broad base of individuals as well as local congregations of various denominations contributed funds to the center so that clients who could not afford full counseling fees would receive financial assistance. The professionals who worked there did so for lower salaries than what they could have earned in private practice. They were committed to helping people to heal in an environment that would respect their spiritual, as well as emotional needs.

Instead of the cold clinical office space I had expected, Jim's counseling room was cozy and comfortable with a small sofa and several chairs. One chair was a cushioned and well-worn rocker that was clearly Jim's. A coffee cup, file folder, tablet and pen crowded the top of the small table beside of it. A handmade round rug with an outline of an androgynous human figure, arms raised high in joyful freedom, decorated the floor. One entire wall was lined with shelves stacked with books. Delicately curtained windows on either side of the small room added a sense of spaciousness.

I was so fearful about seeing a therapist that I had not allowed myself to form a mental image of what Jim might look like. But when I met him, I had a sudden flash of recognition. I had seen his photograph with a newspaper article about the counseling center several years before. I remembered feeling wistful as I looked at the photo and read the story even though I was adamantly opposed to seeking therapy at the time. Accordingly, the information was tucked away in a box inside my mind and faded from everyday awareness. I had not made this connection when I wrote to Jim or even when we spoke on the phone. It was not until I sat on the sofa in the counseling room across from him that, with a startled sense of deja vu, I recalled the newspaper article.

The only way I could get through the first therapy session was to recall the many brave Salvadorans who had shared their experiences of war, capture, rape and torture with our delegations through the years. By telling us their stories, poor people gained a link to the U.S. media and to the U.S. Congress, who had the power to cut the flow of funds to the Salvadoran military. But there was also clearly a healing component in the telling of stories of surviving atrocities. I admired the courage of people who not only articulated their own violations but also were able to put their experiences into a broader social and political context. A survivor of torture would usually recount the history of government violence against her community before speaking about her own ordeal, placing her violation into the overall context of the struggle of justice. This linking of the personal and political seemed to come naturally in El Salvador. It was the way I wanted to approach therapy.

But as I shared portions of my own story with Jim during our first session, I noticed that the strong, competent and capable image that I worked so hard to present to the world began to crumble. Despite my desire to be as brave as a Salvadoran and tell my story in a dignified adult way, his careful questions penetrated my defenses. I expected him to concentrate on the experience of molestation when I was five and the later rape. Instead, he was gently exploring the lack of protection and nurture that seemed to characterize my childhood.

When he asked about my relationship with my parents, it was as though a blanket of wet fog had been thrown over my mind. It had never occurred to me that I lacked protection. The concept of protection was one that I applied only to other people, especially to the poor peasants in El Salvador. I never considered that I had a right to protection as a child, and I had no real understanding of what it meant to be nurtured. My parents kept a roof over my head and food on the table, and I had piano lessons, even though I did not like them. As my father earned more money and prospered in the quest for the American dream, my parents provided nice clothes, toys and summer vacations, reminding me of how lucky I was compared to children living under communism and starving in China. I thought this made them good parents. That my father stopped talking to me after Tommy molested me or that my mother stripped and beat me regularly did not seem to me to be out of the ordinary.

When the session ended almost two hours later, I was completely exhausted and felt as fragile as an eggshell. Although Jim was not intrusive, it seemed as though he had traveled to a place in my inner self where no one else had ever gone. I felt the stirrings of the beginning of the clamor from the long-silenced child who had been hidden inside of me and was yearning to be heard. Locked away in internal war zones, this part of me held the vulnerability and pain I would need to face in order to heal.

Still in a daze but trying to shift back into an adult state, I asked Jim if he would be comfortable working with me. He was silent for a moment. Then he said, "No. Not exactly comfortable. Listening to your pain makes me feel like you do when you listen to the suffering of Salvadorans."

I gave him a poem that I had written and asked if I could come for sessions every three weeks. My budget was strained from the trips to El Salvador and the work associated with education and advocacy. Jim said I could draw on the scholarship fund established by the counseling center's supporters; he didn't think it was a good idea to wait three weeks before coming again. I made an appointment for the next week and quickly left. I was feeling dizzy and sick. On the way home, on familiar roads and in territory where I have lived all of my life, I got completely lost. It was as if a child who had no knowledge of cars or roads took control. It took hours to find my way home.

*   *   *

Despite the fact a part of my brain had stored the memory of Jim's newspaper photograph for several years, I would not have recognized him if I had seen him on the street at any time during my first few months of therapy. The therapy visits made me feel as if I was skirting the edges of a bottomless pit of pain. Every survival instinct I possessed warned me not to fall into this abyss.

I became intimately familiar with Jim's shoes, which is where I most often directed my eyes. His shoes were dark brown with the kind of wear and scuff marks that most often denote a pair of old and comfortable favorites. He usually sat still, with both feet firmly planted on the floor. This was good, because the slightest movement on his part scared me. Like many survivors of sexual violence, I carried the shame that rightfully belonged to my perpetrators and could hardly look at Jim's face. I was sure that some time soon he was going to be completely disgusted with me and tell me not to come to sessions any more.

I left each session disoriented and feeling as though I was living in two time zones: my childhood and the present-day reality. The lines between the two were increasingly blurred. At times, there seemed to be several child parts within me. Eventually, I could identify three.

The one who appeared to hold the potential for healing despite her shattered state I eventually came to simply call "the Child." She held tremendous pain but also carried within her seeds of hope and resistance that had never been entirely snuffed out. She was the one who usually surfaced with Jim, drawn by his patience in letting her approach him only if she chose to do so. She was terrified, yet fascinated, by this adult-person with power who did not want to hurt her and expressed sadness at her suffering. In her experience, most adults were not safe to be around. They inflicted pain and ignored her wounds. The Child existed within me and yet was separate from me, seemingly capable of speaking without my consent. I cannot explain how this is possible.

The other two child parts were less defined, more like fragments that existed for specific and limited purposes. The stronger part held an absolutely forbidden emotion that I would understand much later to be anger. It was her job to keep this emotion from being felt or even acknowledged. She accomplished this in several ways, one of which was abruptly closing up the air passage in my throat so that any rage threatening to escape would be pushed back into its cage and familiar numbness by the imperative to breathe. Bewildered, I would at times find myself gasping for air and holding my throat, not knowing what happened except that for a few seconds, something completely foreign to me had suddenly entered my awareness. I did not recognize this emotion as anger, since I did not know what anger felt like. I called this child part Amy. Her second method of controlling anger was to hurt herself. "Accidental" bruises, burns from a hot stove, cuts from kitchen knives and broken dishes appeared mysteriously in her wake. Amy craved punishment and claimed to like pain. She was quite secretive and rarely talked directly to Jim.

The third and most ethereal child part spoke to no one. She was mute and frozen in the past. She did not interact with the world, but she viewed it with eyes that reflected a shocked emptiness sometimes evident in the eyes of children exposed to the horrors of war. She manifested in absolute stillness and silence. She felt nothing. This child part had no name.

I do not comfortably wear any of the designated psychiatric labels for people with my experience, and I do not believe I have multiple personalities. I am dissociative. I suffer from post-traumatic stress. But there are many more ways of surviving trauma than are defined by medical diagnosis. Jim's philosophy was that human beings are a mystery, each of us unique. And whenever we try to fit one into a diagnostic box, we lose some of that person's essential nature. My diagnosis was of no great importance to me; rather, the imperative was to heal. And that turned out to be a constantly changing, evolving process.

*   *   *

After each session, I would journal furiously, trying to capture the emerging pieces of what seemed to be a giant puzzle. I desperately wanted to heal, and I feared that if I did not write the details quickly, the memories of what had transpired in the therapy room would evaporate like so much of the rest of my life. I would need to concentrate on what was happening in therapy in order to heal. Although Jim encouraged me to slow down and let the therapeutic process take its natural course, I felt a constant sense of urgency. I had to make the pain stop. I was sure I was running out of time.

In the beginning, Jim drew on my Salvadoran experience to help me develop a framework for healing. He asked me what I would suggest to a Salvadoran peasant who had been tortured by the military. I answered like an activist: I proceeded to outline a process of public denunciation of the violation, filing reports with human rights groups, perhaps organizing a protest march.

"And what about you?" he asked softly. "What kinds of things would you propose to do about what happened to you?"

At a total loss, I fumbled. He pressed on: could I come up with a plan, even if it seemed completely implausible right now? Grasping at straws, I rambled on about writing letters to the newspapers and organizing some sort of survivors' march.

He said that those were good things and they could certainly be worked on later in my recovery. But initially, he wanted to propose three primary goals: tears, protest and anger.

There was a silence in the room, and I wanted to disappear. To the person who has not experienced severe trauma, emotions such as sadness and anger are basic. Protest over being unjustly hurt is a natural response. But to me, these goals sounded terrifying and unachievable. I sat miserably on the sofa, trying to figure out a way to explain that these were not reasonable goals for me.

He listened carefully to my defensive reactions. When I was finished, he asked one question: "Do you want to heal?"

The river of pain that had carried me this far suddenly swept through my consciousness in a torrent. I knew I could not survive in its currents indefinitely. I was growing too exhausted and weak. My choices were to heal or to die. Feeling as though I was making a commitment to enter a wilderness from which I might never return, I looked at Jim and nodded.

"Yes." My voice was a strangled whisper, but it sufficed as enough commitment.

"Good," he said. "It's important to *want* to heal."

He looked at me with compassion and appeared to measure his words carefully. "Tears, protest and anger are what you will need to experience in order to heal. We'll make those our goals. Is that all right with you?"

I felt like I was falling into what I would later come to define as child space, leaving behind everything that is familiar. In child space, everything looks huge and unfamiliar, and I experience terror, chaos, and pain. I nodded. Tears, protest and anger lived in child space. They would now be my goals. I desperately wanted to heal.

*   *   *

In the early 1980s, I briefly entered into a counseling relationship with the pastor of the church I attended. My husband Steve and I were increasingly estranged from each other, with our sexual life being one of the major areas of conflict.

When I met Steve at sixteen, I was intrigued with his gentleness. He was quiet and shy, so distinctly different than the jaded older men in the drug culture who I had been acquainted with since I turned thirteen. His family had moved to Pennsylvania ten years earlier when the coal mines in the mountains of their native Virginia shut down and his father, like thousands of other miners, migrated to the factories in northern states to find work. We met by chance one night at a bowling alley where I was waiting for a friend to show up and go to a party with me.

I had never heard of Steve. But my reputation for wildness was a local legend, and he told me later that he had heard a lot about me, including the fact that I was an "easy lay" and good drug connection. Steve had little experience with the drug scene or with women. Although he was three years older, he seemed like a babe in the woods as he tried to impress me. I was attracted to his innocence and naiveté as much as his green eyes. Within a few weeks, we began to see each other regularly. For the first time in my life, I was with a man who wanted a relationship with me instead of just sex.

After being raped when I was twelve, I had taken a promiscuous route, not uncommon with survivors of sexual abuse who frequently go to extremes with sexuality—indiscriminately engaging in casual sexual encounters or completely avoiding sex. Rather than interact with boys who were my peers, I gravitated to men who were much older. By the time I was sixteen, I had been sexually involved with so many men I could not begin to remember their names. I deluded myself into believing I was taking control when men found me desirable and wanted to have sex with me although I know now that I was merely a toy to them. At the time, however, I was obsessed with being extremely compliant and performing well during sex, no matter how degrading or violent, and was perfectly obedient to whatever perverse command was given.

I never stayed emotionally present during sexual activity. I felt pleasure, but only in an animalistic sense that was made possible by my deliberate disconnection from the human being I was coupled with. Although I was often under the influence of one or another kind of drug, in reality I did not need chemicals to obtain the necessary emotional distance.

I thought of other things and let my body function on a kind of automatic pilot. When sex was over, I felt briefly triumphant: I had proven once again that my body could be penetrated and yet "I" was not touched. I made great distinctions between "me" and my body. My body was like a foreign object and I felt no connection to it; what happened to it was of no great concern to me. If necessary, I could numb myself to whatever pain was inflicted on it. And I believed that my body existed primarily for the purpose of being used—and hurt—by others. Following the brief moment of triumph, I inevitably was flooded with feelings of dirtiness.

Despite the years of casual sex, I had never become pregnant even though I had never used any method of birth control. It was ironic that I would become pregnant with Steve's child within a few months after the beginning of our relationship. We married when I was barely seventeen and still pregnant with our first son.

When I asked my pastor for advice, Steve and I had been married for about ten years. My desire for sex had diminished with each passing year until I literally had to force myself to endure sexual activity. Steve felt rejected and frustrated, and I felt close to panic that I could not make the kind of emotional connection he seemed to think was natural when two people loved each other.

To me, sexual activity and emotions had to be completely separate. I loved Steve because he never hurt me and was gentle and patient. Therefore, I could not enjoy having sex with him. In order to have sex, I required either complete emotional distance or humiliation and pain. Although I was not conscious of it at the time, experiences in my earliest childhood had resulted in an internal split in which I was forced to separate the mother who loved me from the one that sexually abused me in order to psychologically survive. A child cannot bear to fully know that the parent upon whom she depends for nurture and love is also the one who violates her. The mother who nurtures cannot be the same mother who rapes. I cemented this deep disconnection between love and sexuality in adolescence and carried it into adulthood and marriage. When I had sex, emotional involvement with Steve with the last thing on my mind. My head was filled with dark and violent images that would not be banished.

After we had been married about a month, I was horrified to find that each time Steve touched me, my mind flew to a fantasy I had not had since first grade. The first time it came careening into my brain as Steve and I made love, I was physically ill for days. I could not understand why it was surfacing now that I was safe in a loving and secure relationship

I can remember sitting in my first grade classroom, squirming on the hard chair as I masturbated during class by squeezing my legs together, actions which resulted in multiple orgasms. Several times during the day, my mind would leave the classroom, and I would find myself in a strangely familiar place I could not name with a woman whose face I could never see. She was someone I both loved and hated, and she held unlimited power over me.

The fantasy never varied. It was dismal in its sameness and required no creativity on my part: the woman always took off my dress, pulled down my underwear, laid me across her lap and spanked me. I knew she spanked me because I was dirty and she was trying hard to make me clean. I hated the fantasy but felt powerless to stop it.

More than 20 years later, I felt helpless in the grip of this strange fantasy. I was unable to have intercourse with my husband unless I imagined that I was being punished by a woman. I was deeply ashamed of myself for these thoughts, but it seemed that allowing the fantasy to run its course was the only way I could tolerate sexual activity. Pain and pleasure seemed to be deeply linked within my body.

Without being too explicit, I told my pastor that I needed to imagine I was being beaten in order to have sex with my husband. After a short discussion, he came up with a suggestion: why not act out the fantasy and see if its power would be diminished by making it real? As long as

I was not going to be seriously injured, he saw no harm in it. And perhaps it would restore our sex life.

I had no frame of reference to understand that I had just received very dangerous advice by an incompetent counselor. I was anxious to save my marriage, and I was convinced that my husband would leave me if I could not respond differently with the sexual aspect of our life. It seemed wrong to ask Steve, who never lifted a hand against me, to hit me so we could enjoy sex. But since my pastor suggested it, I rationalized, it must be a good course of action. I gathered my courage to talk to Steve about it.

At first my husband was shocked at this suggestion. But eventually he agreed to try it in the hope it would improve our sexual relationship. On an Easter weekend in the early 1980s, we took our pastor's advice and entered into a journey toward pain so that we could once again enjoy sex. And the child who learned not only to tolerate but crave punishment was resurrected that Easter.

Unfortunately, our move to sadomasochism, popularly known as S&M, did not have the effect that our pastor predicted. The fantasy was not lessened by the reality of being beaten, and I was horrified and shaken to find that my body actually responded sexually to the pain. I begged Steve to hit me harder, and I had orgasms simply from the pain; sex was not even necessary. I learned I could tolerate the sex if I was punished first. I took cold pleasure in making my husband hit me until my body became numb and my mind floated free, completely distanced from what was happening to my flesh. It seemed essential to me to be able to control the pain.

Occasionally Steve would pick up pornographic movies or books that focused on topics of sadistic pleasure and pain. I understood we were both searching for some way to normalize our experience, and the pornographic materials made it seem like we were two more consenting adults engaging in S&M, a not-uncommon choice. I tried to convince myself that we were simply having modern and liberated sex. This was not difficult because our culture portrays sex as a commodity that sells everything from cars to jeans, and music videos showcase women being whipped in cages while magazines like Playboy and Hustler that degrade and exploit women are no longer considered hard-core porn because so many other publications have surpassed them in the depth of depravity that is depicted in their pages.

Steve never liked hitting me although he did like the sex that followed. I felt filled with despair and increasingly suicidal following each time we acted out these roles of perpetrator and victim. Yet I was compelled by some inner force to continue. Every few weeks, I would feel as though I "had" to be punished, and once that craving surfaced, I could think of nothing else. There was a terrible feeling of dread and a desire to get the punishment over with. It was as though a powerful negative energy entered me against my will and grew steadily stronger and more dangerous until it felt as if I would implode if I could not find a way to release it. And the only way I knew how to do that was to be beaten. Afterwards, the relentless energy impelling me toward pain would be gone, leaving in its place a sense of desolation and despair at having once again been helpless against its force.

I told myself that I was in charge of the scenario and that I could choose to stop at any time. But the reality was that I was no more in control than I was when I was a child. Of course, I was not ready to admit that yet.

*   *   *

Five years later, I began my journey of accompaniment of the Salvadoran poor. Like most North Americans who travel to Central America to "help" the people there, I quickly discovered that these poor uneducated peasants would become my teachers in faith and in life. What they had to offer was equally as essential as the protection that I could offer to them by my presence in their war-torn communities. I underwent a profound spiritual transformation and developed a political consciousness that was rooted in viewing the structures of the world from the perspective of the most vulnerable.

I attended church regularly as a child. Each Sunday morning, our family had dressed up in clothes we could not afford and went to worship at a church where seating was predicated upon social class. The town's elite sat in the front rows by unspoken common assent. In the car on the way home, my parents would inevitably begin to fight. It was as if the tensions that ran just below our surface appearance as a respectable Christian family were magnified by this weekly ritual.

As an adult, I continued to attend worship services out of habit. I instinctively honed in on the ugly realities behind the masks many parishioners wore. Racism, greed, and contempt for those unlike themselves were evident by peering behind only the first layer of pretense. My childhood had trained me well for this observation and led to the cynical conviction that no one actually tried to follow the Jesus who loved children and the poor; who lived without material possessions; and who made it clear that blood ties were not the only definition of family. Despite what was preached from the pulpit, this Jesus was not taken seriously.

In El Salvador, I discovered a God who walks and suffers with *El Pueblo*—with the *people who suffer and who struggle for justice*. From the Salvadoran poor, I learned the values of hope, community and resistance to unjust power. Values imposed by my parents and reinforced by culture and church such as obedience to authority, the privacy and privilege of the nuclear family, and submission to suffering were slowly transformed. I began to understand that God was not in an irrevocable alliance with the powerful.

I immersed myself in studying the writings of Oscar Romero, the bishop who had been murdered because of his defense of the poor in their struggle for liberation from economic, social and political oppression.

I listened carefully to the testimonies of people who struggled for a just peace without resorting to the kind of violence they were daily subjected to. I watched in helpless fury when I saw that U.S. and European teachers, doctors and church workers among the poor invited suspicion, and I saw how the military arbitrarily arrested Salvadoran community leaders who risked their lives to help their people. Poor peasants who served as health promoters, reading tutors and pastors who were traveling among various communities in zones known to be supportive of the FMLN, were frequently murdered. Like Romero, they became martyrs and inspired others to take up their work and continue. In this war-torn land where life was so easily taken, I began to understand that each human being has value and is cherished in the eyes of God.

Accompaniment goes beyond solidarity in that anyone who enters into it risks suffering the pain of those we would accompany. As it is commonly understood in the United States, solidarity is mostly expressed in political actions ranging from protest marches to pressing for changes in law and policy to going to jail for civil disobedience out of belief that a certain law is unjust and that one must follow a higher moral authority for ethical integrity. Solidarity generally operates on the assumption that our actions can eventually bring about the changes we want.

Accompaniment may include all of these actions, but it does not necessarily share the assumption that we can fix, save or change a situation or person by what we do. It calls for us to walk with those we accompany, forming relationships and sharing risks, joys and lives. We enter into the world of the one who suffers with no assurance that we can change or fix anything. The primary purpose is to be fully present so that the pain is not endured alone. In El Salvador, we understood the path of accompaniment might lead to death—our own or of those we accompanied. This would be a great tragedy but not failure. Accompaniment is based on hope despite evidence that there is little reason for optimism.

When Salvadorans spoke of being in solidarity, the term encompassed both political action and deep relational connection. As a value, solidarity stands in sharp contrast to the value of individualism, which is held in high regard by the culture of the United States. Solidarity respects each individual, but it does not promote basing personal actions solely on self-interest. When we live in solidarity, we understand we are an integral part of a relational web of connections, and each of our actions has impact upon the web. When we live in solidarity, we drop our masks and see each other's true faces. We practice values of honesty, openness and community.

As I watched people tenderly care for bodies and spirits of others who had been wounded by bullets, rape, hunger or torture, I began to question my own willingness to have harm inflicted on my body. The dichotomy between the values of hope, resistance and courage that I was learning in El Salvador and my need to be hurt, as well as the secrecy and shame surrounding it, became glaringly painful. The Salvadorans were struggling for liberation from external oppression. After several years of work in El Salvador, I made the decision that I would not permit myself to be beaten any more. My struggle would be for liberation from the internal forces that bound me to pain.

When I told Steve about my decision, he was somewhat relieved. He had never been able to enjoy the violent and abusive role he was asked to play. He wondered what would happen to our sex life, and I assured him I was going to do my best to try to be "normal." I naively imagined that sheer will power could transform me into a person who enjoyed a healthy sexuality rather than one intricately woven with pain. But within a few months, our sex life stopped completely by mutual, but unspoken, consent. Although I tried to stay sexually active, it was clear to both of us I merely endured this aspect of our relationship. I could not tolerate sex without pain. The linkage was too deep.

* * *

I agonized about telling Jim about this aspect of my life. Talking about what I had experienced as a child was one thing; but the S&M was an adult choice, an activity that I freely entered into—or so I thought at the time, not yet understanding the power of unresolved childhood trauma to compel re-enactment of the abuse.

Yet I was firmly committed to truth-telling in therapy. I knew Jim could not help me unless I opened even my most painful and wounded places to the light of his care. I prayed that he would not hate me and that I would not see the disgust I dreaded in his eyes once he knew this about me.

Gathering my courage, I finally told him about the link between pleasure and pain and how it had played out in my married life. I emphasized that the choice to be punished in this way was my decision, not something Steve imposed or even wanted.

When I finished my story, I was trembling from head to toe. In the short time we had worked together, the Child was already making deep connections with this gentle person who seemed almost parent-like but did not want to hurt us. The shame that I felt was immense.

Jim was quiet for a while when I finished. He checked to be sure he understood correctly: I was no longer engaging in S&M and I was not currently being beaten. I nodded.

He said that was good, and the situation needed to stay that way. Unlike the pastor I had counseled with years before, Jim did not think that acting out violent fantasies was therapeutic.

I kept my eyes focused on his shoes. I was waiting to be told that he could not see me any more; that I was too sick, too perverted to be helped. Instead, to my utter amazement, I heard him say that I have a gift for articulating my story. And that he was deeply grateful for my sharing something so intimate and obviously painful with him. It was a measure of the trust I was developing for him. He reaffirmed that he was moved by my suffering and courage and that he wanted to accompany me as I healed. I looked up at him as he said, "Your life has been like a war zone. I can understand why you are so at home in El Salvador."

For the first time, tears almost leaked by my defenses. I heard the steel door quickly slam—my reliable defense mechanism that kicked in when dangerous emotions got close to the surface. Tears might be on the list as one of our stated goals. But I wasn't ready to cry.

Trying to find words to describe my internal reality, I told Jim about the sensation of tears being close to the surface and then being suddenly shut down. I remembered the sound of that door slamming from times when my mother slapped me hard across the face and I had to react quickly by remaining expressionless. Most of all, I had to repress my desire to cry because tears only enraged her more. But Jim was not critical that I allowed the door to slam shut on my tears. "When you're ready, you'll have your tears," he assured me.

I literally squirmed on the sofa. There was so much happening inside of me. I heard the voices of what seemed like children all talking at once. I opened my mouth and closed it. There were no words for the chaos that I felt just beneath the surface. Jim said, "The child is surfacing quite a bit now, isn't she?"

She was, and I was terrified of her.

PRISONERS OF WAR

Where did you go when they took away your innocence
destroyed your trust
crushed your spirit
violated your human rights?

Where did you go when they urinated on you
penetrated your body with dirty fingers
and spoke of tying you up on a table
so you could not move when they
stuffed things in your mouth?

Where did you go when they pretended you did not exist
made you play music only for them
when you turned into an ice cube
small, hard and cold
your only options freeze or melt?

Where did you go
when they kept you isolated
put you in the hospital
and warned you never to speak of it
outside of the walls

> *of a torture chamber in El Salvador*
> *Surely, woman, you were held by the military*
> *named by Amnesty as*
> *a world class violator of human rights*

this is just one more instance
that will be denounced, reported to the press
we'll have a demonstration in the capital city......

No. Don't speak to the woman.
Speak to the child
who saw it all and fled
to a place inside her mind
where they could not follow.
It was not the walls of a prison that held her
but the walls of a middle-class house
traditional family
made in the USA
and a child has no human rights to speak of within those walls.

There will be no demonstration
no great march
no international outcry
only lies and silence and smiles
to cover up the evil that lies at the heart
of the great sacred institution of "family"
upon which this nation is built

Weep for the woman held by the military in a foreign land
Weep for the child held by her family in the United States
prisoners of war
they share common ground.

Somebody should tell Amnesty.

Chapter 4

Remembering What I Needed to Forget

In 1990, I visited a community called Comunidad Ellacuria in the rugged mountains of northern El Salvador in the Department of Chalatenango. Its residents were part of the re-population movement, returning to reclaim the land and rebuild homes after spending years in refugee camps. Their strategy was to develop schools, clinics and small businesses with the help of churches from the United States, transforming refugee settlements into thriving communities. Many of the re-populations were in Chalatenango, long considered a part of the country with strong support for the FMLN. The military was furious that these lands, from which people had been driven years earlier by the scorched earth campaigns, were once again being inhabited. As visible signs of resistance to the government, they were targets of frequent harassment by the military. In order to travel to a community such as the one we were visiting, *salvos* were required.

Comunidad Ellacuria had been named after Father Ignacio Ellacuria, one of the six Jesuit priests murdered in 1989. Father Ellacuria was a brilliant scholar and professor well known for his incisive political and social analysis. Although he traveled the world and his opinion was sought by bishops, heads of state and occasionally members of the U.S. Congress, he spent as much time as possible in poor communities, particularly those involved in the re-populations. He was passionate about the right of the *campesinos* to reclaim their land.

Those who knew him well talked of how intimidating he could be when in the presence of powerful officials or visiting dignitaries. He was outspoken in his denunciation of the repression against the poor and unrelenting in his calls for justice. Yet when he visited poor communities, this fiery intellect became gentle and humble. He believed that God was manifested in the struggle of the *campesinos,* and the brilliant theological treatises that flowed from his pen were always grounded in the perspective of the most vulnerable. Since theology, like history, is usually written from the viewpoint of the powerful, this was a radical departure from centuries of tradition. This kind of creed, which developed and flourished in Latin America and South Africa, is known as liberation theology. Salvation is viewed holistically and takes into account aspects of the economic, social and political context in which people live.

The government wanted to annihilate these communities of re-population for reasons that went far beyond their physical presence. In Comunidad Ellacuria, as in the other villages, there was an irrepressible spirit of resistance that sustained hope. The people were committed to living cooperatively, sharing their goods and possessions as did the early Christian communities described in the New Testament. If any one was suffering emotionally, he or she was listened to and comforted by the community. Solidarity, rather than competition or individualism, was the highest value. Children were treated as precious gifts to the community and raised by the whole village. Beautifully painted murals decorated public buildings, attesting to a love for art and creativity.

The kind of resistance demonstrated by reclamation of the land and the construction of new social and economic structures on a small scale was a threat to the prevailing order. The fact that communities took on the names of martyrs such as Ignacio Ellacuria testified to their belief that the spirit of those murdered in the struggle for justice was resurrected in the poor. And it is precisely this kind of hope that repressive powers cannot abide.

Although Comunidad Ellacuria had been settled only a few years before, the people had already accumulated a tragic history. A recent attack by the Salvadoran air force meant to intimidate the villagers had left four children and one man dead. A brightly painted mural on the lone remaining wall of a small hut depicted helicopters with fire streaming down from their metal bellies. Tiny figures on the ground were bursting into flames. Small crosses made of sticks and decorated with brightly colored ribbons were planted in the earth beneath the wall in memory of the children who had died during the bombardment. Aprons and tablecloths embroidered by the women's sewing collective reflected scenes not of domestic tranquillity but of homes exploding from bombs and children's broken bodies. Like survivors of the Holocaust in Europe in the 1930s and 1940s, the Salvadorans were determined their stories would be told and their suffering would be remembered.

In the community's small church, a hand-crafted wooden cross loomed as the focal point of the bare sanctuary. It was unlike any cross I had ever seen: it was not empty nor did it bear an image of the crucified Jesus. The Salvadorans placed on the cross dozens of photographs of the mangled bloody bodies of the small children killed during the recent strafing of the village. The photographs had been taken by a U.S. church worker who was living in accompaniment with the community when it was attacked; she took the photos with her Polaroid camera not only with permission but also the urging of the people.

The large cross stood in silent rebuke to the madness of war and to the artillery shells, made in the United States, which had been carefully collected and placed at its base. As in most wars, it is the children who suffer the most and pay the highest price. They have no choice about the choices of adults.

During one therapy session, I described my visit to this community to Jim. He asked what symbols I would put on a cross to bear witness to my own story. I could not think of any symbols. I wanted clear, stark pictures of my reality as a child—like the ones the Salvadorans placed on the cross. But unlike atrocities in war, violence within middle-class families is usually carefully hidden. There are no photographs of the rapes, beatings and tortures that children endure at the hands of their parents. There is no community to grieve over lost innocence, broken bodies and wounded spirits.

Where are our crosses for the tens of thousands of children whose bodies and spirits have been crushed by the very people entrusted to take care of them? Who remembers the suffering and losses of survivors of incest and abuse and gives the suffering a central place in our communities? In 1992, there were more than three million reported cases of child abuse in the United States. Will these children be told when they grow up that their memories are false? How many will recant and deny their own history in order to pacify their families and the wider culture?

Unlike the Salvadorans who placed the photos of the children in a public place so no one could ever forget, we do everything we can to hide the ugly face of family violence and to silence the voices of survivors. Denial is so much more comfortable than truth.

*   *   *

Jim believed that I was moving very rapidly in therapy. At times, he urged me to step back and take some breathing space. But the movement of pain within me was inexorable; it felt as though I would die if I could not relieve some of the terrible pressure coming up from the deepest reaches of my soul. Stepping back did not feel like an option.

One afternoon, I decided to tell Jim every detail about the day my mother beat me all the way down the road from my grandmother's house. The Child wanted him to know how she stripped and beat us when we got home and then forced us to play hymns on the piano for her. This was an incident I had always remembered vividly, although I worked hard to forget it and to minimize the damage inflicted on me by my mother's violence. For the last few weeks, memories of the afternoon the music died seemed to be constantly present. I hoped that talking with Jim about it might somehow make the memory go back to its place on the shelf of history. However, I was to discover that it took many renderings of a traumatic experience until the memory began to lose some of its power to intrude uninvited into my daily life.

Toward the end of the session, Jim was reflecting on how we could not seem to find any nurturing presence in my life as a child. After Tommy molested me, my father, who was my source of physical affection, stopped holding me. My mother permitted me to have very little contact with my father's relatives. I had no real interaction with the outside world, other than school, up until I was twelve. Awkward with children my age and unable to play easily, I did not make many friends. My sister and I seemed to exist in different worlds, although we lived in the same family in the same house.

The only nurturing presence I could recall was my third grade teacher, Mrs. Shreiner. A matronly, plump woman, she was kind and soft spoken to her charges. One day, she asked us to write a short story, which in third grade meant about two or three pages. She seemed stunned when I turned in twenty sheets of yellow notebook paper neatly printed in pencil. I had written a story about a frightened, abandoned girl and a magic boy hero who escape the world of adults to live on their own deserted island. They thrived and had a wonderful life eating fruit, living in a tree house, and swimming in the ocean. The girl never wanted to go back to the other world.

I remember she praised my writing ability and thereafter encouraged me to write for her. She told me that one day I would be a famous author. I liked Mrs. Shreiner. The next year, a school redistricting transferred me to a different school. I did not see Mrs. Shreiner anymore.

I shrugged off this loss, as well as the lack of touch and nurturing as though they were not important. More than that, it was something I did not want to even think about.

But Jim persisted. "How about your mother?" he asked. "Did she ever hold you?"

"Only when she was hitting me."

The words were out of my mouth before I could stop them, and I was horrified at their stark truth. This was the only kind of touch I could remember receiving from my mother.

The room was silent. I felt a huge wave of fear begin to build upwards from the pit of my stomach and my head suddenly hurt. It was as though I was opening a door to a place that I had needed to forget in order to survive. I was sure I did not want to remember what was locked away there. I twisted my hands and focused on Jim's shoes. I didn't care if anybody held me or not.

"Only when she was hitting you," Jim said the words slowly and in measured tones.

Shame so deep that it seemed part of my essential nature streamed through my body. I felt the dirtiness surely had to be visible. I desperately wanted this line of questioning to stop. Our time was almost up, and I was relieved. Then Jim said, "I want you to hold that image of her beating you until the next session."

I risked a quick look at his face. I saw the stern quiet anger that was evident when I had earlier described the day when my music irrevocably left me. I was silent. I felt like I was falling into the dreaded child space, and I did not want to be there as the session was ending.

"We'll talk about it more next time," he said firmly. "OK?"

I nodded reluctant assent, nausea rising in my stomach. I most definitely did not want to hold this thought until the next session. To the contrary, I wanted to stuff it back into the box inside of me and jam the box into the furthermost corner of my mind. Those kinds of thoughts are the source of nightmares.

*　　　　*　　　　*

Three days later, I fell into what seemed like a waking nightmare. I remembered an incident that helped me understand the fantasy that had dominated my married life. In psychological terms, the waking nightmare might be called a flashback, which is common as memories awaken within survivors of trauma. Flashbacks are more than remembering a terrible incident in an intellectual way and being able to verbally recount what happened. Instead, the survivor literally feels as if she is re-living the experience, entering into all of its sensory pain and terror as though it is happening in the present.

Trauma is encoded differently in the brain than normal memory. At times, when pain and fear are so overwhelming that a child is unable to adequately process what is happening, the traumatic experience is split into a separate place in the brain's memory and body's memory. Inaccessible to the child, the traumatic memory remains sealed— much like time in a bottle, captured intact, too painful to remember and too difficult to emotionally integrate. However, a memory can be inadvertently triggered by a sight, sound, smell or any part of an ordinary experience that is reminiscent of the original traumatic experience. Survivors usually have no control with this regression, and a large part of healing is learning how to contain the traumatic material and also be able to step in and out of the traumatic material in a more conscious way.

✳   ✳   ✳

As I drove to work on a Tuesday morning, still upset about being asked to hold the thought of my mother beating me until the next therapy session, the first of many time capsule bottles burst. My breath caught in my throat, and my hands gripped the wheel tightly, more as an anchor to hold than to steer the car. It felt as though I was being bombarded from the inside with memories hurled like jagged stones against soft flesh, tearing without mercy through walls built many years ago to contain them.

The images of this time capsule that had been compressed for so long began rushing into my brain, and I almost swerved off of the road. Instead of the four-lane highway where I was traveling at high speed, I saw myself at the age of five, standing before my mother in the parlor of our tiny house.

*   *   *

Remembering...

It is night time, and I am wearing my pajamas. I am in my bed. Mommy calls me into the living room. The TV is on, and she looks pretty. I am sleepy. She is drinking a bottle of beer. She tells me she is going to spank me because I am a bad girl. She says, "Come here!" and I walk over to the sofa. I am afraid. She is mad at me, but I don't know what I did. I'm not awake yet.

She pulls down my pajama bottom and panties and puts me over her lap. I wait a long time for her to hit me. She is telling me she is going to spank my bottom until it's really red. While she talks to me, she rubs her hands all over my bottom and between my legs.

I feel dizzy upside down. The TV is close to my face, and it is too loud. She begins to spank me with her hand, and it hurts. I am crying. She finally stops, and rubs my bottom all over. Now she is gentle. She tells me in a soft sing-song voice that I am dirty and a bad girl and I have to be spanked hard. I am really crying now. There is a beer bottle to the left of my face on the floor. Mommy reaches down and picks up the bottle. I hear the noise of her drinking, and, then she puts the bottle down and starts hitting me again.

There are times of spanking and times of rubbing. My tears are splashing into a puddle on the linoleum floor. But she is telling me that my bottom isn't red enough yet, and she has to spank me until it gets to be the right color. I twist around to try to see for myself. But when I see my mother's face, I forget about trying to look at my bottom. Mommy's eyes are shiny and bright, and her face is all happy in a terrible way. I am terrified of her; she is not my mommy, she is someone else. She sees me looking at her, and yells at me to put my head down.

I know now there is someone else in this room—someone is standing along the wall watching us. I can't see who it is. He has green pants and shoes like my Daddy wears. Finally, she is finished. I run to the bedroom that I share with my mother, father and younger sister and jump back into bed.

*   *   *

I came back to the present, inching down the highway in a daze at about ten miles per hour. Cars whizzed by, blowing their horns. I managed to pull over and park by the side of the road, shaking and heaving. I wanted to die. In the midst of the horror and shock, I was experiencing sexual stimulation. I felt so overwhelmed with shame that it seemed to seep through my skin and drip from my body, a visible sign that I was a vile creature and did not deserve to live. With a rush of awareness, I understood that my mother was sexually stimulated by spanking me. I had remembered being stripped and beaten by her many times when I was older, such as the day she beat me for visiting my grandmother instead of practicing the piano. But this was a memory rooted in an earlier time, and it had a clear sexual component.

I was gagging, nauseated and shaking like a leaf. All I could think of was that I had to get to work. I pulled out into traffic without even looking. Horns blared again. An angel must have protected me that day on the highway because I was able to get to my place of work safely. At work, I locked myself in the bathroom and curled up on the floor in a small ball, my knees tucked to my chest. As I rocked myself back and forth, I felt a welcome white shield fogging my mind. The rocking and blankness were my old friends. Slowly, the memories and shame began to recede. My breathing slowed and became shallow. I pinched my arm as hard as I could, and felt nothing. When the numbness was complete, I came out and went to my desk. I knew how to function, no matter what. I logged into my computer to check my e-mail messages and find out what the overseas financial markets had done during the night.

The next session with Jim was more than two days away. I was still light years from being able ask him for extra help. Calling him was not a possibility; it was unthinkable to the frightened child who now took control within me to need anybody or anything. In her experience, needs were too painful to ever acknowledge since they were never met, and it was better not to need at all. The images that had spilled from my time capsule bottle would not be banished. They now haunted me every waking moment. Sleep was impossible. To my horror, my body was flooded with unbearable sexual stimulation at the memories, which only proved to me that I was totally disgusting, beyond redemption.

By the following night, I was almost overcome with the need to hurt myself. I walked around the kitchen with knives in my hand, shaking and crying. If hurting myself could stop the images and floods of stimulation I was perfectly willing to hurt myself. I clutched my bottle of prescription sleeping pills in one hand and a knife in the other as I paced. If all else failed to stop the pain, these pills were my final solution.

Susan called. She could tell something was wrong by my voice, which she later told me sounded strangely young. She asked me immediately what was happening. I managed to convey I had been flooded with terrible memories about my mother, but I was too ashamed to give her any details. When I told her I had to hurt myself because I could not stand the pain anymore, she implored me to call Jim, but it was beyond me to need him that much. I was totally intransigent about it and close to being hysterical. Understanding quickly she was dealing with a terrified child and not an adult, she talked to me for hours, persuading me to not hurt myself and telling me that I was wonderful and good and brave. She promised that it would not always hurt this much. Somehow, I survived the night.

          *   *   *

The first night that I spent in the Salvadoran community of Panchimilama I did not sleep at all. The village of several hundred refugees had been the target of military harassment since it had been settled with the help of the Lutheran church several months previously. Church and community leaders had been "disappeared" by shadowy men in civilian dress in dark-windowed vans. Although the government disclaimed any connection with the death squads, these men traveled openly through army-held territory and carried military weapons.

Recently the community had been subjected to psychological terror as airplanes bombed the perimeter of the village. Medardo Gomez, the Lutheran bishop, personally assigned our delegation to Panchimilama when we arrived for that trip. When we asked him why, his response was simple and direct: "You will protect the people if the military comes."

As I lay in my straw-mat cot during the long, sleepless night, I heard gunfire coming uncomfortably close in the surrounding jungle. I knew that the FMLN resistance protected this community from the army to the best of their ability; I also knew that the FMLN was no match in firepower for the Salvadoran military. Uncomfortable and cold, I wondered what was happening in the jungle as I twisted and turned on my thin mat. I understood that the military watched our every move and would know that our delegation was sleeping in Panchimilama that night.

On one hand, I felt vulnerable and fragile in the dark jungle night. I did not feel as though my physical presence could possibly offer much protection to the people of the village. On the other hand, I was outraged that in fact it did—that in the eyes of the world, I was a U.S. citizen which meant that my life and well being was so much more valuable than the life of a Salvadoran peasant. If a hundred poor farmers were killed in a bombing raid, it hardly made a blip on the news. But if a U.S. church volunteer was blown to bits by a bomb paid for with U.S. tax dollars, it could create an international incident and jeopardize military funding by Congress.

With more outrage, I remembered the time that we had arranged for a sympathetic U.S. Senate aide to telephone the commanding officer who would be interviewing us during an appointment to receive a safe conduct pass at the *Estado*. I had been at the office when the aide's call came through. The deferential attitude immediately assumed by the commander, who moments before had been arrogant and hostile, was almost amusing to witness. After hanging up the phone, he barked orders for our passes to be issued. He wanted to keep the U.S. dollars flowing and his budget intact.

I was up at first light. I walked to the nearby hut of our hostess, a woman named Santos. She was a remarkable woman, having survived the destruction of her village during the military's scorched earth operations and subsequent years in Mesa Grande, the refugee camp in Honduras. She was thrilled to be back in El Salvador, making a new home in Panchimilama.

Santos, a slim woman with long dark hair, showed a beautiful face that was lined and tired. I believe she was in her late twenties, although it was often difficult to judge the age of most Salvadoran women I met. Poverty and its deprivations often stole beauty before it had a chance to bloom. Because of nutritional deficiencies, back-breaking labor and harsh and primitive living conditions, many Salvadorans in their twenties looked much older.

Highly articulate, Santos was one of the community's leaders and had been given the privilege of hosting us. We quickly learned that Salvadorans would go without food in order to feed us; any protest on our part was an affront to their hospitality and caused hurt feelings. There is a deep generosity among the poor in El Salvador I have never experienced with those living in abundance in the United States.

In the early morning, she was quietly grinding corn for the tortillas that with beans were the main staple foods in the community. She ground the corn in an old metal contraption that she turned by hand, her strong arms working hard as the yellow mush emptied into a clean basin-shaped stone. She was quite proud of her grinder since most of the women in the community ground the corn by hand, smashing it again and again between stones. Adding a little water to the corn mush, she deftly patted the mixture into thick round tortillas, tossing them on the hot iron plate on the wood-burning stove just outside her straw hut.

When the low buzz of approaching army planes broke the quiet of the dawn, Santos quickly looked up. A shadow crossed her face, but she did not stop her work; instead, she began to sing. As the planes passed over the village, flying low in a show of power, Santos sang louder so her sleeping children would not hear the planes and wake up in fear.

We had hot tortillas with salt for breakfast. Margaret, the Catholic nun, translated for those of us whose Spanish was fledgling at best so we could talk as we ate.

I requested that Margaret ask Santos what she wished for most. Without hesitation she replied, "To be free." She said she would remember every minute we spent here in the community for the rest of her life. It was a great joy to her that people from the United States comprehended her story and the plight of her people. Like many Salvadorans, she was careful to make a distinction between the actions of the U.S. government and the values of its citizens, recognizing that there was often disagreement. I asked how she could stay so calm in the face of great danger.

I will remember her reply for the rest of my life. Patting the wet ground corn into round tortillas for baking, she said, "Death is behind us, around us and before us. On the other side is peace and freedom. We

WILL reach the peace. But first we must pass through the death. This we will do—for our children."

*   *   *

I trembled as I sat in the waiting room at the counseling center. The thought of telling Jim about what I remembered about my mother during this recent flashback caused me great distress. I felt flooded with shame, and waves of nausea crashed over me in an unrelenting storm whenever the reality of the memories hit me. In desperation, I had frantically written in my journal the night before, hoping to alleviate some of the intensity of the pain and shame by writing. Instead, more details and clarity poured out on the page until I was so horrified by what I saw there that I shut my journal and jammed it under the bed, trying to get the awful words out of my sight. But I could not shut down my mind, and I could not make the memories go away.

When I sat on the sofa across from Jim's chair, I felt my throat beginning to constrict. I was wearing a black skirt with yellow flowers, and I focused all of my attention on one yellow flower as though it could transport me to some other place where I did not have to face this horror. He knew that something was disturbing me and gently encouraged me to tell him what was happening. I finally opened up my mouth to begin to recount the memories that had come flooding back as I drove to work two days ago.

Instead, I found myself telling him the story of Santos and how she sang to her children so they would not be afraid. Somehow, I needed the reminder of a Salvadoran's courage in order to face my own pain. It was only years later I would understand that Santos had been modeling something very important, which is why I intuitively knew to share the story. The singing to her children was demonstrating the importance of being able to soothe my inner children in the face of threat. I was a long way from being able to do that, and I needed Jim to fill that role.

Jim was moved by her story. We talked for a while about her quiet bravery and her desire to protect her children. I fell silent again; the contrast between Santos and my own mother was excruciatingly painful. And the idea of my own mother singing filled me with a nameless terror.

My voice once again left me, and I looked at Jim helplessly. He asked me what was the worst thing that could happen if I told him what was wrong. The Child had an immediate response: "You will hate me."

I was shocked; it was as though someone else had spoken the words. The voice did not even sound like mine.

But Jim took it in stride. He looked directly at me. "I will never hate you," he said. "It's OK to tell me whatever you need to."

In a broken, strangled voice that was not much more than a whisper, I began to tell him what I had remembered. I prefaced it by saying I was not sure it was actually abuse. But as I talked, the room seemed to shift and change. Suddenly, I was reliving the experience one more time. I was dizzy as I described being turned upside down over my mother's lap, the beer bottle on the floor next to my face. I fell headfirst into the terror when I recalled twisting around and seeing her face—a face filled with a terrible joy at my pain and humiliation. A sound like thunder pounded through my head, and I could not continue. I twisted my hands together so tightly that they would hurt for days afterward. Muscle spasms were moving through my neck, causing more physical pain. I felt like I was drowning in the vortex of a whirlpool, sucked deep into waters from which I would never emerge alive.

Suddenly, I heard Jim's voice saying, "Linda, it's OK."

His voice went straight into the child space where I was reliving the terror. No calm and reassuring voice had ever been there before. I felt the inside space abruptly change, and I gradually swam back to my adult reality. Slowly, I brought my eyes from his shoes to his face. I held my breath, praying his face would not be changed like my mother's and that I would not see hate and disgust in his eyes.

I was tremendously relieved to see that his face had not transformed into the face of a stranger who wanted to hurt me. And the hate and disgust that I feared were nowhere to be found. Instead, there was a compassion coming from him that seemed to fill the room.

"It seems like it is sexual abuse, but it can't be—she was my *mother*."

Even as I spoke the words I knew they were a futile protest against the reality of what had happened to me. I tried again.

"She was drinking. She must not have known what she was doing."

"It *was* sexual abuse," Jim said quietly. "The fact that she was drinking is no excuse for what she did. And when you told me about it, there were at least three people in this room—you, me, and the child who experienced it."

*   *   *

Along with the tremendous relief at having survived the telling of what I remembered to another human being, there were floods of emotion and body memories that raged through me in the weeks that followed. Fragments of new memories—pieces from the lost years—rushed into my consciousness at any time of day or night, threatening to overwhelm what felt like my fragile hold on sanity. I felt as though I was not real and only loosely connected to the earth. I wrote in my journal as the memories and feelings washed over me. Somehow it seemed if I could only get the words outside of me and put them on a page, they might have less power to hurt me.

This strategy worked to an extent. Pouring the pain onto the paper, I shut the journal when I was done and willed the horror to stay in the book's pages until I could see Jim again. Sometimes, I forgot what I wrote almost immediately and it was not until I opened my journal during a therapy session that shock of the remembered trauma was once again conscious. I often handed my journal to Jim to read when I could not bear to read it myself.

Bladder and urinary tract infections struck repeatedly as though my body was protesting its role in remembering, at times leaving me so incapacitated I could not get out of bed. I periodically experienced sharp pains in my genitals and buttocks that felt more connected to the fragments of memory which were emerging than to any current medical condition. It seemed that my body was remembering the trauma as well as my brain.

Even with my medication, sleep was restless as I struggled to feel safe. I was often jolted awake by some nameless terror in my dreams I could not quite remember but which left me both drenched in sweat and shivering in the middle of the night. At times, I doubled the recommended dose but rarely slept more than three or four hours each night, hardly giving me strength to work my ten-hour day at the office. In this exhausted state, concentration was difficult and I had headaches almost all of the time. I took sick and vacation days when it became impossible to continue to function, but only at Jim's insistence. I would have worked until I collapsed. My husband took over the bulk of household chores, including shopping and cooking, because I crawled into bed or curled up on the sofa at every opportunity.

Steve had little difficulty believing I had been abused. We had been married for several years before my mother's suicide. During that time, he witnessed her deteriorating mental state and listened to her accounts of having the phone tapped and being followed in her car by government agents.

Steve confided he was shocked when, a few weeks after we met, I told him about cutting my genitals on the "potty chair" and needing stitches to repair the cut. He said he could not fathom how a child could be cut so badly on a potty seat or why I told him this information when we barely knew each other. It was my turn to be shocked; I had no recollection of having spoken about this incident. He revealed that in fact I had relayed the story not once but several times throughout the years of our marriage.

It was also Steve's opinion that my father was a "strange bird." He and my father had worked in business for about 10 years, and he was often embarrassed by my father's angry recitation of how "those bastard doctors tried to take our daughter away" to business associates and prospective clients as he recounted his version of what we called "the hospital story" to anyone who would listen. Steve had endured many of my father's tirades about sin and judgment according to his interpretation of the Bible, some of them quite loud and delivered at restaurants and other public places. My father could quiet an entire dining room as he pounded his fists on the table, his face flushed with anger, and pontificated on the evils of homosexuality, which he seemed to consider a sin worse then murder.

Like me, Steve was also troubled by the symbiotic relationship that he observed between my younger sister and father. Although she was now in her thirties, Diane had never left the Big House. Subject to frequent nightmares and severe mood swings, she worked only part time and most of her social life revolved around my father and his relatives.

A quiet man of few words, Steve tried his best to be supportive by allowing me to rest as much as possible and read several articles and books about the healing process that I recommended. What neither of us imagined at this point was that the process would take years.

*   *   *

I did not believe Susan at first when she talked about an "inner child." The term sounded silly to me. I associated such language with what I considered fuzzy popular psychology focused on making spoiled bored people feel good. I had no use for such unscientific concepts.

However, now I was increasingly aware of the presence of the Child within me who seemed to carry the memories and the emotional and physical pain. She also seemed to hold the keys to healing. She was not an abstract concept when I suddenly plunged into a time warp and re-experienced trauma through her eyes and in her body. She had nothing to do with popular psychology's emphasis on feeling good when she surfaced. It was her voice, not mine, that whispered secrets too appalling for me to voice. This child was alarmingly real.

She also brought with her enormous needs for physical and emotional nurturing, most of which were directed toward Jim. Ashamed of her volatile emotions and her needs, I was terrified to unleash her.

One night, I woke up drenched in sweat and shaking in terror. I could not recall dreaming, but I was so frightened I could not even move from the bed to get up and turn on the light. Suddenly, inexplicably, I heard Jim's voice call my name. "It's OK, Linda." The words I heard so many times in his office were somehow now coming from deep inside of me. "It's OK."

Amazed, I sat up in bed, hugging my knees. The voice was so real. My heart gradually stopped pounding, and I could get up more easily. I got a drink of water, turned on a low light and got back into bed. I listened for Jim's voice, and I heard it again. A feeling of security and comfort washed over me. As I drifted toward sleep, I was hazily aware that he was responding directly to the needs of the child. And that when she heard his voice, she felt safe. We slept. Jim's voice calmed us just like the song of Santos soothed her children.

*　　　　　　*　　　　　　*

Despite the emotional turmoil created by finally facing my history of abuse, I continued work with Project *Via Crucis*. This work involved the attendance at monthly board meetings to coordinate the increasingly complex planning of providing economic aid to several communities, among them funding for a tiny medical clinic, supporting a start-up of a carpentry business and providing dairy cows to produce milk and cheese to improve nutrition in a poor village. In addition, I helped to train and educate each delegation we sent to El Salvador.

We decided to invite a Salvadoran pastor we knew to visit Pennsylvania for a few weeks and talk to various churches and community groups about his work in El Salvador. I volunteered to host Pastor Walter Baires, his wife and their three young children at our house. I took time from work and immersed myself in providing meals, hospitality, transportation and translation. I was finally proficient enough in Spanish to translate, provided the speaker had a clear and moderately paced articulation. Although Pastor Baires did not speak English well, he understood enough to correct me when I translated something inaccurately. It seemed Salvadorans were always teaching me.

Despite my exhaustion, I also was able to contact that part of me who functioned like a well-trained robot. She took care of all the administrative and organizational details that I was too exhausted to cope with. When she took control, she overrode the Child as well as the depleted adult. This part was the part primarily present at my corporate job. Her voice was strong and forceful; she was a savvy negotiator; she could read and absorb huge amounts of complex material such as Securities and Exchange Commission regulations in a short amount of time; and she was good with math.

One afternoon I took the Salvadoran family to spend a few hours relaxing at our community pool. The Salvadoran couple's eight-year-old daughter, Atzen, emerged from the water shivering and cold. She darted toward her mother, holding out her arms. To my surprise, she changed course at the last minute and threw herself on my lap, snuggling close in order to get warm. As I held her small wet body, tears filled my eyes. She was so small, so vulnerable, so trusting, so deserving of protection and love. How could anyone betray a child like this? How could anyone rape and beat a creature as fragile and beautiful as Atzen? She reminded me of a high-spirited colt, her limbs lithe and brown and her long dark hair streaming behind her when she ran with a peculiar combination of agility and awkwardness that promised to evolve into pure gracefulness.

I felt anger well up within me at the very thought of someone hurting her, a rage that I still denied for the violence that had been done to me. It was so hard to admit that I had been just as vulnerable and innocent as Atzen when my mother violated my deepest places. Unlike Atzen, I had never run to anyone with wide open arms, anticipating acceptance and comfort. I had learned not to expect love from adults and to tend to my needs by myself.

*　　　　　*　　　　　*

Jim asked me to draw a floor plan of the house where I lived when I was growing up and bring it to the therapy session the next week. He wanted me to note the places in the house where I felt safe. I was not happy about doing this assignment, but I trudged to the mall to buy large sheets of paper, a box of crayons and colored pencils. Later in the evening, I sat at the picnic table in the back yard, sketching the outlines of the Little House, where I had lived for my first nine years. The house, which was remodeled into a garage when we moved into the bigger house, consisted of a parlor, a kitchen and one bedroom. My sister Diane and I shared a bed that was positioned at the foot of our parents' bed. There was no curtain or screen dividing the room so that whatever took place in my parents' bed was completely in view of the two of us.

I felt an eerie foreboding as I drew in the outlines of the furniture that I remembered in the bedroom. Particularly troubling was my parents' bed and the small dresser with the mirror. I moved on to the parlor. I drew the piano and then I erased it. I didn't want it to be there. There were too many painful memories. Taking a deep breath, I began to color the kitchen table with a brown pencil. Suddenly I threw down the pencil and took up a blue crayon and quickly shaded the whole house in blue. Blue was my mother's favorite color. As I drew, I realized that she filled every inch of that space. The house was hers. There was no safe space for me.

I gathered up my drawing materials and ran into the house. I felt on the edge of panic. My teen-age son was playing the electric guitar in his bedroom. The amplifier was turned up, and the walls seemed to vibrate with the sounds of hard rock music. Usually, I enjoy hearing his music; it is completely his, and he plays it wild and free. But this night, the music seemed to invade me, tearing at my insides. Holding my hands over my ears, I bolted to my upstairs bedroom and shut the door. But even this sanctuary seemed unsafe. The music—like my mother—was everywhere. A whimpering sound that I had never heard before filled the room. It took a while until I realized it was coming from me. One thing was paramount in my mind: I needed to find a place to hide.

With trembling hands, I locked the bedroom door. I pulled a woven Salvadoran blanket around me and huddled in a far corner of the room. I honestly expected to see my mother materialize at any moment. It was as though she was given power by the music to come inside me. I pulled the blanket over my head and blanked out. A long time later, the music stopped. I discovered to my embarrassment that I was sucking my thumb and holding a stuffed animal. The Child sought comfort in ways I never would have dreamed of.

It was the Child rather than the adult self who showed Jim the floor plan. After she asked him to sit next to her, he sat on the sofa with us to see the picture, careful not to sit too close. He examined each room, asking questions about what it was like to live there. I felt myself slipping into child-space. I heard the Child tell him that there was no safe place in that house for her. The house belonged to her mother. All of her safe spaces were outside.

Struggling to pull myself out of the domain of the child, I said that I did not understand how I could go into such a panic in my own house after completing the drawing. I haltingly told him of the whimpering, thumb-sucking, and intense need to hide that the sketch had precipitated. I wanted him to give me a psychological explanation for what I had experienced. Most of all, I wanted his assurance that it most likely would not happen again. Instead, he looked at me as he held my sketch on his lap and said quietly: "It's not such a long way from there to here, is it?"

It was not. And the distance between the two places in time seemed to be getting shorter.

*   *   *

From my journal…

I woke up with memories of my father tickling me with his mouth. I feel his mouth and breath on my chest, my stomach, between my legs. I hear my laughter turn to sobs. How is it possible that tickling hurts? He is playing a game with me. I have just had a bath and I am wearing a white cotton T-shirt and panties. I am on the floor, and he is holding my arms up above my head and tickling me with his mouth. He makes a loud noise; he says I smell good and he is going to eat me up. I am screaming and crying but he does not stop. He is laughing. But his whiskers are hurting me and I am afraid.

*   *   *

I leaned over the bed, dry heaves shaking my body. The minute I awoke, these images, always remembered but deftly ignored, flooded my mind. I hit wildly at my body, trying to push my father away. The feel of his scratchy whiskers grated against my skin, and it took a few minutes until I was able to understood that I was safe, that this tickling was not really happening right now but was another memory related to my childhood.

I sat up in bed, trying to calm down. What kind of a man would hold down a small child and tickle her, his mouth between her legs, until she screamed and cried? Immediately, a sneering internal voice accused me of being too sensitive. It was, after all, only a game. At least he was paying some attention to me. I tried to imagine how old I was, and I realized that the tickling must have taken place before the molestation incident with Tommy. My father stopped touching me in any way after that incident.

I drifted back in time again. Once, I got too close to our collie, Pal, who was tethered to a chain on the maple tree in the back yard. The dog, always eager to play, pushed me on the soft grass and then stood over my body, wagging his tail and licking my face. Although I loved Pal, I became hysterical. I started to scream, and my father came and pulled me away from the dog, which seemed reluctant to give me up to him. Later, he told my mother how I screamed over and over that he was going to eat me. But it was not Pal I feared as I lay pinned on my back in the soft green grass.

Body memories flooded through me that day. Dry, sharp pains kept shooting through my vagina. Thoughts of, "The angle is wrong, it hurts me," kept racing through my mind but I could not connect the pain to any visual images. I kept feeling my father's breath and scratchy whiskers on my belly and my inner thighs. I refused to link the pain and terror I was feeling with my father's ticking games.

When I got to therapy a few days later, I was at first too ashamed to bring up the story about my father. After all, this was only a game. It seemed too trivial to talk about. But the Child wanted to tell Jim how much she hated this game, and we talked about it. As he listened to us describe and then defend my father's game, his face grew dark. He told me in no uncertain terms that fathers do not pin down their small daughters and use their mouths to tickle chest, bellies and inner thighs. His response was clear and stark: it was not a game. It was sexual abuse. And to make it worse, it was couched in terms of "fun."

Like many survivors, I did not name these traumatic experiences as abuse because I did not understand my body belonged to me and that no one had a right to invade and hurt it for their own pleasure or in pursuit of domination. I had described being beaten, molested and raped to my friends at the retreat center without ever naming what occurred as abuse or feeling a sense of outrage about what happened. I simply did not recognized abuse when I was the victim.

I felt a brief, but quickly smothered, flare of anger—not at my father but at Jim. I did not want to know that I had been abused by both parents. It was only a game. My father meant well. It's not fair to say it was abuse. The defensive thoughts rushed through my mind, but I was silent. Jim was giving a name to what had been nameless for me.

He asked me what I thought it meant when Pal held me down, I was not afraid of being eaten by the dog but of my father. I stayed silent, hoping he would move on. He didn't. The room grew pregnant with expectation as Jim waited patiently for my response. I was sure he would wait as long as it took.

I closed my eyes. I saw a little girl, crying and screaming, pinned down on the floor as her father's head is buried between her soft legs. I asked myself how I would react if someone did that to one of my children and I felt a quick flash of protective rage. I thought about the terrified state I woke up in after dreaming about the tickling game and the subsequent days of experiencing sharp vaginal pain and the feel of scratchy whiskers on my inner thighs. My body was confirming what my conscious mind knew but still wanted to deny.

Denial has its place. It protects us from what we are not ready to handle psychologically. And when its numbing comfort has served its purpose and we are ready to deal with reality, we still cling to it like a child to her security blanket. We are angry at anyone who begins to tug at it gently, encouraging us to let it go. We are not sure we can navigate the world without its protective mantle.

With a bottomless sadness, I knew my father's tickling could not be classified as a game. I opened my eyes, and drew a deep breath.

"It means he abused me too."

A shudder ran through my body. I felt as though I had lived at least a hundred years—way past my allotted time. But I had never been a child. Childhood was stolen from me. In the end, all I could do was to survive.

Notes From El Salvador: A Woman Tortured, A Woman Healed

One day I visited a tiny Salvadoran community of about seventy five people who had been displaced by the war. They were struggling to survive on a scrap of land at the edge of a zone of conflict, living under shelters of plastic and tin. When their homes many miles to the north were destroyed by the army, they fled toward San Salvador. However, upon hearing from other travelers about the crowded, dirty, and disease infested squatter settlements inhabited by tens of thousands of refugees on the outskirts of the capital city, they decided to set up camp about thirty miles outside of San Salvador.

The rural area they selected was desolate. Most of its prior inhabitants had fled military bombardments a few years earlier. Yet the people believed that the land held promise for yielding food, despite the damage that had been done to it by the army's "scorched earth" campaign. They decided they would try to survive on this small piece of cleared earth, nestled in the shadow of a volcano and surrounded by mountains, rather than seek shelter in the capital.

Most everyone who was physically capable of hard labor worked all day tilling the soil and planting crops. One man was an experienced bee keeper, and applied his skill to cultivating hives so the community would have honey. The elderly residents tended to the babies while the others worked, and prepared tortillas for the community from the scant corn meal they had managed to carry on their backs when they fled the bombing of their homes. For months, their sole diet consisted of tortillas. They had no beans or corn, nor salt to flavor the tortillas.

After months of carefully tending the fields, the campesinos were rewarded by a good harvest. Color returned to weary faces grown pale and wan with malnutrition, and children started to play again as their energy returned. The people prudently put some of the harvest back for lean times, and soon began another cycle of planting. The bee hives began to produce honey, and there was enough to provide a small cash crop they could sell in San Salvador, enabling them to buy cooking oil, salt and other necessities.

One day, the army came to the small settlement, rounded up all of the people of the community and began to interrogate them. Despite the fact that the majority of the people were women, children and elders, the military accused them of being part of the FMLN resistance. Their suspicions were aroused since this particular group of refugees had not continued on into the capital, but had stayed outside its perimeters.

After several days of occupation and harassment, the soldiers finally left. They took the community's meager food supplies and farming tools, leaving the refugees completely desolate. They also took some prisoners. One of the prisoners captured was an old woman, a grandmother who tended the babies while others worked in the fields.

She was imprisoned for several months at an "unofficial" clandestine location used by shadowy para-military groups who often worked in complicity with the armed forces. During her captivity, she was badly tortured. A bag with lime dust was placed over her head during interrogations. She was stripped and sexually tormented and humiliated. Sometimes when she did not respond to questions in the way her torturers wanted, electric current was applied to her genitals.

Eventually, she was released and returned to the community as a living reminder of what would happen to anyone suspected of supporting the resistance movement. This kind of strategy—a tremendous deterrent with select use—was a favorite tactic of the death squads: torture suspected so-called subversives to the limits of their endurance and then send them back to their families. The horror of knowing what kind of torture had been inflicted during the imprisonment of these captives as well as observing the devastating long-term effects of physical and mental damage served to terrorize whole communities. To make the point even more bluntly, the bodies of the captives who did not survive torture were dumped on country roads or city sidewalks during the night so that their brutalized corpses would be visible to all those passing that way the next morning.

After her release and return to her community, the old woman could no longer function. She sat and stared blankly, or mumbled to herself about things no one could comprehend. At times, she became suddenly terrified of men she had known since they were boys as some phantom vestige of her torturers seemed to pass over their faces and she cowered before them, trembling and pleading. She could not perform even the task of making tortillas. She was unmoved by the soft bodies of the babies she once loved to hold as mothers wedged them into her stiff arms, then sadly took them away when she showed no emotional response.

The trauma of the torture had resulted in severe psychological damage. She was filled with guilt because she had made false confessions under torture, agreeing that she and everyone else in the community who her interrogators named were connected to the armed resistance movement.

Like many survivors of trauma, she could not sleep at night. Holding a small candle, she stumbled from shelter to shelter, begging forgiveness from each family she might have betrayed.

I asked, "What did you do? What happened to this woman?"

A peasant in a worn and faded shirt answered quietly: "We healed her. It cost us a lot, but we healed her. "

I caught my breath. Here was a community of poor uneducated peasants who somehow had accomplished what highly trained professionals often cannot—they healed a severely traumatized torture victim.

The man explained that no one knew exactly how to respond, but they were certain of two things: she needed to be listened to and she needed to be held. Working with that simple framework, the people of the community organized themselves so that someone would be literally a companion to the old woman 24 hours a day so that she was never left alone.

They talked to her, encouraging her to spill out the pain, the rage and the grief that she was carrying. They held her like a child, rocking her. They let her cry. Eventually, she recovered from her trauma and was healed. She once again prepared food for those who worked in the fields and tended children with the other grandmothers.

It cost that community a great deal to heal their wounded member. Their very survival depended on the labor of each person in the fields where their crops of corn and beans were cultivated. Every day that someone sat with the woman was a day of lost labor, which meant less food for all in the community. And they were taking a huge risk as they had no assurance that the time they were investing in her recovery would be successful and restore her.

They also did not have the comfortable distance that we in the United States have when listening of survivors of childhood sexual and physical abuse recount what are often litanies of torture at the hands of trusted family members. If you dare to risk opening yourself to the pain and potential heartbreak of accompanying a survivor of abuse as she is healing, you may feel shaken, sad or angry yourself as you listen to her tell how her father came into her room at night and forced his penis into her mouth. You may even have difficulty sleeping later as you remember the vivid images. But it is fairly certain that you will listen with the security of knowing that her father is not going to come into your room that very night and do the same thing to you.

The cost of listening to the old woman's ordeal went far beyond the economic factors involved in loss of labor in the fields. Death squads and soldiers could invade the community at any moment. The people, armed only with their faith in a God of life and justice, had no weapons of defense. The fate of the grandmother could befall any member of the community at any time. To accompany the old woman in her healing, the community members who held her and listened to her fully entered into the raging torrents of her pain. They allowed themselves to become the targets of her displaced anger, shame and fear. They refused to abandon her even when her fragmented mind imposed the images of her torturers upon the compassionate faces of her friends.

Recovery from torture requires plunging into the depths of both the remembered and forgotten horrors. Many trauma survivors eventually drown or simply give up in these treacherous waters because they have no one to hear their pain and accompany them. Some, like Virginia Woolf, finally fill their pockets with stones and walk into the ocean.

It is those who are lucky enough to be heard and held who survive the remembering.

Chapter 5

Pain, Need and Touch—
the Forbidden Combination

The wounded Child who was surfacing with the memories of child-hood horror brought with her tremendous pain and need.

These two experiences had been mutually exclusive for all of my life. It was forbidden to have any need whatsoever, and it was particularly dangerous to have a need surface when I was experiencing pain. To have hope in the midst of torture when there is no possibility of rescue only intensifies the agony. The Child who lived through the pain coped by fleeing her body, traveling to safe places deep inside her mind where no one could hurt her. When she was not able to reach this safe harbor, the fragmented part that I identified as Amy took over and converted pain into pleasure, embracing her own violation and desperately drawing nurture from rape.

In her wisdom, the Child learned to shut off any small fragment of need for love and kindness. When she began to surface with her mem-ories, the dangerous combination of pain and need rushed to the sur-face. The pain was intense and immediate. Remembering the abuse involved living the traumas once again with all their concomitant agony, panic and shock.

And the need for nurture and comfort, which had been silenced but never destroyed, was directed toward Jim. I could not ask my husband

Steve to hold me because of the unresolved sexual issues in our relationship. The Child needed to be held by someone with whom there had never been—nor would ever be—any chance of sexual encounter. This was the kind of safe holding that she had been denied since her earliest years.

In many ways, Jim was re-parenting the traumatized Child. During some sessions, the child was withdrawn and unreachable, justifiably suspicious of any interaction with a parent-like person. If the tension became too severe, the "no-name" child surfaced. Silence and stillness were her shields, and the shields served to effectively block any interactions with the outside world. But there were periods of time when the Child's desire for a mother and motherly nurturing outweighed her fear. She turned to Jim with all of the expectations, fears and needs, especially the need to be held and comforted physically. This relentless child-need became a stumbling block over which Jim and I both fell and were bruised until we learned to see it as a gift and a challenge.

It was, in fact, the gateway to healing.

*   *   *

In the early 1980s, I took yoga classes for several years. Most of my classmates struggled to enter states of meditation, finding it difficult to still the mind and shift into an altered state of consciousness. Having learned how to enter trance states in order to survive my childhood, however, I easily achieved deep meditative states in which my breathing and heart rate slowed significantly. My teachers were excited about my abilities and told me that most students worked for years to be able to enter the level of trance that I seemed to naturally achieve within minutes.

But I became increasingly fearful of what was happening to me as I practiced yoga meditation. Each time, the same image came into my mind and refused to budge. It was huge: shaped somewhat like a heart and dull red. Although it was quite complex with many wrinkles and crevices, it also seemed strangely stylized with a haunting surreal quality. It pulsated slowly and had a yellow center that was terrible in its familiarity. It filled me with fear and revulsion, and my usual reaction was to allow my body to become numb and to begin to let my mind drift away. It never occurred to me that I could stop the meditation. Feeling powerless and trapped, I responded in the same way I did when I was a child, using my mind to flee to another place.

One night during yoga class, the image grew larger and larger in my mind. I was overcome with terror and I could not bear to know what it was. Everything went blank. Suddenly my eyes popped open, and I found myself floating close to the ceiling of the gymnasium, looking down with wonder at the bodies of students on the floor, including my own. I was free of the awful image at last! I felt an exhilarating sense of release and a reluctance to return to my body. In fact, I was not sure I even knew how to come back to my body from such a long distance.

As I was puzzling about how I would get down to the floor, I felt a quick rush of disorientation and dizziness, and blankness enveloped me once more. Suddenly, it was as though my spirit was slammed back into my body. When I opened my eyes, the room was out of focus. As my vision cleared, I could see that both of my yoga teachers were crouched on the floor beside of me, their faces showing concern that I had not responded to their repeated requests to open my eyes. They gently asked me what I experienced. Trembling, I shook my head. I told them only that somehow I had ended up on the ceiling, looking down at my body. I could not speak of the image that haunted me. They were astounded; out-of-body states were generally obtained only after years of disciplined yoga practice and training.

I returned to class for a short time after this disconcerting and frightening incident, but I never again allowed myself to meditate. Within a few weeks, I decided to quit yoga altogether. I needed to get away from the terrible picture that came into my mind each time I slipped into a trance state. I had no way of knowing that it would re-surface more than a decade later as one of my earliest memories of abuse by my mother.

*   *   *

I had been in therapy for about six months when I began to notice a strange and unidentifiable taste in my mouth. No length of time of brushing my teeth or amount of mouthwash could keep the taste from recurring. At times I felt as though something was covering my mouth and cutting off my air supply, causing me to choke and spit. I started to whimper in my sleep and sucked my thumb in every secret moment I could find. To my consternation, the image that had frightened me out of yoga class ten years before reappeared, constantly hanging in my mind like a still-life picture, a snapshot surrounded by dead, flat, dense space. I did not yet know what the image represented, and I had no desire to find out. I said nothing to Jim for weeks about the strange sensations I was experiencing or about the picture I could not purge from my mind. I feared I was losing my sanity.

One evening when I was doing my weekly grocery shopping, I felt inexplicably compelled to enter the aisle where baby food and supplies were sold. As though I was on a mission, I went straight to the shelf holding the pacifiers. With shaking hands, I immediately snatched up a yellow pacifier, tucked it in my cart beneath the groceries and headed for the checkout lane. I was completely baffled by my impulsive actions and I had no clue why I had just purchased a yellow pacifier. I hid the object in a drawer in my night stand when I got home, feeling ashamed and extremely anxious.

Two days later, I went into the bedroom, locked the door and unwrapped the pacifier. Sinking down to the floor, I placed it in my mouth. I curled up in a ball and began to suck, drifting into child space as the rubber became soft and pliable in my mouth. Suddenly, the terrible picture exploded in my mind and the strange taste flooded my mouth. Gagging, choking and crying, I flung the pacifier across the room. I pulled myself up on the bed and began hitting my face and tearing at my hair, trying to make the flood of images stop. But it was no use. With a sick certainty, I knew exactly what the fleshy heart-shaped orifice was. And I knew why my yellow pacifier was pulsating in its center.

The picture that hung in my mind and filled me with such dread was a child's view of an adult female vagina: huge, red and pulsating with a terrible yellow center that was my own beloved pacifier. The pacifier was used by my mother to accustom me to the taste of her genitals and to turn my attention from sucking on my pacifier to pleasuring her with my small tongue. Her vagina loomed as huge in my mind as it did when I was a two-year-old child placed on the bed just in front of her spread legs, crying with frustration because my yellow pacifier was mysteriously being swallowed by a strange-tasting place belonging to my mother.

*　　　　　*　　　　　*

From my journal (Thursday)…

*Just came from a session with Jim. I got to the car and could not drive. Had to sit in the parking lot until I felt stronger. The world shifted for me when I told Jim about the picture in my mind of me as a small child in front of my mother's genital area, touching her with my tongue and crying over my pacifier. Everything looks different; there are colors I have never seen before. I have crossed some irrevocable line. **I told this.** Jim said to let it be for now and to rest. He is always so calm, even when I am sure that the world is going to end. He said that healing and remembering will take its natural course. I was scared, but I asked Jim if he would read a story to me on a cassette tape so that when he goes on vacation, I will be able to hear his voice. He immediately said YES and smiled at me. He said it is*

*very good to ask for what I need. I am so relieved; maybe somehow I will
be able to survive his two-week absence after all.*

*   *   *

From my journal (Friday)...
*I feel like somebody died. I am walking slowly, silently in the house. Any
noise jars my system. I cannot eat. I could not go to work. The picture of
my mother's vagina and the sensation of my tongue tasting her genitals is
horrifying. There is a terrible grieving about the pacifier. It was something
that was supposed to be mine, and she took it and perverted it for her own
pleasure. I don't think I could stand this except for the simultaneous event
of asking Jim for something the Child needed (his voice on a cassette tape)
and having him respond in such a positive way. To allow myself to need
something in the midst of pain is a totally new experience for me. I think
I can learn a lot from the Child.*

*   *   *

The reality of asking for and receiving what I needed when I was vulnerable and in pain unleashed a new level of emotion from the Child.
We listened to the cassette tape of Jim's voice every night during his
two-week vacation. We began to imagine being held and rocked by him,
being tucked into bed and hearing his soothing voice telling us everything was all right. The sensation of receiving the imagined nurturing,
however, was painful. At times my stomach would seem to drop to my
feet as another little chink of fear dropped away and a drop of kindness
and acceptance landed in its place. The Child and I spent hours under
the covers, sucking our thumb and imagining that we were being held.
By the time Jim returned from vacation, the need for his touch was
equal to the terror about what would happen if he did touch us. It was
the beginning of a lengthy internal and external struggle, which would

lead to the depths of despair for the Child before any glimmer of hope could be realized.

In the meanwhile, I was scheduled to participate in a delegation to El Salvador in two months. Since I would take a leadership role, I focused on the task of immersing myself in the most current political reports so that I would be informed about the events in the rapidly changing post-war environment brought by peace accords signed earlier in the year.

On January 16, 1992, the Salvadoran government and the FMLN signed a complex peace agreement negotiated by the United Nations. It called for a gradual disarming of the FMLN, purging of the military officers responsible for the scorched earth policies and human rights violations, land redistribution, dissolution of several of the army units widely known for their crimes against civilians and military reform. The accords included a specific timetable for completion of each segment, with the entire process to be completed by October 31, 1992. In the nine months that had passed, very little had been done by the government to comply with the provisions for purging, reducing and reforming the military. We would enter El Salvador two weeks before the deadline. Tensions in the country ran high, and some believed war would begin again if October 31 passed and the military remained intransigent.

I attempted to brush up on my Spanish by listening to language audio tapes in my car during my work commute and poring over Spanish textbooks while I grabbed a bite of lunch in the company cafeteria. I made efforts to help with the myriad of details involved in coordinating a delegation. But I was unable to give the upcoming trip my full attention. What was more important than anything else in the world at that time was my desire to be held by the only parent-like person I had ever encountered in whose presence I felt safe and protected. And Jim, who had called the wounded child to life back from the land of the dead, was drawing the line at holding her. To the Child, it seemed the ultimate betrayal. To be coaxed back to life only to encounter memories of the pain and horror of her mother's abuse —and to once again not be held and comforted—was beyond her endurance.

Jim seemed genuinely perplexed at how to handle this emerging need for safe touch. He assured the Child that her need was legitimate and that she was not wrong to ask to be held. He said he needed time to consider her request. Several times, he asked for clarity on exactly how she wanted to be held. This was a question that proved impossible to answer. It was incredibly difficult to have this child need out in the open. To try to articulate exactly how holding should take place was way beyond what even the adult part of me could describe.

During this period of time, additional fragments of memory were surfacing. I remembered sitting on my mother's lap at the kitchen table. I was about six years old. Her hand was beneath my panties, and she was gently rubbing me with petroleum jelly. It was a warm good feeling to be held by her. She allowed me to relax against her body as she massaged my genitals. Eventually, her manipulation would result in an involuntary spasm, what I now know was a tiny orgasm. However, at the time, it was an overwhelming sensation for which I had no name. My mother, however, had a name for it. She called it "peeing on mommy's hands."

Each time it happened, she would withdraw her fingers in feigned horror. Quick as lightning, the gentle mother would be gone, and the angry mother took her place.

"What did you do?" she would shout, holding up her wet finger and shoving it in my face. "You dirty, bad girl! You peed on mommy's hands!"

She would throw me upside down over her lap, jerk down my panties and pound on my bottom until her hands seemed to tire. Terrified, I was sure I had done something awful. She said I was disgusting. I believed her.

An insidious thing about repeated abuse by a parent is that the child grows up internalizing the messages of the parent, however abusive or distorted. Deep within my body and my mind, I felt disgusting and dirty. My mother had touched me gently and I responded by "peeing" on her fingers. What worse thing could a child do?

When I began to remember the times in the kitchen when she stimulated me to orgasm and then punished me for it, I regressed to the level of a six–year-old child as I told Jim about it for the first time. I fell headfirst into the terror and completely lost any connection with the current reality.

The Child, spent and drained, was huddled on the floor, desolate about the crime of "peeing" on her mother's hands. Jim rose from his chair and sat on the rug. He began talking directly to the Child. As he had done in the past, he assured her that she was not disgusting or dirty; that she was good and beautiful and her mother was very, very wrong to treat her in that way.

To my amazement, I heard a young voice that was not mine ask him who he was. It was as though the adult part of me was locked out of this conversation, relegated to observer status.

He quietly but firmly said that he was an adult, and it was up to him to make boundaries so that I would be cared for and protected. He reassured the Child that her mother was not there and that she was safe.

He reached out and gently touched my shoulder. His touch went straight to the deep wounded place that had just been exposed. I could not understand most of his words as he continued to talk, but I could feel his hand gently rubbing my shoulders and neck. My child self could understand the compassion in his touch. She accepted what she could and then began to recede into the depths from which she came. Slowly, I returned to the present time, bringing with me yet another piece of the puzzle that had been my fractured childhood.

When each session was over, Jim would hug me gently. The Child instinctively knew his touch and his scent. With her eyes blindfolded, she could have picked his hug out of a thousand hugs given to her. She could have sensed his presence close by. The intimate physical bonding that usually takes place between a mother and child was mysteriously happening between Jim and myself. At times, those few seconds of contact were the most important part of the sessions. It was only his touch that could assure her she was not disgusting. And she needed much more than brief hugs to be convinced.

In subsequent years, I have spoken to and corresponded with a number of women abused by their mothers. The need for touch and holding seems to be particularly strong in these survivors. When you are brutally abused by your earliest caretaker, the luxury of safely laying your head on your mother's chest and listening to her heartbeat has been denied. Reestablishing safe human contact on a physical level becomes a crucial element in healing in later years. One woman wrote to me to say that the first two years of her therapy were primarily devoted to her therapist holding her. She needed to hear a human heartbeat to feel safe and reported that talk therapy could only begin after she had established physical connection and security.

But at the time my needs for safe touch were surfacing, I did not know that other women hurt by their mothers also struggled with this huge issue of safe touch. I thought I was the only person on the earth who was so needy, dirty and disgusting. I craved what I could never have: the safety of a nurturing mother's touch. And it was somehow wrong to need this. If it were right, Jim would hold me. And that still had not happened.

*   *   *

My friend Susan began to work with a therapist named Kate. Susan's visits to El Salvador had reactivated abuse-related issues that she thought had been resolved in therapy sessions a decade earlier. Because Kate was also trained as a body worker, she was able to include massage in Susan's treatment as well as talk psychotherapy. Although the touch was very difficult at first, Susan was convinced that it would bring the kind of deep healing and body connection that had been absent in her earlier therapy. She was a strong advocate of the Child's need for safe touch from Jim.

One night during a telephone conversation, I was running through a litany of self-blame and hatred for what I perceived as my unacceptable weakness in needing Jim to hold me. The Child felt neglected, dirty and untouchable. Yet every time Susan criticized Jim's lack of touch, the adult part of me rushed to defend him. Even though I was not convinced that the traditional therapeutic no-touch rule was justified in all circumstances, I also understood that it serves a good purpose most of the time and is generally accepted as a standard of professional conduct meant to insure safety for both client and therapist. Yet there are situations in which therapists may be able to provide some form of safe touch without violating their own boundaries or their clients' boundaries. Each case depends on the particular client, the maturity and professional support community of the therapist and the healing which could take place as a result of including touch in the therapeutic process. It is a complex decision, and I understood that Jim was wise to be cautious in considering the implications.

But I did not voice my doubts about the validity of the no-touch rules to Susan. Instead, I defended Jim by supporting him with arguments I did not fully believe. The adult part of me understood that the child would choose to die unless this need was met. At a deep level, I instinctively sensed it was more important to save her life than to adhere to a set of rigid rules. But I did not have the strength to protect her. If she were to be spared, the initiative would have to come from Jim.

Sensing the futility of the argument, Susan finally bypassed the adult and spoke directly to the Child. "Listen to me," she said firmly, "Sometimes grown-ups are just plain stupid. You have every right to be held."

The Child inside heard her and held on to a small hope that she was right. The adult quickly ended the conversation and hung up the telephone.

*　　　　　　　*　　　　　　　*

As my youngest son's sixteenth birthday approached, I began the preparations for the traditional family gathering that was expected by my father at each holiday. In addition to my immediate birth family, the guests would also include my father's five siblings and their grown children. I never questioned the necessity of dutifully hosting the entire clan as each birthday or holiday rolled around, but I always became so anxious that my physical health would suffer for weeks after these mandatory celebrations.

This year, I particularly dreaded having my cousin Tommy in my home. Now in his forties, he continued to live with his parents, never having married. From time to time, there were family whispers about his periodic "involvement" with children. But these conversations always ended with the solemn collective agreement that "Tommy is a good boy."

Although I had always remembered the summer he had molested me, I had never felt the emotional pain of the experience until recently. Now, the thought of having to serve cake to Tommy and socialize within the family system that had closed its eyes and ears so many times to the pain of a little girl in its midst provoked great anxiety.

When I told Jim about the upcoming event which I felt I was duty bound to host, he challenged the assumption that I was required to continue the obviously painful tradition. He said that we could choose to celebrate holidays and birthdays in other ways. Despite my dread and the heavy feeling in my chest, his suggestion to cancel the gathering seemed absolutely unthinkable. Saying no to the wishes of my father was something I could not yet imagine.

Steve also dreaded the convergence of my relatives at our house on holidays and birthdays, but for different reasons. The relatives were noisy and always insisted he play board or card games, which he disliked. He always agreed to play to keep the peace, but he resented feeling coerced into participating.

Steve's family did not place much importance on birthdays and did not mark them with rituals such as gift giving and decorated cakes. Although he appreciated celebrating, he wished we could celebrate without my relatives. He knew the ordeal of hosting Tommy was going to be particularly difficult this year, given my newfound ability to be upset about his molestation of me as a child. However, we both felt bound by the force of tradition to plan every major celebration around my extended family. Both of our sons enjoyed the presents showered on them by their grandfather, aunts and uncles. Neither Steve nor I could call a halt to a practice that both of us resented and did not enjoy.

Our culture is replete with images of traditional extended families celebrating special occasions. From advertising sales pitches to admonitions from church pulpits, this nostalgic notion of family is used to persuade us to buy and to bond. Until we are aware that blood ties are not the most important aspect of what constitutes real "family," most of us believe the myth that we are obligated to sublimate our own pain in order to preserve attachment to our biological families. At the time, I still believed the myth.

I prepared for the birthday party in a haze. I felt detached from my body and distant from everything around me, including my husband and children. I moved through a thick fog no one but me could see, its cold mists swirling around my legs until I no longer felt my feet touch the floor as I drifted through the chores of cleaning, shopping and preparing the food.

Tommy was one of the first guests to arrive. Heavy and lumbering, his step on the porch caused panic to rise in my throat. As I opened the door, I felt my body grow numb. With more of a leer than a smile, he said hello and brushed past me, collapsing his bulk into the nearest chair. I quickly escaped to the kitchen and let my husband greet the other guests.

Several times during the hours that followed, I fled to the sanctuary of my bedroom and wrote in my journal, trying to cling to my rapidly diminishing equilibrium. I pleaded a headache and was grudgingly released from the task of playing cards and board games as the afternoon turned to evening. It was not an easy decision; games were extremely important to these family members who played with great seriousness and competition, often provoking shouting matches and accusations of cheating. When I had refused to play cards after Christmas dinner a few years before because I was exhausted, my father ordered my sister to get their coats and they left in an angry huff. This time, I was careful to emphasize I did not feel well, rather than refuse to play. This allowed me to escape to my bedroom without causing a scene with my father.

Periodically, I came downstairs to serve food and refill drinks, making an effort to be gracious when my son opened his gifts and cut the birthday cake. When the last guest left, I collapsed on my bed. The Child was strangely silent. She felt cold as death. I took several sleeping pills because I was quite sure I did not want to dream that night. I fell asleep with the giant prescription bottle and a glass of water on the night table by my side. It gave me great comfort to know that my final option was only a gulp away.

*   *   *

In the weeks that followed, I began a downhill slide. The strain of having my extended birth family inside of my house—one of my few safe spaces—felt like an invasion that had violated my spirit. I poured energy into the upcoming delegation to El Salvador, scheduled to leave in less than three weeks. Meanwhile, the Child was still desperate to be held by Jim, and the matter was far from any sort of resolution. The two weeks of his vacation seemed like an endurance test rather than a brief break from therapy.

Although I was struggling to stay present, I constantly lost chunks of time and was often unable to account for hours of a day. I regularly became lost while driving in familiar territory. At times I regressed to child states behind the wheel, suddenly waking up in the driver's seat in a state of terror—I had no clue how to drive a car. I could hardly see over the dashboard and it seemed as if my feet were barely able to reach the pedals on the floor. Once I stopped in the middle of a four-lane highway, unable to overcome my confusion enough to pull over to the side of the road. If I approached a traffic light, I could not comprehend the signals. Did red mean stop or go? Looking back, I know that in this state I was a real hazard on the road and it is only by the grace of my guardian angel that I did not hurt myself or someone else.

One sunny weekend I walked to a park several miles from my house. The uneasy silence and alienation I sensed from the Child was of grave concern. I hoped that by spending some time outside I might reconnect with this wounded part of me that had so recently emerged after her long exile.

I sat down beneath a towering elm tree. I felt the strength of its trunk against my back. I snuggled in close among the roots and shut my eyes. When I was a little girl, all of my safe places were outside. Trees were special friends, and I often imagined they reached down their leafy arms to me as I huddled next to rough bark, pretending I was being held.

Gradually, I felt the Child stir. She brought with her an inexpressible sadness. She had lived through hell. She had been frozen in time for many years and had finally risked resurrection. She emerged into a world in which there were no warm arms to hold her or hands to stroke her head. Her question of why she was once again rejected was unanswerable. I knew that if she chose not to face the pain involved in healing, I had no right to stop her. She needed to be touched and held, the same as any traumatized child, and I was unable to provide that for her. Who could blame her for giving up?

Slowly, I let her surface and allowed myself to feel the force of her presence. I needed to hear what she was saying to me. As we sat beneath the tree and watched the sun set, her communication became clear. She wanted to die. There was no reason to live. And she wanted me to help her. I clung to the trunk of the tree. For the first time in years, tears filled my eyes. I had reached for life and failed. I had reentered the horror chambers of my childhood, and I still only had trees to hold me.

*   *   *

From my journal…
This is important. I reached down deep and found the truth: I have no value. There is too much damage to heal. This doesn't frighten me. I am relieved to discover the truth. I am untouchable. I am not human. This explains why I can't be close to people and why I always feel unreal and disconnected. I have no value. Knowing this helps me to understand why Jim will not hold me.

Susan called to tell me that Kate wanted her to take off her shirt or shorts for her massage yesterday. Susan felt a little tense but took off her shirt. Said it actually felt wonderful to feel Kate's hands on her bare skin. Susan is human. I am not. Now that I understand that I have no value, it doesn't hurt so much that Jim isn't willing to touch me as part of therapy.

*   *   *

Jim continued to encourage me to talk about my need for touch. He said we would find a way to respect boundaries and meet the Child's needs, but that he still needed time to figure out how to best do that. I began to withdraw, thinking that words without actions were meaningless to the Child. She stopped asking to be held. I felt detached, numb and very calm.

I planned to leave for El Salvador shortly. Secretly, I hoped I would die there. I told myself that my death would be for a good cause, that martyrs abounded in this small country of so much suffering, that people drew strength from the sacrifice of others. Being a martyr would save me from having to hurt myself, and I would be honoring the part of me that rebelled against walking the suicide path. Suicide had been my mother's choice, and I abhorred the idea of being like her in any way. Ironically this rebelliousness kept me alive and struggling for another solution. It was given to me in El Salvador. But not at all in the way I expected.

*   *   *

At the beginning of a therapy session shortly before the trip to El Salvador, Jim said he wanted to bring up an agenda item. This was rare. Usually, Jim came to wherever I was in the healing process and accompanied me as I struggled to find the next step. Seldom did he place a specific topic on the agenda unless he thought I was refusing to deal with something he considered essential.

As it turned out, he was afraid for my physical and emotional safety. He knew I was going to El Salvador at a time when great tension and uncertainty gripped the country. He wanted to know how I planned to take care of the Child. He was concerned that the trip was coming at a difficult time for me; he understood the struggle it was just to hold on to life. He also knew the ongoing issue of touch had triggered depression and withdrawal from him to a certain extent. He wanted to be sure that the Child was not further damaged by the stress of the trip.

While Jim was supportive of the work I was doing with the churches there, worry was evident in his eyes. The deadline for completion of the fragile and complex peace process was drawing near. New tensions had erupted in recent weeks as each side accused the other of bad faith, and the time frames so painstakingly negotiated for demilitarization were ignored. Peace is much more than the absence of war, and El Salvador was still a volatile and dangerous place. The cease-fire was barely holding.

I felt a torrent of mixed emotions. The Child deep inside stirred. The experience of being cared for by someone who was protective and gentle while also making rules, setting boundaries and imposing limits was so new that the feelings evoked were raw and painful. Part of me wanted to soak up all of Jim's nurturing presence, but another part wanted to run away screaming because getting what I needed also hurt. And although the word "love" was not spoken, I had never in all of my life felt as loved and valued as I did within this relationship with Jim, despite its limitations and frustrations.

I had given careful thought to how I would handle the Child in El Salvador. I felt a keen responsibility as a person in a leadership role to work with delegates and the Salvadoran communities who would be hosting us. But I now knew enough about the Child to understand that if I did not pay at least some attention to her, my ability to function in such a demanding environment could be severely compromised. And that could place not only me but also other people at great risk.

I promised Jim I would indeed take care of the Child because I certainly didn't want her wrecking the delegation or its mission. I had already packed in my suitcase the stuffed bear the child needed to sleep with at night, the tape of Jim's voice telling a story that he recorded for me before he went on vacation and two new blank journals. I only hoped no one would discover the bear. I planned to keep the Child's existence hidden as well as I could.

Jim was relieved to hear that the Child would not be ignored. At the end of the session, he held me for a few extra seconds in a warm hug. He predicted that it would be different for me this year in El Salvador. For the first time, I would go there with an awareness of my own wounds.

Notes from El Salvador: The Real World

When I traveled to El Salvador for the first time in 1987, a Latina woman in a seat near mine sobbed inconsolably during much of the flight. Another passenger occasionally turned around to speak with her, periodically offering tissues and words of consolation. I learned that the weeping woman was returning to El Salvador to claim the body of her daughter, a college student and advocate for social justice for the poor, who had been killed by the army as a suspected collaborator with the FMLN.

After our brief stop in Guatemala, the jet headed for its final destination in El Salvador. Very few people, mostly wearing business attire, remained on the plane; a country at war is not a popular travel destination. To increase our delegation's chances of being allowed to enter the country, we were dressed in similar fashion. Business travelers were welcomed in El Salvador as they were usually connected to the interests of the wealthy. Church delegations were viewed with suspicion, and at times detained at the airport by the military. One recent group that included prominent church leaders was forced to return to the United States after being held at the airport for several days. Our best chance of passing through military security was to appear to be either wealthy tourists or business travelers.

Scrutinizing my conservative suit, the woman who had been dispensing tissues turned her attention to me. With piercing eyes, she asked me in heavily accented English if I had been to El Salvador before. I told her I had not. She asked why I was going there.

Painfully aware that I dare not disclose my true intent, I muttered that I was in banking, and had business interests in the capital.

Her face turned to stone, and she uttered words I have never forgotten. *"You have not seen the real world until you have seen the Third world,"* she said.

Then she turned her attention back to her sobbing companion and left me to puzzle over her pronouncement. After a few days in El Salvador, I was no longer perplexed. I understood what she meant.

Chapter 6

To Touch is to Heal

"Security is still an issue in El Salvador. On February 1, 1992, the cease fire went into effect. However, death squads are still active and this means that Salvadoran leaders need to be cautious. Leaders include church and community leaders, leaders in cooperatives and peasant organizations, etc. Because our sister parishes are composed of poor people who are in the process of moving out of oppression, they pose a threat to those whose interests are not favored by change.

We enter a happy new time in El Salvador when there is no active war. The tension seems to be less but for the sake of the people we are visiting, we must be cautious."

From "Security Guidelines for El Salvador"
Share Foundation, 1992

*   *   *

By 1992, El Salvador felt like my spiritual home. I had grown to love and deeply respect this small struggling country comprised over-whelmingly of poor people who struggled against huge odds to build their communities and help their children realize the dream of a just and peaceful society.

It was clear that Salvadorans peasants loved children. Many of the poorest families took the children of parents who had been killed or who had fled to the mountains to become resistance fighters during the twelve years of war.

When I visited many of the country's rural villages, I witnessed a gentle collective form of child rearing unlike anything I had ever seen in my own country. Children were touched often with warmth and affection and held by members of the community. They were treated with respect and gentleness. When a child cried for whatever reason, the nearest adult was ready to comfort and wipe away tears. I never saw an adult strike a child, and it was rare to see children fight with each other. Because the adults modeled non-violence and cooperative living, the children copied these core values that were reflected in play with each other. I was amazed at the way a group of children could share a few worn-out toys without arguing. Children when treated with respect learn to respect the rights of others.

This form of child rearing was most evident in the communities that had gone through a long process of what Salvadorans spoke of as "becoming conscious." It was somewhat similar to the consciousness-raising process popular within the U.S. feminist movement in the 1970s when women started to make connections between the personal and the political. In small groups, women began to talk about their experiences of domestic violence and rape. Shocked to learn that many others had been similarly victimized, they slowly came to understand that sexual violence and battering were not private traumas but aspects of their lives that could become potent political forces for change if they shared their stories and organized.

Many Salvadorans in Christian-based communities located in regions of the country such as Chalatenango and Morazan experienced this same kind of evolution in thinking when they began to comprehend that it was not the will of God that their children die of hunger and they bear the crushing burden of poverty despite their hard work.

Strengthened and inspired by studying the Bible through the lens of their daily reality, they organized themselves to demand political and social changes to end these injustices. Because much of the consciousness-raising with Salvadorans took place in the context of community and family, it naturally expanded into areas of life such as raising children with non-violence, respect for basic human rights and changing family structure as part of a political process of transforming social structure from a hierarchical to cooperative model.

My newly awakened internal child was not oblivious to this environment in which children were so evidently loved and cherished. As I reestablished friendships with our hosts, I felt the Child who I was determined to keep in the background rise to the surface, demanding to be a part of this experience. She watched with anguished longing when a child's hair was being tenderly stroked by her mother or when a toddler fell and hurt his knee and was quickly scooped up in loving arms before his second indignant wail of pain could be fully voiced. These were the kind of simple touches the Child craved but was always denied. The pain of wanting what could not be obtained was acute.

This was a very different dynamic than my previous method of coping with the challenges posed by spending time in a country at war. In past trips to El Salvador, I focused intently on the social and political issues in a broad context. Now, I found myself wanting to spend time just being with families involved in the daily chores of cooking, tending children, carrying water, and sharing life. Instead of immediately launching into a political discussion when I sat to eat a meal, I found myself quietly watching the others at the table, suddenly realizing with amazement that people also told funny stories, joked and laughed as they shared a meal and the company of each other. These were the places of simple human connection I never paid attention to previously.

It seemed as if the new consciousness—the awareness of my own wounds as Jim had said—allowed me a level of emotional connection with other people that I could never have experienced when my own pain remained sealed within me.

I understood well my role as a perpetrator of violence through my payment of tax dollars to a government that used them to fund the war against the poor in El Salvador. I knew that as a citizen of the United States, I consumed far more than my fair share of goods in relation to the rest of the world, and this consumption contributed to the desperate conditions of poverty in Central America. The relatively inexpensive cup of coffee I drank during a break at work was picked by peasants who toiled in the hot sun all day for less than the equivalent of three dollars. The clothes that I bought at department store sale prices were sewn by dark-skinned women who were paid just a few cents an hour. I accepted my responsibility to find ways to protest destructive U.S. military and economic policies and to stand with the people hurt by their implementation. I understood my political and social power.

But until I permitted myself to feel the pain about the ways in which I was personally violated, I did not comprehend that I, like the Salvadorans I accompanied, had also suffered injustice and oppression. I did not realize that torture is torture, whether it takes place in a military prison or in the kitchen of a middle-class home in the United States. I did not understand my own powerlessness to prevent what had happened to me.

I would discover during this trip that each step of opening myself to my history of abuse and violation and allowing my wounds to be seen and healed by others was an agonizing endeavor.

*   *   *

This year, Gary was to meet us at the airport. As the delegation made its way through the hundreds of people waiting for arriving passengers just outside the huge glass doors at the far end of the terminal, I eagerly scanned the crowd for him. Tall with light hair, he was easy to spot in the throng of dark-headed and bronze-skinned Salvadorans, who also tended to be much shorter than *gringos*. Pushing my way through the crowd and trying to keep the other delegates with me, I finally made my way to Gary. Although he was in his 40s, with his slim frame and boyish face he looked 20 years younger. His face lit up in a grin, and he embraced me with an enthusiastic hug. "Welcome to El Salvador!" I hugged him back, hard. As we threaded our way through the crowd to the curb for transportation, I introduced new delegates and smiled at the warm reception given him by returning delegates who already knew him. Gifted with a magnetic personality, Gary was a strong person who attracted the attention of others in a positive way.

As the delegation leader, Gary had arrived in the country several days earlier to make appointments for delegation visits and handle the myriad of details involved in shepherding a group of North Americans in El Salvador. Since part of the purpose of the trip was education, it was important that delegates be exposed to a wide range of cultural, political and social issues. Project *Via Crucis* groups were diverse and could include teachers, doctors, executives, engineers, students, retirees and pastors. Devising a schedule that would meet the needs of the Salvadoran communities and yet provide the delegates with a solid sense of the historical context and current situation of the country was a daunting task at which Gary excelled. When he handed out our detailed itineraries and maps, we knew the visit would be two weeks of intensive activity.

When I first met Gary six years before, I felt a strange and powerful bonding take place and knew that an important person had just come into my life. As years passed, I had grown to respect this openly gay man and fellow activist, admiring his courage in refusing to keep silent about his identity in a world largely hostile to anyone outside the pale of heterosexuality. By speaking candidly of his sexual orientation, he helped to pave the way for others still too frightened to disclose their true identities to families, friends and employers.

Gary had lived in El Salvador in the mid-1980s, giving up a financially lucrative career in real estate to work in poor communities. Much of his work for the church centered on human rights issues. In 1987, he and Nat, another U.S. church worker, came to the Lutheran guest house to meet with the initial Project *Via Crucis* delegation when I him for the first time.

Gary and Nat described in detail the desperate situation of the peasants in poor communities who organized themselves to demand rights as citizens, laborers and human beings from the government. To ask for fair wages for work, schools for the children and freedom of political expression was condemned as communism by the government. To denounce police surveillance of church activities invited the wrath of the military that primarily served the interests of the elite.

Nat spoke with quiet passion about his work of accompaniment. He described living with *campesinos* from whom he learned how to plant corn and dance between bombing raids. Accompaniment was an ongoing process of living in relationship with the poor, celebrating their joys, sharing their risks and suffering pain with them. Nat said many in his own Mennonite faith did not really understand the work of accompaniment. They were more familiar with traditional mission work such as building churches and spreading the Gospel. Conversely, Nat believed that it was North Americans who needed to be evangelized by the Salvadoran poor. As he accompanied them, he felt the presence of God.

Gary talked about U.S. involvement in the training of Salvadoran officers in torture techniques as a clandestine instruction manual with graphic "how-to" illustrations was passed in the group. As he spoke of his encounters with survivors of torture, I saw that tears glistened in his eyes. Most long-term international workers I met distanced themselves from their emotional responses to the human suffering in order to function in an environment of terror and constant crisis. I did not fault them because I understood the necessity of detachment in chronically stressful situations. At the same time, I was intrigued that Gary somehow had the inner strength to operate at a high level but still feel the pain of the people he worked with.

When I arrived in El Salvador that October 1992 with a stuffed bear hidden in my suitcase, Gary already knew that I was struggling with childhood abuse issues from telephone conversations and letters. I found him easy to talk with, especially since he listened intently and asked careful questions that often helped me clarify my own feelings. Perhaps because of his own wounds from living in the homophobic culture of the United States, he was able to empathize in a way that communicated to me that my pain mattered to him. I considered Gary to be my friend.

He had made the decision to identify himself publicly as a gay person after he moved from El Salvador to the United States several years before, continuing the solidarity work on the north side of the border and traveling to Central America frequently to lead delegations. He had suffered repercussions for his honesty. The church congregation which he served faithfully for many years in various ways would no longer allow him to read scripture aloud during worship services, a form of participation he deeply loved, and he was banned from holding any leadership role in the church.

Recently, he had become involved in a relationship with Joe, a man he loved deeply and with whom he hoped to spend the rest of his life. I celebrated the joy of this commitment with him because it seemed like a healthy, growing relationship filled with respect and caring. From the deep happiness that shone in his eyes whenever he talked about his partner, I knew Gary had found someone to cherish.

The Child instinctively felt Gary was a safe person and wanted to tell him about all of the things that had hurt her. She liked to be close to him and usually found ways to sit near him during meetings or meals. I was still determined not to let my own issues distract from the work at hand in any way and firmly told her that El Salvador was not the place to try to get any of her needs met. She would have to be satisfied listening to the tape of Jim's voice and holding the stuffed bear at night.

Our schedule was quite demanding. Project *Via Crucis* was now actively involved in developing "sister church" relationships between parishes in El Salvador and Pennsylvania. Gary had carefully divided our time between meetings in the capital with political, labor, human rights, and social movement representatives as well as trips to the countryside to spend time with rural communities. Up before 6 a.m., we often collapsed in exhaustion after the last meeting ended twelve hours later. Meals were sporadic, sometimes consisting of granola bars and chocolate as unreliable transportation fell through and schedules were juggled to make up for delays. Everyone was talking feverishly about the peace accords. Most were pessimistic about the prospect of a lasting cease fire agreement and construction of real peace.

Yet repressing my internal desire to connect more fully with Gary by sharing personal information began to take a toll in a few days. I started to emotionally withdraw and feel completely drained of energy. Under cover of darkness in my bedroom at night, the child with no name surfaced, smothering all thought of drawing comfort from something as useless as a stuffed bear.

I excused myself from evening reflections with the delegation one night, pleading exhaustion from the heat. I felt the numb detachment beginning to creep through my body, and I could not tolerate being around other people. I retreated to my room to sit and stare at the wall until my mind carried me to a place of vast and empty whiteness where I felt nothing. Early the next morning, Gary came and slipped his arm around my shoulders as I stood drinking coffee in the kitchen of the church's guest house, trying to jolt my sleep-deprived system awake with caffeine.

"How did you sleep?" he asked.

I mumbled something about being really tired from the heat and the heavy schedule.

He just held me closer and waited.

"What are you feeling?" Each softly spoken word fell into the early morning silence and seemed to form a solid crystal. There was no question I dreaded more than this one. Conversely, it was exactly what I wanted to be asked.

The forbidden needs for physical touch and closeness rushed to the surface, dissolving my carefully constructed intellectual defenses and freeing my frozen emotions. One of the reasons Gary represented the ultimate in safety for me was his sexual orientation. I was terrified to be touched even casually by a woman, and I understood that many heterosexual men would have a difficult time with their own sexual feelings if they had been asked to touch an adult woman as freely as they would a small child.

In the tranquillity of the open courtyard bordering the kitchen, I finally began to speak. My words formed slowly at first, then rushed to the surface in torrents as I tried to describe my experiences and revelations during the past months. I told him how overwhelming it was to actually feel the long-denied emotions about being molested by my cousin and raped by Rick. I confided the sense of lingering violation I felt about having Tommy as a guest in my home for the birthday party. My breath caught in my throat as I whispered that I had remembered being hurt by my mother. My body trembled, and I instinctively huddled closer to Gary for protection. The boundaries between me and the Child began to crumble. As physical and emotional intimacy were finally brought together by Gary's gentle words while he held me against his body, his arm now wrapped firmly around my waist, I knew the Child was being irrevocably released. For better or worse, we were in El Salvador together.

Other delegates began to congregate for breakfast. Gary asked if we could spend some time together that evening to continue the conversation. Unanimously, the Child and I agreed.

*   *   *

Following customary evening reflections and prayers, Gary and I found an empty room in the rambling guest house where we would not be interrupted. We sat on the floor between two cots in a small windowless room. The night was stiflingly hot and humid, and we turned on a fan to provide cool relief. Leaning against the beds for support, we faced each other.

At first, my words came out haltingly. I had remembered so much in the past year and had begun to feel emotion for the first time about the abuse I had always remembered but consistently minimized. I did not intend to tell Gary about the dilemma with Jim over the issue of touch and felt deeply ashamed about wanting to be held. Despite assurances by Susan, I remained convinced that Jim was right not to hold me and that it was wrong and stupid of me to allow such a child-based need to surface. It made me feel dirty and unclean.

But eventually, the intensity of his listening and the insistence of the Child on telling him everything won over my determination to keep the conversation on an adult level. I heard myself tell him, as though from a great distance, that Jim would not hold me. I shared the conclusion I had reached as I wrote in my journal about why he would not. With a certain amount of detachment, I explained I was not really human, and that I had no value. This is why Jim would not touch me like Susan's therapist touched her. I knew that it was wrong to want to be held and that I would just have to get over it.

Gary's face reflected the pain I refused to express. He reached out and took my hand. Rubbing it gently, he told me that I was a wonderful and good person and that he was sad that I did not value myself as a human being and a creation of God. He said that the relationship with his partner had taught him the necessity and the value of being held. As he talked softly and stroked my hand, I heard him say that being held is a basic human need.

I felt as though my body had turned to ice. His voice seemed to be coming from far away. Inside I heard the Child sobbing. She wanted

Gary to hold her. She was frightened of the need and even more terri-fied to ask for it to be met. Too many times, her need had been denied.

I opened my mouth but no words came out. I heard Gary say, "Give me your other hand." I did, and both of my hands were enveloped in his warm grasp. With great effort, I looked into his face. For a long moment, there was a pain and love that passed between us without words.

In a barely audible voice, the Child asked the question that always led to greater pain or rejection. "Will you hold me?"

His answer was an immediate yes. There was none of the agonizing dis-cussion that I inevitably faced with Jim about how I wanted to be held or what being held would mean to me. He simply reached out and pulled me into his lap, cradling my back against his chest. He wrapped his arms around me, held both of my hands and began to rock me gently.

Huge waves of fear flooded through me. Although the Child desper-ately wanted to be held, she also feared closeness with another human being. Tremors ran through my body, and I was freezing in the tropical night. My hands jerking in spasms, I felt as though I could not breathe. Gary held me tight and kissed the top of my head. With his gentle encouragement, I slowly relaxed and began to take in the sensation of being held in a completely safe and non-sexual way.

For hours, in the soft Salvadoran night, Gary gently rocked the trau-matized Child. At times, he would talk to me about his own experiences of rejection by people who believed he was less than human because he was gay. He understood in a profound way the importance of having your deepest identity and self affirmed in an unconditional and loving way by trusted people. He firmly insisted that my need for touch was legitimate and that I deserved to be held. He was outraged that my mother stole even my tears. Echoing Jim's conviction, he promised that one day I would reclaim my ability to cry. He agreed that tears, protest and anger were worthy goals.

In the early morning light, when we finally headed for our beds to get a few hours of sleep, I felt a sense of being loved and valued in a way that touched the core part of my being. By his ready acceptance of my need for touch, Gary had helped me to take a giant step toward life and healing.

We had been friends for some time. But that night, this gay man who suffered from his own wounds and yet reached out to heal others became my brother. Like Jim, he also would walk with me through the wilderness that lay ahead on my long healing journey. I could have chosen no finer accompaniment.

*   *   *

My acceptance of the presence of the Child in El Salvador and acknowledgment of the legitimacy of her needs freed the adult part of me to go about the work of the delegation. As long as I was careful to allow the Child her fair share of time, I was able to participate in the activities that filled each day's schedule. Being physically close to Gary was enormously important. Without touch, I could not keep myself from sliding into withdrawal and numbness. I needed frequent hugs and reassurances to keep from disengaging. Without making it a central issue, I was able to share briefly with the delegation that I was in an active process of healing from childhood sexual abuse. I explained that Gary was helping me to cope with many abuse-related issues that were surfacing in El Salvador. Like the Salvadorans we were accompanying who did not wish to be alone as they struggled to rebuild their shattered lives, I needed friends to walk with me.

I was also grateful for the presence of Susan. Although I was very uncomfortable with any kind of touch from Susan because of her femaleness, we did share a special closeness through our commitment to the Salvadoran people and mutual histories of childhood abuse. We each had a terrible point of reference inside of us for what it is like to be raped and tortured. Their stories were like our own in many ways and I know that the suffering of the Salvadoran poor affected us both on very deep levels.

One of the ways in which Susan's abuse shaped her adult life was that she was constantly seeking a protective and loving mother. During the past few years, she had developed a deep affection for Felicita, the woman who ran the church's guest house that was our home base during our visits to El Salvador. Although I was more distant from Felicita, I found myself looking forward to her smile whenever I arrived on the doorstep of the guest house for another visit.

Felicita, whose name means "joy" in Spanish, was one of the most gentle people I have ever encountered. From dawn to dusk, she took care of the cooking, cleaning and laundry of the many delegations placed under her care every few weeks. With her young children at her feet, she somehow always found time to talk with Susan and me, inviting us into the small room off the kitchen where she lived to help with our Spanish or to explain some point of Salvadoran politics that mystified us. I believe she sensed the wounded child within Susan and me and did what she could to provide a safe space for us. She taught us how to make beans in a special way. She wrote down lyrics of songs in Spanish so we would not stumble over words in church services. She ironed our skirts after she dried them in the sun, despite our protests, saying she wanted us to look nice when we went to our delegation appointments.

Susan sought out Felicita's touch and thrived on the mother-like intimacy she offered. Although the slightest touch from Felicita triggered panic within me, I did allow a limited form of affection from her. But Felicita's dark eyes mirrored puzzlement and concern as my body stiffened whenever she pulled me into her embrace. She always hugged me briefly and then released me. I never answered the unspoken question in her eyes about my fear.

Susan and I assumed that because Felicita never spoke of her past, she had somehow escaped the direct impact of the war. Yet we knew she was originally from a community in Chalatenango where there had been much conflict. We noticed that sometimes when she held her daughter Rosa, her eyes filled with an unfathomable sadness. One day she told us why.

*   *   *

Felicita worked in the fields of corn and beans each day. But when the military planes loaded with bombs darkened the skies of the village, Felicita had not yet left for the fields and was in her small house with two of her children. Her husband and oldest son were already at work, and Felicitia was packing tortillas to feed her family as they labored to harvest the crop.

As bombing started over the fields, people were screaming and smoke was filling the air. Following the bombardment, ground troops swarmed through the village, killing its residents and burning what had not been destroyed by the bombs. Grabbing her two younger children, Felicita fled to the mountains with other members of the community. She did not know what happened to her husband and oldest son. All she could do was pray for their safety and try to stay one step ahead of the army that hunted them.

Felicita's flight was slow because she was nine months pregnant. After two days of running on bare feet through formidable mountain territory, she could go no further. Her child was about to be delivered.

She left the straggling group of refugees and collapsed just inside the entrance of a small cave, her two frightened and exhausted children at her side. She was already in hard labor, the deafening sounds of heavy artillery nearby barely distracting her from the contractions. Chewing on a rock to keep from crying out in pain, she began to give instructions to her children on how they might help with the birth.

Suddenly, an old woman, who had been traveling with the group of refugees, appeared at the doorway of the cave. Moving with firm determination, she set out to assist with the birth in the most difficult and primitive of circumstances. Calmly, she explained that she simply could not continue with the group knowing that Felicita needed help. She was old anyway, she reasoned, and if she were to be killed by the army as she made her way back to the cave, so be it. No woman should have to give birth to a child assisted only by other children.

Rosa was born a short time later, and the old woman wrapped the infant in a precious clean towel. It was the only thing from her house she had carried with her, tucked deep into her pocket when she fled the village. Foraging food and water from the forest around them, the women, children and newborn baby huddled in the cave for several days until the sounds of the battle faded into the distance. When it was safe, they headed for one of the church-sponsored refugee camps that were dotting the country as a sad consequence of the military operations.

Felicita was reunited with her oldest son after a few months. However, her husband had been captured by the military. He was automatically considered a FMLN collaborator because he was a male in his prime and was imprisoned and tortured. When he was released more than a year later, he searched for his family, and they were joyfully reunited.

But Felicita soon discovered to her horror that this was not the same sensitive, considerate man she loved and married. The torture had totally changed his personality. He had nightmares and could not sleep. He became violent with his wife and children and at times he thought he was back in the prison, suffering agonizing pain as his body remembered being penetrated, poked, cut and shocked with electrical currents.

Once again, Felicita took her children and fled, finding the job with the church as a guest house coordinator. She grieved deeply for her husband and prayed every day that his mind would be returned to him and that they could again live together. Periodically, she went to visit him at his parents' home. But although more than nine years had passed since his torture, the nightmares and fits of rage remained, as fresh as they were the day he was released from prison.

Felicita's brown eyes filled with tears and she began sobbing as she spoke of her continuing love for her husband. We sat with her, stunned by her story and trying to find words of comfort for her pain. Finally, she composed herself and dried her eyes. "I have forgiven the torturers of my husband because God teaches us we must forgive," she said with fierce dignity. "But I will never, never forget what they have done."

*   *   *

Listening to Felicita's story moved me immeasurably. Her quiet strength and cheerfulness as she attended to the needs of delegations staying in the guest house belied the multiple traumas she had suffered. I had let myself believe that Felicitia had been spared the horrors of war as I watched her play with her young children with the variety of small toys that Susan had stuffed into her suitcase. I did not realize until the moment she told us her story how much grief and loss was held inside this woman whose care-taking role and nurturing gestures I both feared and wanted. As she served a meal, she would sometimes caress my cheek or lay her hand on my shoulder briefly as she moved deftly around the large dining table. Although her touch was light, my body would react with a quick involuntary jerk. I usually managed a small smile to let her know I was not offended. But I could always see the puzzled concern in her dark eyes.

I had heard many accounts of military atrocities like those suffered by Felicitia and her family through the years of work in El Salvador. Until I began to connect with my own pain, my response to the stories of survivors was limited to the political action I undertook on their behalf. But I had crossed an irrevocable line when I began to allow the previously buried parts of my history to become part of my conscious knowledge. The inclusion of the child in my Salvadoran journey left me much more vulnerable and yet strangely more resilient For the first time, I considered sharing my own story of suffering with a Salvadoran person.

Susan and I discussed this idea of sharing extensively. We both wanted to develop relationships of mutuality and respect with our Salvadoran friends. Increasingly, we realized that unless we were also willing to allow them to know of our own pain and accompany us as we struggled for healing, our relationships would lack an essential integrity. We decided we would talk with Felicita about our childhood abuse.

Late one night, after other delegates had retired, Susan and I met Felicita in the kitchen. She spoke no English, and Susan's Spanish was fairly limited. It quickly became clear that I would have to translate Susan's story in order for Felicita to understand. I steeled myself to detach emotionally. I concentrated on doing my best to convey the childhood horror of nightly molestation by her father. Although my Spanish was more advanced, I was not fluent and often had to struggle for the proper words. The language of this particular kind of pain was not yet part of my Spanish vocabulary.

Felicita listened intently, nodding her head occasionally to let us know she understood and occasionally interrupting to ask for clarification when my Spanish became garbled. Her outrage and indignation about what happened to Susan was apparent as she reached out to touch her frequently, patting her shoulder and murmuring words of consolation. Although the subject of family violence and incest had not been raised in our prior visits to El Salvador, Felicita's response made it clear that domestic violence and child abuse were significant problems that were largely denied and rarely discussed in her country.

Many Salvadorans whose rural communities were destroyed were herded by the army toward the capital city of San Salvador, where the strength of the government was greatest. The shelters provided were abysmal and could accommodate only a small number of refugees. Thousands of people resorted to living on the outskirts of the city, erecting shelters of plastic and tin and scavenging for food in garbage dumps. These sprawling urban slums were potent breeding ground for hopelessness. Separated from the land they loved and the communities that formed their identities, many succumbed to drinking and then to alcoholism. Soldiers returning to civilian life often brought the violence of war back into their families. Trained to kill and rape as part of their military campaigns, they continued to function in those roles long after they turned in their uniforms. Women and children were battered and sexually abused.

When it was my turn to tell my experiences, I felt a cold sickness in the pit of my stomach. I began to haltingly describe the environment in which I lived in as a child. I could tell that Felicita was expecting that my story would be similar to Susan's as we had both identified ourselves as incest survivors at the beginning of the conversation. But when I disclosed that it was my mother who sexually and physically abused me, there was an audible gasp, and Felicita's calm demeanor cracked.

"*Tu propia madre?*" she questioned, obviously shaken and perhaps doubting my Spanish.

I nodded miserably. "Yes, Felicita. My own mother."

She swore. It was the first and only time I have heard her use that kind of language. I could see the sudden understanding in her expression as she reached out to touch me, then quickly drew back when I reflexively flinched. Her eyes filled with tears, and her face was dark as I related a short story of my mother's sadistic abuse. When I finished, we sat in silence in the darkened kitchen. Finally Felicita spoke.

Linda C. Crockett

"It is true that God calls us to forgive," she said. "But what your mother did was a great evil, and it is beyond forgiveness. For this kind of crime, we must never forgive."

*   *   *

I discovered that the gentle Salvadoran woman who insisted on forgiving the army that destroyed her community and tortured her husband was adamant on this point. A mother-child relationship was sacred. For the abuse of her daughter, a mother could never be forgiven.

Chalatenango *

She reached her hand toward earth
and plunged into the rich red soil of
Chalatenango
soft firm pliant earth, womb to corn
and wild purple blooms.
She kneaded and touched and dreamed
into being the mist-covered mountains
the white rocky cliffs
the eagle to soar in deep blue
a rainbow to play with fleecy clouds
and she knew it was good.

A people gentle and brown
who lived the dance and loved the land
were placed in this holy land of mists
to be a hope for the earth
a light for the world
though they knew it not.
They knew only the delight of warm wind
perfumed tropic air
the cry of a newborn baby
the shelter of each other's arms

---

*Chalatenango is a province in Northern El Salvador that primarily supported the resistance movement during the country's civil war. It was home to thousands of displaced refugees who repopulated the area against the wishes of the government.

the joy of the corn
and the dance.

One day, there came a man riding
face pale as death
eyes like blue ice
carrying death and destruction
to turn land into wealth
his dream
and the people's nightmare.

They came with barbed wire and fenced in the fields
soldiers filled the hills and guns echoed in the mists
planes spewed death from the sky
and fire consumed the land
vultures circled
where eagles once soared
the people could no longer dance
and the corn died.

She looked down and wept,
the cry of her people in her ears,
then she reached her hand toward earth
and plunged into the rich red soil of
Chalatenango
fresh with the blood of her murdered children
she raged and she wept
and she began to knead.

The Deepest Wound

From the fire and the dark and the blood and the pain
she pulled out a dream, gently breathed into clay
her tears mixed with blood
her life for the life
of the children of Chalatenango
and her hand remains.

See the rainbow return
watch the roses burst forth
hear the sound of the laughter of children
feel the mists
walk through valleys grown pregnant with corn

join the dance
hear the cry of creation

Chapter 7

The Cost of Accompaniment

"The situation in El Salvador is critical. All the gains we have made could be lost. It is important that we be vigilant over the life of the newborn Peace Child. It must be the responsibility of Solidarity, which helped us give birth to Peace, to assure that the Child grows to full strength."

Salvadoran Lutheran Bishop Medardo Gomez
San Salvador, October 1992

The bishop used the metaphor of a newborn child to emphasize the fragility of the peace that had emerged after more than a decade of war. In sermons, meetings with delegations and in media interviews, he emphasized that the Peace Child needed nurture, protection and years of devoted attention to grow and to flourish. He bluntly told the Solidarity movement that the Child would be in great danger if they abandoned El Salvador now that the guns had fallen silent. Drawing on the story of the Biblical King Herod who ordered the slaughter of all male infants to eliminate a possible Jewish Messiah, he warned that there were contemporary kings who wanted to kill the newly created Salvadoran Peace.

Bishop Gomez implored the Salvadoran poor, devastated and grief stricken from their many losses during years of war, to gather their strength to parent this vulnerable newborn Peace. He understood that a traumatized people may not have the stamina for the long-term commitment it takes to raise a child, particularly one which powerful forces seek to destroy.

A North American delegate asked the bishop who the Child will become when fully grown. Without hesitation, he said: "The Child has been born of solidarity, hope and resistance. The Child, fully grown, will become Peace with Justice."

A threat to the Herods, indeed.

*   *   *

It became increasingly apparent that people traumatized by decades of fighting were not emotionally healthy. Those who managed to physically survive frequently carried multiple psychic and spiritual wounds. Friendships that had flourished during years of conflict loosened as people tried to cope with the realities of the massive restructuring of the social and economic order that was needed to insure that peace would take root and grow. Families whose relatives had been murdered by death squads entered into a long-delayed process of mourning. Political and religious leaders naively called for forgiveness and reconciliation long before grief and anger had their season.

The result was that people guarded their bitterness and rage like a secret, ashamed to admit that they could not forgive. The child of Peace was born into a wounded and shattered family.

Mistrust and hostility replaced openness and compassion in many communities as people struggled with new alliances and shifting political tides. Thousands of combatants from both sides returned to conditions of poverty and unemployment, their sacrifices not rewarded by any immediate economic or social benefits. Crime, especially assault and rape, rose alarmingly, and the prices of basic goods soared. The initial exuberance at the signing of the peace accords slowly gave way to resigned weariness, evident on the faces of the poor and those who still struggled to accompany them. No one wanted to believe that so many could have died in vain.

Many internationals who came to El Salvador to offer solidarity during the war became frustrated and disillusioned as the currents of rage, confusion, resentment and grief stirred. Organizations began to fray as the lines shifted from the clear life-and-death issues so apparent during armed conflict to the more ambiguous complexities of constructing a just peace. Those who were motivated by the excitement of coming to a country at war, guilt at U.S. involvement with the Salvadoran military or by purely political purposes began to disengage from their commitment to the Salvadoran people.

Even well-intentioned people who began the process started to realize that the emotional price would be high and would affect their continued involvement. They were puzzled and hurt when the relationships they had so carefully built with Salvadoran friends and communities were lost in the confounding maze of the new and tenuous peace which few people knew how to navigate. In some cases, international church and humanitarian workers were betrayed and pushed aside by the very Salvadorans they loved and respected the most. Many who had courageously risked their lives to accompany the poor during the war did not understand that the confusion, anger and disorientation of their Salvadoran friends were normal and predictable responses in the aftermath of prolonged trauma. Raising the Salvadoran "Peace Child" required a different set of skills than those needed for defense during armed conflict.

In the same way, those who would accompany a survivor of childhood abuse may turn back when they realize the length and hardships of the path. Hearing accounts of childhood torture is not easy; it is a daunting and challenging task that calls for great reserves of love, internal strength and compassion as well as willingness to dedicate oneself to listening.

But listening to the stories of rapes and beatings may be less disconcerting than becoming the target of the survivor's displaced rage, fear of abandonment and mistrust. Incest impacts a child's development and sense of safety in the world, and the effects of this betrayal of body and soul are often played out in subsequent relationships decades later.

Much of the popular recovery literature written in the past fifteen years stresses how survivors can support and encourage each other during the healing process. What is generally ignored is the darker side of the aftermath of trauma, and how it impacts relationships among even the wounded who have shared the same experience. Although it may be true that some survivors form groups that offer support and nurture, another reality is that survivors often hurt and abandon each other as they feel the full impact of the pain and betrayal once inflicted on them by a trusted family member.

The process of healing was slowly dissolving my old defenses and ways of coping. The emergence of the child brought tremendous needs and fears to the surface. Gary, who had offered such important healing touch, lived in a city more than a thousand miles away from my home. I turned to Susan, Jenny, Stephen and Emily for support. But my friends grew increasingly unable to respond to my intense need for their physical presence as memories surfaced and I began to feel pain that I had avoided all of my life. At other times, like the old woman tortured by the military, I imposed the face of my torturer on my friends, especially women friends. They were angry and perplexed by my sudden and complete withdrawal from them each time one of them seemed to wear my mother's face.

Like the fragile Salvadoran Peace Child, I needed a secure environment in which to grow. I needed people who could nurture, protect and stay with me during the turbulent years as I remembered my own history, experienced long-delayed pain and struggled to complete childhood developmental tasks that I had not had a chance to master. I needed people who were able to gently confront me when my deeply buried hatred of my mother distorted my current reality.

In addition to the need for personal support, I also found myself seeking support from the society at large. But this was the time when powerful forces dedicated to silencing the voices of abuse survivors were developing in the United States. Like the Herods who sought to kill the Peace Child, these organizations aimed to crush the survivors who dared to tell the truth about the sexual abuse and violence in some middle-class and upper-class American families. A primary strategy was to skillfully manipulate the natural forces of denial about human capacity for infliction of atrocities. Hearing the voices from Soweto, Bosnia, Auschwitz, El Salvador and war zones in the heartland of the United States forces us to face what we would rather not know.

Largely because of my experiences in El Salvador, I recognized the information disseminated by the backlash organizations as propaganda designed to cast doubt on the credibility of all survivors. But I was saddened and outraged when I realized the press and general public believed otherwise. How many survivors, newly born into the possibility of life after emerging from decades of the darkness of denial of their own history, are destroyed by the media barrage of stories about "false memories" and the public's acceptance of unsubstantiated theory? How many perpetrators eagerly embrace the easy avenue of escape from responsibility for their crimes, forever closing the door to their own redemption and healing?

I had learned in El Salvador that when the military destroyed a community and killed innocent civilians, the government propaganda was uncritically picked up by most media and was predictable in its progression.

First, there was firm denial that the incident ever happened. If that did not work, the next tactic was to insist that the victims-witnesses exaggerated and lied. When that became unpalatable, the claim would be made that the civilians were inadvertently killed in the crossfire of a battle between the army and the FMLN. Finally, it would be asserted that those killed were actually members of the FMLN and therefore legitimate targets of war. More than ten years later, the Truth Commission, operating under the auspices of the United Nations-negotiated peace settlement, exhumed the skeletons of women, children and the elderly in El Mozote. When the evidence of execution-style slaying was incontrovertible, the government finally acknowledged the slaughter took place there.

These tactics of denial and distortion are similar to those used by organized backlash groups against survivors. The progression is sadly predictable as that of a government denying atrocities against its own people. The abuse never happened. She exaggerates, even lies. She was disciplined harshly at times but not abused. And finally, the trump card: She is not a competent adult, but mentally disturbed as our family was wonderful. Her therapist, whom we intend to sue, implanted these terrible memories in her head.

Unfortunately, the skeleton of a murdered childhood cannot be exhumed to provide hard evidence.

In the Biblical story of the murder of babies by King Herod, the sound of weeping fills the land at the slaughter of the innocents. I listened for the lament that should have been raised at this further violation of people who have already suffered far more than any human being should have to endure. Instead, there was the sound of silence, broken by an occasional voice on behalf of survivors crying in the wilderness of a nation numb to the pain of its children.

*   *   *

At times, Jim and I talked about the chilling impact the pervasive bombardment of stories on television, newspapers and magazines about "false memories" could have on survivors just beginning to face their own painful history. Jim expressed a steadfast belief that despite the backlash movement, the truth would prevail. His faith was like a solid rock on which I could firmly stand when the media-enlarged cacophony of voices deriding and doubting survivor's memories occasionally rose to a hurricane-force crescendo and threatened to blow away anyone who dared to speak of childhood abuse. Jim maintained that too many survivors had come forward and too much documented research had been done in the last decade to force the issue of incest back into a box despite the efforts of some powerful social forces.

His quiet conviction strengthened my own resolve to keep talking and to keep healing. No one was going to push me back into the box of silence and shame. I had lived there long enough.

*   *   *

Jenny and Stephen were among those people who promised to accompany me on my healing journey. But their understanding of the process was very narrow even though they attempted to inform themselves by reading books on trauma and recovery. Despite their formidable intellectual capacities and high levels of education, they could not comprehend the simple necessity of their physical presence when I was struggling through critical periods. I waited for invitations to spend an evening or weekend with them, a segment of time when I could articulate my experiences as I stumbled through minefields of memory. But invitations rarely happened. Their schedules were heavy with work, community and church commitments. They had no children of their own, although Stephen had partial custody of a child from a previous marriage. On visitation weekends, Stephen and Jenny immersed themselves in family activities with Cora.

One obstacle was separation of considerable geographical distance, which meant that visits and other contacts had to be carefully planned. But contacts that were made were mostly limited to board meetings and occasional telephone conversations regarding our mutual solidarity work. They assumed that I would let them know what I needed from them.

This was a grave miscalculation. Still bound by the childhood mandate of silence and the ingrained habit of isolating myself when I felt fearful or needy, I often failed to articulate that I was bearing the brunt of an emotional crisis brought on by the intense work of healing or integrating a new memory. It is fairly easy to wear a mask of competence at a board meeting when your entire life has been based on acknowledging no pain or depression. No one knew that when I excused myself to go to the bathroom, I often collapsed on the floor in tears at their seeming indifference to my struggle. Nor did they know that during our phone conferences to discuss project administration, I frequently covered the receiver with a cloth while they were talking to muffle my sobs.

Emily, a single woman in her fifties, seemed jealous of the close relationships I had with Jim and Gary. Her view of the world was rooted in a radical feminist perspective that sometimes veered to intolerance of anyone or any action not, in her opinion, appropriately pro-woman. She expressed a low opinion of most men, although she did make exceptions for men like Gary and Stephen who were committed to working on social justice issues and whose politics were largely feminist.

Emily was much more comfortable with females than males. During the six years of our friendship, I discovered that Emily was as afraid to sleep in a dorm-style retreat center room with a man present as I was to sleep in a room with a woman. Eventually, she began to question my commitment to long-term psychotherapy as my recovery began to affect the amount of time I could give to the solidarity project. In her opinion, I was becoming less "liberation minded" as a result of my healing.

Since Emily was an accomplished musician, conversations often focused on themes of women and music. Based on my mother's distorted love of music, this was an unbearable combination for me. Gathering my courage one day, I asked her to not talk with me about these topics. I had shared parts of my story with her, and she knew about the ways my mother had used music as a weapon of abuse and control. Although she reluctantly agreed, she soon became resentful about this new boundary. Her anger at my alienation from my own gender as well as my inability to separate the enjoyment of music from my mother's abuse ran below the surface of every interaction.

Eventually, Emily began to frequently wear my mother's face, and I became afraid to spend time with her. A woman who was angry with me felt extremely threatening. I decided that what I needed from Emily was to be left alone, and I refused to speak with her.

The other community members tried to support her as she expressed her frustration and grief over my rejection of her accompaniment and made pleas for reconciliation and understanding. They were puzzled and disturbed that I seemed to totally ignore the impact of my withdrawal upon her. I felt detached from her obvious pain and oddly triumphant when I made her cry. Her grief meant nothing to me; she was an angry woman who represented female connections and music. From my perspective, she was more like my mother than not.

Unlike Gary, my friends could not grasp that they were frequently interacting with a frightened, traumatized child instead of the logical and rational adult they had grown to know through the work of the solidarity project. And like the international workers who began to disengage from the Salvadoran people when the aftermath of massive trauma began to adversely impact carefully planned projects and relationships, Jenny, Stephen and Emily began to pull back from me. They had not understood nor counted the cost of what it means to accompany a survivor who is beginning to feel and assess her losses.

Within two years, my friendships with women and my work with the solidarity project were shattered in the hurricane force that lies at the heart of all deep healing.

*   *   *

My friendship with Susan was precious to me. It was also the first relationship to fall in the relentless storms that sweep over survivors who traverse the desolate terrain of childhood in a desperate search for wholeness. The loss of relationship with her affected me profoundly, impacting even further my ability to trust women.

As a survivor of abuse who had successfully addressed many of her own issues a decade before, her support and counsel had been invaluable in the initial stages of remembering the abuse. Yet I had the growing sense that Susan had great difficulty dealing with the issue when the abuse came from a mother. She was horrified by the sadistic nature of what I had endured and told me that she often had nightmares after I shared some aspect of these experiences with her. She was searching for a loving and protective mother figure while I was coming to terms with my terror of women and remembering acts of torture at the hands of my mother.

I had never developed a close relationship with a girl or woman, preferring the company of men or solitude. The few female friendships that I cultivated during adulthood were casual relationships, based on mutual interests or activities rather than emotional bonds. But the friendship with Susan was different. Born in the context of war, we drew close in ways that perhaps people only do when they face a common danger. Long before we knew of each other's childhood terrors, we sensed a deep mutual woundedness without being able to name it. Both of us had strong emotional reactions to the suffering of the poor as we repeatedly returned to El Salvador. Both of us formed deep personal ties with the Salvadorans that went beyond the scope of the solidarity project.

Susan's work in El Salvador began to call up unresolved feelings concerning her childhood trauma. Perhaps it is impossible for a survivor of abuse to go to a country at war and remain detached from her own pain, no matter how much healing has taken place. Witnesses to violence often experience vicarious, or secondary, traumatization, even though they are healthy and do not have a history of trauma.

One night the FMLN attempted to liberate political prisoners held at a sprawling thick-walled government complex only a few blocks from where we were staying in the guest house in the city of San Salvador. Hearing a huge explosion that seemed to rock the house, we rushed to the second-floor balcony to see swarms of army troops on the streets below and huge helicopters buzzing in the air above, heading to the prison to quell the uprising.

As watched from the porch, we could hear the noise of gunfire and heavy artillery booming in our ears and feel the wind from the helicopter gunships as they flew without lights like dark, ominous birds of prey. Delegates began retreating back into the house, but Susan was huddled in a small ball, not moving from her spot in the corner of the porch. I bent down to her, noticing that her head was on her knees and her shoulders were shaking. I touched her gently, trying to reassure her that she was safe and to convince her to come inside. But she did not respond. She seemed to be repeating a phrase I could not understand.

Bending closer, I finally caught her muffled words between the sounds of explosions. They had nothing and everything to do with the war being waged just down the street. It was the universal plea of the innocent caught up in inexplicable violence:

"Please stop, it hurts, please stop, it hurts, please, please…"

Her sobs were almost impossible to hear above the din of combat.

*   *   *

It gradually became clear that Susan needed to step back from the work in El Salvador. Unlike me, she did not seem to have a part that mechanically functioned in the world, taking care of job and home details with a detached efficiency. She was not as skilled as I was in wearing masks to hide suffering. She began missing board meetings and removed herself from the daily work of the solidarity project.

During this period, Susan became immersed in the relationship with her new therapist Kate, spending much time at the therapist's house. She explained that by Kate's expansion of traditional therapeutic boundaries, she was having the chance to experience what it was like to be part of a healthy family unit. Kate invited her to stay overnight at her house on Christmas Eve and to spend the next day celebrating with her family. My single hour each week with Jim seemed hopelessly inadequate by comparison.

Although Jim was greatly relieved by the way that Gary was able to meet some of my needs for safe touch in El Salvador, he was still struggling with the issue of holding me himself. Susan's therapist not only held her but offered inclusion in her own family. Although the experience of being held by Gary in El Salvador had literally saved my life, it also opened up a new place in the Child who dared to hope and, at times, expect that her needs for touch could and should be met. She felt resentful about Jim's continuing refusal to provide physical nurture. The careful boundaries he had constructed around our relationship seemed arbitrary and restrictive compared to Susan's work with Kate.

It was painful for me to listen to Susan's glowing accounts of her inclusion in Kate's family. Susan had little time for other relationships, including ours, because she was so focused on her relationship with Kate. Awkward silences now permeated our conversations. Not only did I feel increasingly abandoned, I also found it difficult to be supportive of her therapy process. I could not comprehend how a female therapist could ever be a safe person or how a woman might use power in a way that was nurturing and protective.

Like the Salvadorans whose overwhelming trauma and grief pushed them away from each other as they attempted to deal with massive loss, our pain finally separated Susan and I as we coped in the only ways we could.

Instead of talking on the phone several times each week as had been our pattern, our calls dwindled to once or twice a month. As the Christmas holidays approached, I felt alone, unsupported and fragmented. I needed to be with Susan and the other friends who promised to accompany me, but I was ashamed of the need and remained silent. The cultural emphasis on family ties only intensified the pain because I knew my birth family was not a safe or good place for me to be at Christmas.

*   *   *

Though the holidays and during the following months, I struggled in therapy with the strong but apparently dangerous child-based desire to sit on the floor during sessions. It was now clear that the Child spent as much time with Jim as I did. Sitting on the floor had little to do with comfort or convenience. At home, I often preferred a floor cushion when I watched television.

Sitting on the floor in Jim's presence somehow symbolized the ultimate in safety to the Child. Paradoxically, it also seemed to represent an unseen danger. There was a feeling of impending disaster whenever the urge to abandon the sofa and sit on the carpet surfaced during therapy. I would grow small, and the room would grow large as I looked longingly at the floor through the Child's eyes. Small tears formed as I contemplated what I could never have. The floor was as inaccessible to us as though it was separated from the sofa by a vast ocean.

Despite Jim's persistent questions about what was happening to me during these times when my tears made their first appearance, I was too frightened to bring up the subject of sitting on the floor. I remained silent, knowing in my deepest places that it is not safe for children to sit on the floor in the presence of a parent-like person. The Child and I would rock gently on the sofa, comforting each other and blocking out the seductive danger just below us. We knew better than to go down there again.

The memory of where this knowledge came from would surface before winter allowed the gentleness of spring to soften its edges. With it, the long-forgotten origin of the Lady in White would emerge.

✶   ✶   ✶

The memory of being hurt by my mother in bizarre and sadistic ways made me feel extremely fragile and increased my sense of isolation. I haunted libraries and bookstores, searching for information about abuse of daughters by mothers. Occasionally the topic was given a page or two within a scholarly work on childhood sexual abuse. But books and literature on female-perpetrated abuse and sadistic abuse in general were nowhere to be found.

Finally, in a small bookstore on the edge of the nearby city, I discovered "When You're Ready" by Kathy Evert. When I returned to my car after hastily making my purchase, I sat in stunned silence for a long time. There, in my shaking hands, was a slim blue book subtitled *"A woman's healing from childhood physical and sexual abuse by her mother."* I was not alone. This had happened to someone else. I cried.

I wanted to absorb the entire book at once, but in reality I could only emotionally handle a few pages at a time. In the few professional publications in which I had found brief discussion of sexually abusive mothers, the abuse was generally described as gently seductive and non-violent. But the mother described in "When You're Ready" was brutal and sadistic like my own mother. The realization that I was not the only female child to have been sexually tortured by her mother was both a shock and huge relief. As I read her words, I felt a sense of solidarity with this woman who knew what it was like to both long for and fear her mother's touch.

I took the book to a therapy session to show Jim. His reaction of shock, then gratitude, was similar to mine. We had been groping in uncharted waters, with no navigational map or compass to guide us through the complex issues that arise when a daughter is sexually, physically and emotionally abused by her mother. Now, we held in our hands a book which contents confirmed that we were not walking this path alone. Others had passed through this wilderness before, seeking healing.

*   *   *

During the long season of winter, Susan became almost completely unavailable to me as she was consumed with her own struggle with memories of abuse and immersed in her relationship with Kate. For several months, she had not returned my phone calls or responded to my letters. Finally, one night before a board meeting, she called to say she planned to attend and apologized for her withdrawal. Her close relationship with Kate had finally precluded any effective therapy, and she had been involved in making the transition to a new therapist for the past month. Kate's role would now be focused on providing her with a reparative family experience. She described a recent weekend retreat with Kate's family. I listened in silence. I could not express the rage I suddenly felt at her return to my life after having abandoned me. Somewhere deep within the rage, a fervent wish to make her suffer for hurting me rose to the surface before it was quickly banished to the darkness that mercifully blanketed forbidden emotions. The internal censorship process was chillingly efficient. Amy was ever vigilant.

I did not sleep at all that night. When I got up at dawn, I felt caught in a powerful force I did not control and knew what I had to do. Only one thing mattered: I had to make the pain stop. And the only way I knew how to do that was to remove myself from her world so she could never hurt or abandon me again.

Following the board meeting, I ended the relationship with Susan. In the parking lot behind the church, I silently handed her the key to her apartment. She had given it to me almost two years before as a symbol of her commitment to our relationship. She told me it meant that if I ever

– 173 –

needed to talk or if I wanted a safe, quiet space I could always come to her house. I had never used it without an invitation, but I had been deeply touched by the open acceptance and support it represented. Now, it seemed to mock the covenant she made but could not keep. I could no longer bear to see it tucked in the little box I kept for precious reminders from El Salvador including delicate hard-carved crosses, stones from the Lempa River and hand-woven necklaces made by political prisoners.

Susan's face grew pale as she listened to me say flatly that our friendship was over. That I could not tolerate being hurt and abandoned by her time and again. That part of healing was learning that I deserved to be treated a lot better than this by people who said they cared about me.

When I finished, Susan looked at me with tears in her eyes. "I know I've done a terrible thing," she said finally, holding the key in her still outstretched palm as though she did not want to accept its return. "I abandoned you when you needed me. And I know that there is nothing worse. I'm so sorry."

I fought to retain some measure of control over the chaos within that threatened to plunge me further into child space. Wordlessly, I shook my head, unable to change my course. I had to make the hurt stop. I turned away from her and walked to my car. I felt indescribably cold. As I drove from the parking lot, I looked in my rear view mirror. Susan was still standing there, the key glinting in the sun on her outstretched palm. She was crying.

*   *   *

By their initial accompaniment, my friends had helped to give birth to the child within me who somehow survived years of violation and betrayal. But they were not able to make the long-term commitment to nurture and protect the fragile newborn self who emerged into a world that seemed filled with terror and confusion. Like the solidarity workers who left El Salvador rather than learn to deal with the dysfunction of a people traumatized by years of war, Jenny, Stephen and Emily fled from my unrelenting neediness, anger and withdrawal. Like the Salvadoran families and communities who shattered when the guns fell silent, Susan and I found we could not accompany each other through the valleys of pain that comprise so much of healing.

I grieved the loss of my friends as I mourned my lost childhood. And I began to face a hard and terrible reality: incest had not only stolen my childhood, it also continued to steal my adult life, affecting my relationships in ways I was just beginning to comprehend. A child who has been violated by a parent grows up to be an adult with virtually no tolerance for the ebb and flow of coming together and drawing apart that comprises the complex dance of relationships. To such a child, needs in relationships are dangerous. Silence is the rule that must never be broken. The face of your torturer can appear at any time. Abandonment from those who claim to love you is expected.

The only people who could possibly accompany me as I healed were those people who instinctively or through experience and education understood the difficult and complicated effects of long-term trauma.

And they were few.

*   *   *

Jim was not only relived but delighted about my experience of being held by Gary in El Salvador. He expressed a deep gratitude for this friend of mine he had never met, but who freely offered what the Child so direly needed. He spoke of his own sadness at not being able to meet this need for physical closeness as well as Gary could.

Strengthened by the unconditional love Gary had demonstrated not only with his words but actions when he pulled me into his lap and rocked the Child during a sweltering Salvadoran night, I was not willing to let Jim off the hook so easily. From the beginning of our relationship, we agreed to use the concept of accompaniment to guide our work together. Jim's role was to walk with me, offering support, presence and guidance as I determined the paths I needed to follow for healing.

Yet we discovered that we could not simply export the experience of accompaniment in El Salvador to the process of healing from childhood abuse. For example, at times Salvadoran communities chose to embark on a venture or made a decision that seemed completely wrong, or outright dangerous, to those of us who walked with them. We expressed our opinions and used whatever power of persuasion we possessed to convince them to reconsider. But ultimately, the decision belonged to *el pueblo*, the people. Despite grave misgivings, we would accompany them in whatever direction they determined to travel, even though it involved greater risk to our own security.

As Jim and I struggled to walk through complex and potentially dangerous minefields of healing from deep trauma, I came to understand that he would not permit the Child to chose a path he felt was dangerous and destructive, even if that meant temporarily not abiding by her wishes. It was one thing for a community of adults to come to a decision to take a collective risk, but quite another to allow a frightened and hurt child complete freedom to make choices that could result in great harm.

I interpreted Jim's reluctance to hold me as unwillingness to risk his own personal security and comfort to provide what the traumatized Child needed. Through many halting and painful discussions, he tried to convince me that it was not only himself, but also the Child, he was trying to protect.

Jim sought the counsel of another therapist during this long struggle over physical touch and his role in accompanying me as I healed. Gradually, I came to accept that his refusal to hold me did not mean I was dirty and unclean. Slowly, he came to understand that this Child he had helped to resurrect had the right to have some of her needs for physical closeness met by him.

One day, after more than a year of therapy, I sat nearly immobilized and exhausted in Jim's office. The Child had just re-lived a horrific incident of abuse. My hands jerked sporadically in my lap, and I felt as though the temperature in the room was below freezing. It was a dark afternoon, and thunderclouds filled the sky that could be seen outside window of the therapy room. It started to rain in torrents. Lightning sharply flashed, and the sudden clap of thunder sent what felt like electric shocks through my depleted internal system. The Child raised her head to look at Jim and asked, without much hope, to be held.

Unexpectedly, Jim came and sat beside me. He did not ask how I wanted to be held but simply put his arm around my shoulder. My body shivered uncontrollably, then began to relax as the Child absorbed the comfort of his presence. As the thunder cracked and lightened split the sky, she laid her head on his chest and listened to his heart beat. It was the sound she had been waiting all her life to hear:

The heartbeat of a mother she could listen to without fear.

Nobody's Daughter

I want to hold a rainbow in my hands
and sift through colors caressing my skin
the green, the violet and gold
signs of a promise, a covenant made long ago
given for all time

Never again will I destroy what I have created.

Instead, broken promises, lies and betrayal
slide through my fingers
cold and in jagged pieces
that cut me
as I try to make whole what was broken
perhaps irreparably, a long time ago

innocence and trust
forever shattered
gone the moment you entered my body
violating my small secret places
with your mother's hands

you destroyed what you created
turned the rainbow into ashes and dust
a sign of hope
converted into a symbol of despair

no covenant here.

Some say I will heal
but they don't understand
the depth of the wound

each time I see a rainbow arching in the sky
with its streams of bright colors
its promise of fidelity
mocks my pain

And I remember that from the parent-god
there was no command to honor the children
only the father and the mother

how can I feel safe in the world
how can I trust
when I never knew safety in my own house
or how to relax into sleep in your arms?

No trust here.

There should be a sign in the sky
a warning, a portent
so all of the children would know
of the terror, the danger
wrapped up in the rainbow
and in a mother's hands

I am nobody's daughter
child of the broken promise
I keep my eyes to the ground

but sometimes I dream of holding the rainbow in my hands

Chapter 8

The Good Mother

I had now remembered enough about my childhood to be upset with my father's lack of protection and his complicity in the abuse. He was present when I was beaten many times. He stood by watching when my mother threw me against the wall with such force that I lost consciousness. He also had clear warnings from the doctors who treated me at the hospital that I was being abused by my mother. But I did not yet have the strength to confront him with the knowledge of my hard-won truth and history. Conversations with him that contained even a grain of conflict always deteriorated into a tirade of Biblical quotations, mostly drawn from the Old Testament and replete with warnings of hellfire, brimstone and the coming judgment.

I began to avoid contact with him to the extent possible. Although my brother and sister were now in their twenties and thirties respectively, they continued to live in our childhood house, bound by economic and emotional dependency. They still obeyed the cardinal rule my father proscribed for us during our childhood: "What goes on in this house stays in this house. Our family is nobody's business."

I did not want to lose my relationships with my birth family by confronting my father. Yet as my therapy progressed, it become clear that my only hope of a relationship was to finally confront the truth of our lives, including the abuse by my mother and my father's passivity and denial in the face of it. An innocent man would not have needed to constantly admonish his children to never speak of what went on in their house.

Talking with my father was always difficult. I just did not realize how bizarre and unhealthy the conversations were until I saw Jim's shocked face when I recounted my father's way of talking with me. For example, he asked me one night on the phone how my oldest son was doing at the university he attended in a distant city.

Glad to be talking about a topic with no apparent danger, I described his recent studies, new job and plans to come home for a long holiday weekend. My father made no response to any of this news. Instead, he interrupted me to ask bluntly if he was seeing any girls. Taken by surprise, I said I thought he probably dated a few different young women; there was no one special person in his life.

"Well," my father said darkly. "Just so he remembers this. All those young ladies in the city care about is that thing between their legs. They're nothing but sluts and whores."

Stunned, I felt myself dissociate from the rest of the conversation, which now became a series of disjointed Biblical quotes, focusing on Sodom and Gomorrah. My father's voice seemed to echo as though he were suddenly at the far end of a tunnel, and I could barely hear him. The labels "slut" and "whore," often flung at me as weapons by my father when I was a teen-ager, ricocheted off my brain which had just entered into the frigid internal Arctic zone designed to quickly anesthetize incoming emotional pain. My father's words had struck again, his disdain and hatred of women slicing into what I thought was an innocent conversation about my son and his grandson. In a way, I could not blame him. Any man who lived with my mother for twenty years would have developed a hatred of women as a matter of survival.

*   *   *

I was sitting at the kitchen table drinking a mug of coffee on a winter afternoon when I thought I caught a glimpse of movement out of the corner of my eye in the empty house. The light in the room seemed to shift, and a chill ran through my body. For a split second, I thought I saw my mother standing in the doorway. With my heart pounding, I walked into the living room to assure myself that I was indeed alone and then returned to the table.

I sipped more hot coffee and stomped my feet nervously on the floor, trying to ground myself and to ward off the disquieting silence that seemed to be accumulating in the room. I kept my eyes on the door, where only moments ago I thought my mother stood. But the coffee and my alertness did not protect me. With my eyes wide open, I saw a grotesque image slowly floating across my line of vision. It took a while for me to realize what I was seeing. When I did, I was so frightened that I ran out of the house into the 20-degree air.

I stopped when I reached the street, my heart pounding as I stared back at the house. It was not possible that I had seen what I just thought I saw. Yet my instinctive response was to get as far away from it as possible.

As my breathing returned to normal, I became aware that I was standing in the snow, shivering without coat or sweater, probably looking very strange to our neighbors. We lived in a small town where a number of the houses dated to the early 1800s. A good portion of the residents were elderly people who continued to live in the homes in which they were born and raised. Since many of them were retired and seemed to enjoy sitting by their windows when it was too cold to sit on their front porches, I suspected there were probably witnesses to my strange behavior.

Reluctantly, I walked back to the house, knowing that running into the street would not shield me from the image that precipitated my flight. In the kitchen, pieces of the broken coffee mug knocked from the table in my haste to escape were scattered near my chair. I bent down to pick them up, then suddenly straightened. Leaving the shards on the floor, I backed away slowly, then turned and fled toward the sanctuary of my bedroom. There was no way I could get down on the floor to clean it up. The floor was not a safe place when my mother was there.

For the next three days, the picture of a child's disembodied chest floated through my mind repeatedly. There was no head, no torso—only a small chest, which looked as though it was being carried in someone's arms. A wooden clothespin was attached to each barely formed breast. The whole image was surrounded by what seemed to be a thick fog.

I felt nauseated and unable to concentrate, missing a day of work. I slept only by doubling my normal dose of sleeping medication. I could not dispel the image despite a brisk walk, hot shower and many more mugs of coffee. I spent hours trying unsuccessfully to distract myself by watching television and reading the kind of fast- paced fiction that I usually saved for easy summer reading by the pool when I didn't want to be bothered with complicated plots or complex characters. Steve was accustomed to my silences and self-isolation when I was dealing with memories, and he did not comment on my behavior. He knew from past experience that once I had erected a self-protective wall, there was no breach of my boundaries unless I chose to let down my guard and open the door.

I finally gave up and simply paced the floor throughout the house, wishing either the strange image would go away—or that I would under-stand what it was about. I was learning that if I could connect the image with an experience and talk about it, there would be relief after I passed through the tremendous pain of bringing together what had been split apart for the sake of survival.

My wish for understanding was granted when my husband and I drove home from the shopping mall later that week on Friday evening. I had asked Steve to accompany me on a shopping trip because I felt incapable of driving. I was not sure I could handle facing the crowds alone. Conversely, I did not feel that I could bear another minute at home trapped with the image of the small chest floating in fog. Steve wanted to go to a mall music store, and we agreed to go separate ways and meet an hour later. I wandered through the stores aimlessly, making no purchases and feeling as though I had stepped, like Alice, through the looking glass. Nothing seemed real or familiar. When Steve and I reunited at our agreed-upon location, I was ready to leave.

As we left the mall parking lot and turned on to the expressway, the lights from the oncoming cars began to blur, and I felt disoriented. I suddenly heard what sounded like a door slam inside of my head. My whole body stiffened in fear. I stared out the car window, and the commercial strip that bordered the expressway by the mall was gone. Instead, I saw my mother's raging face reflected in the glass.

*   *   *

Remembering…

I am nine years old. I'm playing with clothespins on the kitchen floor close to the basement door. I'm lining the clothespins in rows and then rolling a little red ball through the rows. Mommy is doing wash in the basement. I'm not supposed to play in front of the basement door because she is busy doing wash, coming up and down the basement stairs. I'm not supposed to get in her way when she is busy. But I forget, and I line up my clothespins right in front of the basement door. I don't hear her coming up the steps.

The basement door opens and knocks down my clothespins. She slams her wash basket down on the floor and steps all over the clothespins. I look up at her face and I am afraid. She is so mad at me. I am not supposed to play close to the door. PLEASE MOMMY I'M SORRY I'LL BE GOOD/////Blank White Space. ///////// don't remember what happened next. Somehow I am on my feet and my shirt is pulled up around my neck. She is behind me now.

Searing/burning pain in my chest...my hands are twisted way up behind my back...pain/hot my right hand is going to break//// PLEASE MOMMY PLEASE MOMMY I'LL BE GOOD PLEASE///there is a clothespin on each of my breasts/// I don't know how they got there////she is screaming in my ear, "How do you like that? Did I tell you to stay away from that damn door? How do you like that?"/// white space all blank...I am falling...no pain...then I see a lady all dressed in white...she holds out her hand to me and I go with her...she takes me to a place with flowers and water and holds me...she talks to me without words...no one can hurt me now...

*　　　　　*　　　　　*

I came out of the memory scene gasping and choking. My husband was looking at me with alarm. I started to shake, and my teeth chattered. I could not move my right hand and cradled it with my left hand as though it were broken. I became aware of a terrible burning pain in my breasts, and I began to helplessly flail at my chest. I could not speak about what was wrong as we drove swiftly toward home. I seemed to be caught in a waking nightmare.

Hours later, my breasts still burned, and I could not use my right hand. I refused to call Jim. I could not reach out for help even when I desperately needed it. Somehow, needing him was still shameful and bad. I conceptualized therapy as being one precious safe hour in the week, but if anything bad happened outside that protected space, I was on my own until it was my time to be there again.

I eventually managed to tell Steve what I had remembered during our shopping trip. Understanding dawned in his eyes. He recounted an incident that had taken place a few weeks before of which I had no memory. For some time, we had been sleeping in separate rooms, but he had slipped into my bed one morning and cuddled behind me as I slept. Forgetting my long-standing insistence that he not touch my breasts in any way, he cupped his hand over my chest, intending to sleep for a few minutes more before the final alarm.

What happened next frightened him badly. The instant that his hand touched my breast, I woke and shot from the bed as though I was a missile launched from a canon. He said I growled and snarled as though I were a wild animal, making unintelligible sounds. He had a few seconds of actual fear for his safety because I seemed capable of physically attacking him. He left my bed, deeply shaken at the terror that had been triggered by his touch of this forbidden area of my body.

"It makes sense to me now," he said softly.

It was disconcerting to listen to him tell me this story, even though it also validated what I had remembered. Although it had taken place only a few weeks before, I had absolutely no memory of it. Later, when I discussed it with Jim, he said he was not surprised. My anger was as disowned and dissociated as an adult as it had been when I was a child. It was logical that an incident in which my rage was released, even briefly, would be banished from my awareness.

For the rest of the weekend, my right hand was filled with shooting pain and was practically useless. My breasts burned and ached. I could not stand even the softest material on them at night and slept by holding my pajama top away from my chest. My body jerked with uncontrollable spasms when I lay down. But the image of the headless chest was no longer floating before my eyes. Instead, the memory was now accessible to my conscious mind. I was not sure which was worse. I just wanted the pain to stop.

The pain in my breasts continued to flare up several times a day, receding gradually over a period of weeks. I wrote down pieces of the memory to share with Jim. I was unable to talk about it without becoming terrified and incoherent. I could not say the word "breasts." I communicated by vaguely pointing to that area of my body each time the word was called for, always being careful not to touch myself.

I understood now the roots to my life-long aversion to touching my own chest, even in the shower. I consistently ignored all of the literature and medical advice urging women to periodically examine their breasts as part of cancer screening. I always felt like I wanted to crawl out of my skin at the very thought of touching this area of my body. After my first trip to El Salvador, I abruptly stopped wearing bras, wearing T-shirts under my clothes instead. Although I could not articulate why, I just knew I could not bear to be reminded that this part of my body existed.

Jim encouraged me to share only what I could safely process. Little by little, the incident that gave birth to the Lady in White was whispered, scribbled on notes and talked about during several sessions. Jim asked me once if I thought the Lady was a hallucination. I said I supposed she might have been; but somehow, she seemed more to me like an angel—a creature from another realm whose job it was to rescue a child who was being tortured by her mother.

Jim nodded slowly, his face thoughtful. Trained in theology as well as psychology, he did not always accept the pat medical explanations and diagnostic definitions developed to categorize human suffering. He practiced a way of healing that respected the unique mystery of each human being given to his care. He also understood that not all experiences are easily explained by standard methodology and science.

Whenever we talked about the Lady in White—the only woman who ever held me as a child—he allowed that she was indeed an angel.

*   *   *

My father's birthday and Father's Day fell on the same week in June. For the first time, I did not buy him the kind of card he always petulantly demanded. The more sentimental and idealized the card, the more my father praised it when he opened it. Any card that did not romanticize the wonderful family memories was always laid quickly aside with a curt "thank you." He somehow managed to expunge from his memory the fact that my mother had made no secret of her hatred and disdain for him for most of their years together. That she never forgave him for breaking his promise to take her back to the oceanfront town that she loved, forcing her to live in a community she despised. That they had been in the midst of a bitter divorce at her initiation at the time of her suicide. That one of his daughters had been abused so badly she required hospitalization when she was only 12.

To please him, I usually searched for days for the perfect card. Even Hallmark did not make many cards syrupy enough to suit my father's need for affirmation that our family was, indeed, quite wonderful. He was a master of denial and insisted that those close to him participate in the game.

On this particular Father's Day, I stood in the kitchen of the house I lived in from the time I was nine until I left at age seventeen, when I was pregnant with my first child. My two sons were downstairs playing table tennis with my husband and brother. My sister bustled around the room, getting birthday cake and ice cream and trying to gloss over the chilled silence that was precipitated by the noticeable absence of any card from me for my father. I had broken one of the unwritten rules, and everyone was off balance.

When I visited my father's house, I quickly became disoriented and felt as though I were stepping into a bad dream. But today was different. I felt grounded and centered, as though I existed as a separate person and not just as a part of a sick but powerful family system. Since remembering the brutality of my mother's attack with clothespins, which had taken place in the kitchen where I now stood, I had made a decision.

The rooms of this house absorbed lies, betrayal, secrecy and denial for years. The time was approaching when the truth, no matter how unwelcome, would be spoken here. I vowed to myself that the next time I returned to my father's house, I would come to speak that truth. I would confront my father.

*　　　　　　　*　　　　　　　*

The aftermath of remembering the traumatic moment I first encountered the Lady in White dovetailed with the grief I was plunged into as I mourned the loss of Susan. I felt numb and inconsolable. At the same time, the memory of this sadistic violence perpetrated by my mother formed the beginning kernel of a strong resolve to confront my father with the reality of what happened to me as a child. Like many survivors of the Holocaust who harbor greater anger at the bystanders who did nothing rather than the guards who actually carried out the tortures, the resentment I felt at my father's lack of protection and denial of my situation twisted my insides like a poison. I was through with protecting him and the illusion of a happy family by my silence.

Jim supported my decision, but he cautioned me about how difficult confrontation would be. Many survivors wait until they are further along in the healing process before taking this risk. Some survivors never confront their abusive families. The experience of confrontation can be shattering since most abusive systems will protect themselves at all costs. Denial of the incest, accusations of fabrication and refusal to allow the survivor to be considered part of the family unless she recants are common.

The primary reason I decided to confront my father with his complicity in the abuse was because I could no longer tolerate remaining silent. My silence allowed me a place in the extended family, but it came at great emotional cost. It was clear that in order to heal, I could not remain immersed and docile within a family system that permitted the abuse to escalate and continue for so many years. The first step was to speak the truth about what happened.

Jim helped me to prepare for what he feared would be a wrenching experience by encouraging me to practice during therapy sessions what I would say to my father. I asked Jim to sit beside me. I needed someone in my corner. Pretending my father was seated on a chair in the room, I tried to form the words I needed to tell him about what I had remembered about my mother, and how I continued to suffer from the devastating impact of her abuse. Haltingly, as though each word was being pulled up by tweezers from the muck in which it was mired, the language began to come forth in the protective space of the therapy room. But even there, I began to shiver with anxiety after a few minutes and I could not utter another word.

Jim laid a firm hand on my shoulder. "Linda, it's OK," he said. The combination of his warm hand and his calm voice, speaking my name with words of assurance, burrowed deep down into the decades-old muck where the words were lodged, freeing them to flow again.

*   *   *

The Child began surfacing regularly with Jim. Reclamation of the memory of being punished for playing at the wrong spot on the kitchen floor freed me from my previously incomprehensible fear of sitting on the carpet in the therapy room. Despite Jim's repeated assurance that I did not need his permission, I was still always careful to secure it before I ventured from couch to the floor during sessions. Sitting on the floor in his presence was a sign of the growing trust the Child felt for him, and she began to sit there regularly. The first day I sat on the floor without asking him if we could sit there was a milestone in healing.

One day, he left his usual place on the chair and joined me on a floor cushion to look at a drawing I had done. The grief over losing Susan was something I could not adequately put into words. In a desperate attempt to articulate my pain, I had spent hours the night before filling sheet after sheet in a huge white tablet with crudely crayoned symbols of my pain at her betrayal and my devastation at her abandonment.

Jim carefully examined a sheet I laid before him. A small broken figure lay on a desolate gray landscape. A bottle labeled "HOPE" was buried deep beneath the earth; the carelessly flung shovel gave testament that the job had just been completed. Huge rocks were piled on top of the ground where hope lay buried, ensuring that resurrection would be difficult or impossible. A bottle of pills stood starkly on a small table in the corner. A chair was pulled out as though in invitation to the tiny shattered figure laying beside the buried hope. A rainbow and sun in the far upper corner stood in bright contrast to the scene of death and mourning below. But they were not actually part of the picture; a thick wall drawn with black crayon separated them from the world in which a child's best friend is that which has made her numb.

Jim asked me to tell him about the drawing. As I did, tears streamed down my face. The relationship with Susan was gone. There was no more hope of connection with her or any other female person. They all betrayed, abandoned and hurt me. The only relationship I could expect to keep was the one I had with the medication for sleep I had become addicted to over the last six years. There was always a place at the table for me with my trusted bottle of pills. They offered not only sleep but also the option of death if the pain of living became too great.

Without minimizing the justifiable hurt I felt over Susan's long silence and her lack of attention to our friendship, Jim tried to help me to see that there might be another way of handling anger and disappointment in a relationship. He said that it was not always necessary to completely cut ties when things go wrong. He speculated that it would take quite an expression of pain and anger from me to Susan in order to restore the relationship. I looked at him in horror. There was absolutely no way I could ever tell Susan I was hurt or angry. That would mean she would know I was vulnerable. And to the child whose only means of defense was to develop a detached numbness in the face of her mother's torture, that was unthinkable. I put my face in my hands and sobbed. Even Jim could not understand this. He continued to talk, but I no longer heard him.

* * *

From my journal…
*Tomorrow I confront my father. I am filled with dread, but I am ready. I wrote a letter to Gary to let him know of the confrontation and to say I will need his support in aftermath. Jim would say that it's **good**—I reached out and asked for help. May God give me courage tomorrow. There has been too much silence for too long. What happened to me mattered.*

*　　　　　*　　　　　*

I called my father and told him I needed to talk about something important. During the conversation, he kept saying, "Aren't you still my sweetheart?" I did not respond, refusing to be drawn into the sickly sweet affectionate talk that so often served as a cover for the darkness we lived in but refused to acknowledge. I told him I would see him at 2:30 Saturday afternoon. When I hung up the telephone, I was drenched in sweat and the child inside was crying.

I woke up early on Saturday morning and went outside to the back yard. A maple tree towered over the lawn, its branches thick with green leaves offering shade and protection. A tall privet hedge sheltered us from the bustle of neighbors. Flowers and blooming bushes circled the sidewalk. The back yard was a sanctuary for me, and I needed to draw strength from its beauty and serenity today. I lay for a long time on the soft grass, looking up at the leafy arms of the tree above me. I pressed my palms firmly against the earth, and imagined I felt its resilience and nurturing power flow through my cold body.

I turned my face to the sun and let its warmth penetrate me. I took comfort in knowing that when I returned from my father's house this afternoon, the tall maple tree with its deep roots, graceful branches and sheltering shade would be here for me—just like when I was a child.

*　　　　　*　　　　　*

When I walked into the house at 2:30, I felt as though time was shifting. A cold chill passed through me as I walked by the basement door just off the entrance to the kitchen. My mind flicked to the memory of my mother's raging face when she came up the stairs to find me playing with the clothespins. I pushed the memory away. It was important I keep my wits about me if I was not to dissolve into complete incoherence. This house had a way of doing that to me.

I passed by the breakfast counter where my mother's body was discovered after she swallowed quantities of medication prescribed by psychiatrists during her one and only hospitalization just before her death. I remembered her phone call to me early that morning as I was hurrying to dress my young son for day care and get to my part-time job.

"I've decided to end it all," she began when I had picked up the phone at 7:30 a.m.

Having had this conversation many times before, I impatiently brushed her off, saying, "I've got to get to work. I'll call you later." I picked up my son and his diaper bag and flew out of the house, worried I would be late for my job. I was tired of listening to her threats of suicide. At first, I had taken her words seriously, often rushing to the house to be sure she would not harm herself. I knew she had the means to kill herself, given the formidable array of psychiatric drugs that she had on hand.

While she was hospitalized, she had not swallowed the medications she was given, but had furtively spit out the pills and hoarded them, taking for granted I would keep her secret.

"You of all people know I'm not crazy!" she whispered while I stood by her hospital bed. She triumphantly showed me the proof of how she tricked the nurses, drawing on her lifelong assumption that I was simply an extension of herself and could have no opinion but hers.

Gripping my shirt, she pulled my face close to hers. "You know I don't need these damn pills."

My mother left the hospital with enough medication to kill several people. She never failed to remind me of this whenever she talked of ending her life. But as the months passed and there were no actual suicide attempts, only relentless threats, I began to feel manipulated and resentful.

When my younger sister Diane came home from school that afternoon, she found my mother's body slumped beneath the breakfast bar. By the time I arrived, the paramedics were loading a sheet-draped stretcher into the ambulance. I was now passing the spot in the kitchen where she drew her last breath as I headed toward a confrontation that was more than two decades late.

My father and sister sat solemnly at the kitchen table. I had requested that Diane be present. I wanted her to hear what I had to say because I knew it was impossible for her to be unaffected by growing up with a mentally disturbed mother, even if it turned out she was not directly abused as I was. Although in her thirties, she still lived with my father, and I knew she would be deeply distressed by the impact of my disclosure on him. She had assumed a care-taking role with my father, catering to his whims and allowing her identity to be swallowed up by his needs.

My younger brother Jack, who also continued to live in our childhood house, was somewhat less emotionally bound to my father. A few years before, he had married and briefly moved away from our childhood home. When the marriage fell apart, he returned to live with our father, even though he had a good job and could have easily afforded an apartment. My sister, on the other hand, had never lived anywhere else. I planned to meet with Jack privately at a later time. I did not fear the impact of my disclosure on him as much as I worried about the ramifications for my sister.

When I began to talk, my voice sounded shaky and close to breaking. I tried to ease into it. Drawing a deep breath, I began to speak. My voice was so soft I was not even sure I was making any external sound at first. My throat felt constricted, and I could not seem to take in enough oxygen.

I looked at my father. "I know you've been wondering about why I didn't want you to take me shopping for a dress for my birthday in March."

Silence. *Was I really talking out loud?*

"And why I haven't come over to visit lately. Or called you on the phone."

Silence. *Could they hear me?*

My voice began to shake. It sounded close to breaking. I took the plunge quickly, before I was once again reduced to the terrified silence of the child who had been tortured not more than ten feet from where I now sat in the kitchen. "The reason is that I've been remembering some very painful things that happened in my childhood, and I came here today to talk about them...."

My sister drew in her breath sharply and winced. My father remained stoic and expressionless.

But as I continued to speak, I felt strength returning to me as the truth about our lives in that house was spoken into the silence of the kitchen where my mother hurt me so many times and where she finally acted as her own judge and executioner.

When I confronted my father with his abandonment of me at the age of five in the aftermath of being molested by Tommy and his friends, he shrugged it off as "kids fooling around." Not meeting my eyes, he refused to answer the question of why he stopped touching me afterward. When I demanded to know why he had not stopped the physical abuse by my mother he witnessed so many times, he admitted he thought she was "too hard" on me and said he talked to her privately about it.

I asked him what her response was. He looked at me with eyes that were veiled.

"She told me to go to hell and to mind my own damn business," he said. A slight shrug of his shoulders completed his statement as if to say he had no other recourse.

I began to cry. "And you did. How could you let her hurt me like that?" I was no longer afraid of my tears. I wanted an answer.

His answer was one that he was to repeat in response to almost every incident of abuse I recounted that day.

"I thought she was a good mother," he said.

It was his defense for his lack of action in response to the concerns of the doctors in the hospital who suspected that something terribly abusive was happening in my home and that my mother was involved. It was what he said when I told him of the sexual abuse that began when I was not yet in school. His logic was simple: if he believed she was a good mother, he was not to blame for what happened.

In excruciating detail, I described the day she dragged me out of my grandmother's house and beat me all the way down the road, escalating her assault when we got home. I told him how she forced me to play hymns for her on the piano and how my music irrevocably died on that day.

Completely ignoring what I had just said about my mother's mistreatment, my father made just one comment. "I know you took piano lessons. For eight years, I paid for them."

Despite my best efforts, I felt myself begin to fall into the numbness in which I lived as a child. Holding on to any sense of the reality of my experiences was difficult with my father who was so rigidly attached to his version of reality.

From deep within me, I heard Jim's voice. "Linda, it's OK." It was a voice of firm assurance in the midst of the insanity of this house of denial and pain. Feeling strengthened, I began to recount what I remembered about the incident with the clothespins.

When I finished, my sister let out an audible gasp. "Was I in the house?" she asked fearfully. It was the first time she had spoken, and her face was white. I looked at her, and my heart felt like it was breaking. Only four years younger than me, she had never known life outside of this house. Haunted by nightmares and given to extreme changes in mood and personality, she played the role of the faithful daughter, taking care of her father as her own life slowly passed her by.

Given our social isolation and the fact that she was a sickly child, it was likely she had been in the house that terrible afternoon. But I had no memory of anyone other than my mother and the Lady in White during the incident.

I shook my head. I could not answer her question with certainty. "I don't know. Why?"

She was visibly shaken. "I have always been so afraid of clothespins," she murmured softly. "I can't stand to see them. They terrify me."

My father stared off into a distant place only he could see. He began to talk about the vacations in the mountains that we had taken when I was a little girl. With an air of near defiance, he reminded me of how hard he worked so we could have good clothes and a nice house. I cut his reminisces short and reminded him that these things were not the issue. That my mother physically and sexually abused me was the issue.

After more than an hour, I was spent. My father's face seemed made of stone. He would not look at me. He began to speak slowly. "This is what we need the good Lord for—they drove nails into His hands so he could pay for our sins…" My sister sat quietly at the table, wringing her hands and rocking herself.

Standing up, I steadied myself for a moment, trying to pull air down into my lungs. The room suddenly seemed devoid of oxygen. There was nothing more to say. I turned and began walking toward the door. My father called out my name, and I stopped.

For a moment, I thought maybe he would be a real father; maybe he would acknowledge my pain and hurt and apologize for his lack of protection. But my hope was dashed within a split second of its birth. My father's voice was flat. "When you said you were coming over today to talk, I hoped when you finished we would be like father and daughter again, and you would let me buy you pretty dresses at Christmas time. But nothing you have said here today makes me feel any closer to you."

Through my tears, I looked at this man who was my father in biological terms only. He equated fathering with the buying of trinkets and sentimental birthday cards to gloss over painful realities. To secure any crumb of affection from him required my silence about any deviation from the perfect family of his fantasy. I had come speaking of incest, rape and beatings. He was disappointed because I had not made him feel closer to me. He saw himself as the victim.

I turned again and walked away. This time, my father did not call me back.

*　　　　　*　　　　　*

As weeks and months went by with no response from my father to my disclosure, the reality of my situation became chillingly clear. As in childhood, my punishment for calling my father's attention to my suffering would be his silence. By unmasking the truth and tearing down his illusions about a happy family life, I had committed the unpardonable sin. For this, I was banished to the realm of invisibility. It was a familiar place.

I knew well his capacity to refuse to acknowledge my existence. It was his response to the molestation when I was five. It was his way of dealing with the beatings he watched my mother give me. It was not unusual for him to refuse to speak to me or look at me for weeks if I had committed some unnamed misdeed. When he decided I was to be invisible, even common mealtime courtesy was suspended. If he needed the salt from the end of the table where I was seated, he would get up and walk around the table to get it rather than ask me to pass it.

I was only his "sweetheart" when I played the role he assigned to me: a smiling girl-doll who paraded for him in the beautiful dresses he bought her. A prop in a scene which supported his delusion that all was well with our family. A crying child, needy and wounded, was not allowed in his fantasy. If the child was soiled and her innocence destroyed by the adults in her world, it was not his fault.

His responsibility ended with making sure I had a good mother. And once he was convinced of that, no amount of evidence could change his mind. What he could not bear to see, he rendered invisible. Even his firstborn daughter.

Butterflies Are Free

You wait, trembling
for the pain to begin
hoping your heart
will not burst with the wild beating
      of fear

the first blow you will feel
but by the second or fourth
you'll be sailing away
to a place in your mind
where the butterflies live

      if you are lucky

no clothes to protect you
no one to save you
from hands known too well
that deal pain mixed with pleasure
in their own special form
of private hell

      you've been pulled in

but butterflies are free
and they sail on the wind
so the hands cannot hurt
your child's body

The Deepest Wound

from outside or in....
your spirit has gone

    to be with the butterflies

who live
with grace and color
free
for a short time

Chapter 9

The Language of Silence

It was a season of loss. My relationships with Susan and my father were shattered. My connections with Jenny, Stephen and Emily were disintegrating. I crawled into what I viewed as caves within myself, withdrawing from the outside world that seemed to hold only pain. The only voices I could hear belonged to Jim and Gary.

The habit of seeking safe space within a small dark cave was developed in my childhood. About a mile from our house, the surrounding woods gave way to a country meadow, filled in the spring with colorful wildflowers and all manner of small animals. Many times I wandered through thick trees and brambles until I came upon the pond that bordered the edge of the meadow. Several huge boulders formed a small but deep cave-like structure at the edge of the water thick with lily pads. I would creep inside the cool shelter of the rocks and imagine myself to be safe in a home made just for me. I spent hours watching butterflies dance and frogs leap as I peered out at the pond and the meadow beyond from the snug sanctuary of my little cave. The coldness of the rock shelves where I huddled, and the music of the water rushing by just beneath them lulled me into welcome numbness in the aftermath of one of my mother's abusive rituals. In this place, I was often joined by my imaginary friend Peter, who assured me that the tall trees surrounding the meadow stood guard over us. My mother never ventured into the woods. I was safe here.

Internal caves were formed to protect me during the times when I could not flee to the shelter of the rocks bordering the pond. When pain became unbearable, I could sometimes close my eyes and slip away into the darkness of my imagined caves. From within, the world looked foggy, unreal and very unimportant. Most blessedly, if I tunneled deep enough I would become numb and cold. What happened to my body then was of no concern to me.

The Child drew Jim's voice into deep wounded places where no protective adult had ever gone. For one hour each week, I found shelter in the oasis of sanity and security that his presence represented. Carrying little more than a comforting voice which could sometimes sustain me even in the darkness of childhood memories, I returned to the wilderness of healing to try to survive another 167 hours until I could once again find sanctuary in the room at the counseling center that the Child regarded as a magic, protected space. Gary's voice came to me only by traveling along a thousand miles of telephone wire. On the rare occasions I heard it, I clung to it as though I was drowning and it was a lifeline. In a very real way, it was.

Unlike the stories told in popular recovery literature, I found no new "family" to embrace and welcome me as I healed. The past had become present and would not be put aside. My fear of women increased as more memories of my mother's abuse returned, isolating me even further from potential sources of support within survivor groups. The few groups that existed in my area were comprised exclusively of female survivors and led by women therapists. Nothing could have felt more threatening for me.

I slipped deep into the isolation facing many female survivors of abuse perpetrated by mothers. My political consciousness and values have origins within various feminist streams of thought, and I have great respect and admiration for the feminist insistence that the roots of violence must be named and exposed in order to be healed. I was distressed to learn that although feminists were in the forefront in breaking the silence about incest a decade ago, there was little tolerance for any suggestion that women as well as men raped and beat their children. Female sexual abuse was not recognized or talked about. Groups, programs and resources were primarily oriented to women as victims and men as perpetrators. And any survivor, male or female, daring to raise issues of female violence was considered a traitor to the cause of feminism.

I searched for articles in feminist publications on sexual abuse. Virtually everything I found was based on the assumption that men were the perpetrators. There was no substantial discussion about the sexual violence of women toward children. By the consistent exclusion of this issue, I felt as though my experience was not important enough to even be acknowledged by feminist women, and some men, who wrote so powerfully and eloquently about the need the stop male violence against women and children.

I switched my focus from feminist books and articles to psychiatric literature. One day, when pursuing a list of abstracts and titles that seemed impossibly dry and clinical, I came across mention of a psychotherapist in England who was writing about female sexual abuse. I decided to write her a letter. To my great surprise, she called me on the telephone to let me know she was deeply moved by my letter and I was not alone in my struggle.

Ironically, she considered herself a feminist activist. My search had led me back to a feminist source!

In her clinical practice, she discovered a number of women and men who had disclosed sexual abuse by their mothers when they were asked questions about it candidly and felt assured such a topic was not taboo. After several years of working with these clients, generally very isolated from other survivors, she decided to organize a conference on female sexual abuse. She was stunned by the hostile response of the feminist community to her proposal.

Friends who could always be counted on to help publicize and coordinate a conference dealing with violence against women refused to be involved. She was told that talking about sexual abuse by women would damage the "movement" and divert attention from the important issue of male violence. She received anonymous threats. She preserved despite the opposition, securing the funding and organizing the conference. She was overwhelmed with the response by survivors of female sexual abuse. For the first time, many women and men were given a public forum in which their experience was named and validated.

I was greatly dismayed to learn of the fierce opposition she encountered but deeply moved by her courage in bringing the issue of female sexual abuse out of the closet and into public consciousness. I was also struck by her understanding of the enormous difficulty I faced in healing. She told me that those abused by females carried within them a pain that surpassed her wildest imagination.

Those of us who live with this pain should not be shamed into silence or told we will damage women's social progress by speaking about women as perpetrators as well as victims. Any movement for social justice is ultimately weakened by its refusal to examine its own failings and its refusal to challenge violence committed by its core constituency.

In El Salvador, I found the FMLN to be very reluctant to acknowledge the human rights abuses committed by its units, let alone criticize them. Its supporters in the international solidarity movements largely remained silent about this, since atrocities committed by the government backed military vastly outnumbered the occasional abuses by the resistance. Yet this inability to see and name its own evil compromised the integrity and cohesiveness of the FMLN, whose cause was just and whose motives were good.

In the same manner, the feminist movement is compromised by its inability and unwillingness to challenge the sexual violence of women against children. Although the preponderance of evidence to date is clear that men commit the majority of abuses, sexual violation of children by women is not a rare phenomenon.

∗   ∗   ∗

My reliance on the medication that I used for sleep deepened. As my connections with family and community dissolved, I held to the one relationship that I believed I had complete control over: addiction to mood-altering substances. It was a reunion of sorts; we knew each other well when I was a child of fifteen, struggling to numb the pain of a lifetime of abuse. We became reacquainted two decades later in El Salvador, when my body began to remember what my mind could not, bringing nightmares and sleepless nights to disturb my carefully constructed internal defenses against knowing what was written on the deceptively blank pages of my childhood.

The anxiety I felt about the possibility of losing what had become my most reliable friend was enormous as I tried to cope with the turmoil that the returning memories of childhood torture brought to my life. Jim knew of my dependency on medication for sleep, and one day I fearfully asked him if I would have to give up my pills. I wanted to be free of the yoke of addiction, but I was terrified of yet another loss in my life.

Conventional wisdom in treatment of abuse survivors holds that addictions must be addressed before trauma work can be done. Yet Jim and I had been working with deep levels of traumatic memory for almost two years. A survivor's path is as individual and unique as her history. No one can say with certainty what is the proper road to travel when you are attempting to navigate through uncharted territory. Jim understood that I could not face another loss in my life at this moment. He also sensed that some of the worst memories were starting to surface and that I needed to be able to sleep if I were to avoid a complete breakdown in functioning.

His response to my question about giving up the pills simultaneously reassured and terrified me. The afternoon sun shone softly through the windows of this room that had become my one external safe place, illuminating the shelves of books that lined the far wall. There was a peace here that I rarely experienced anywhere else.

Jim looked at me with compassion and said softly, "No. You're not ready just yet. But soon you will be. And then we'll go through it together."

*   *   *

I returned to El Salvador in the autumn to assess economic aid projects in communities where we worked. Although I was not physically or emotionally up to the challenge of travel in the countryside, I agreed to go on behalf of the solidarity project. On a personal level, some part of me continued to reach out to El Salvador for the healing that I so desperately needed. It was undeniably the birthplace of my journey into the heart of the pain that I hoped would eventually lead me to wholeness.

It was to be my last official trip for the solidarity project. Accompanied by one other board member, our time was less tightly scheduled than during previous trips, when we led delegations of up to fourteen people. As we frequently stayed in the homes of Salvadorans in rural areas rather than church-run guest houses, we had ample opportunity to discuss topics in conversations that were not normally part of delegation agendas, including family violence and incest. The topics were inevitably raised by the Salvadoran women who hosted us.

I was stunned by the frequency with which this issue surfaced during our two weeks in El Salvador. During the war, conversations had predominately centered on political issues. Now it seemed that people were talking more about the destructiveness within their own families than the political violence which still swirled through the country, held barely in check by the peace accords.

One night, we sat with a group of Salvadoran women, our feet on the dirt floor of a small thatched house nestled deep within the mountains in the eastern part of El Salvador. The only light came from a small lantern that sat on a rough wooden table in the center of the small house. We had feasted earlier on eggs, beans and tortillas and would soon retire behind the tattered curtain on the hammocks that stretched across the small back room that served as sleeping quarters for about eight people.

Our hostess was Marta, a small compact woman with quick, energetic movements and a gift for organizing. I had seen her in action with several delegations and secretly believed she would make an excellent drill sergeant, affable but demanding. When Marta was in charge, there was no opportunity for lack of participation in singing or in playing *dinamicas,* group games designed to get people interacting. When a new delegation arrived at her church, within ten minutes she had doctors, pastors, professors and activists marching around in circles calling out the names of various fruits in Spanish to place in their imaginary shopping carts.

Marta had been talking with animation about the work she was doing with women in her community with issues of domestic violence. Her common-law husband, surrendering to the climate of desperation and hopelessness that is prevalent in a country in which the unemployment rate runs at more than fifty percent and machismo is every man's heritage, had beaten her repeatedly until she finally forced him to leave.

Marta was using the expertise in grass-roots organizing that she had gained during the years of conflict to bring women together to talk about similar experiences in their own families. She spoke of the feminist conference in the capital city where the issues of family violence and incest were the focal points. Carefully removing a sheaf of papers from a worn satchel, her sturdy brown fingers traced over the papers of the conference agenda in the dim glow of the lantern. Although her reading skills were at no more than perhaps a fifth grade level, she proudly pointed out the workshops she had attended, circled in red ink on her papers.

Tentatively, I began to share that many people in the United States were also dealing with problems of family violence and incest. I described some of the work of the adult survivors movement, such as the Clothesline Project in which survivors design shirts telling the story of their abuse and hang them on clotheslines in a public area as a visual way of breaking the silence. Heads nodded approvingly. Several women spoke enthusiastically of the possibility of a similar kind of project in their own communities. Feeling that we had established the kind of space in which I might be free to tell some of my own story, I haltingly began to speak of the smaller but significant number of women who were sexually abused in childhood by their mothers or other female caretakers.

The room seemed to suddenly become too quiet, and the faces in the dim light of the lantern grew perplexed. Taking an irrevocable plunge, I said that this was my own experience—that my mother physically and sexually abused me as a child, and that I was in the process of trying to heal from these deep wounds. Stumbling through a shortened Spanish rendition of my story, I tried to paint in broad strokes the reality I had lived in as a child growing up with a mother who inflicted pain on my body for her own sexual pleasure.

When I finished, there was absolute silence in the room. Finally, Marta spoke. "I do not understand how it is possible for a mother to sexually abuse her child," she said slowly, her eyes reflecting genuine puzzlement. "I know how a man can rape a daughter. But tell me—how does a woman rape a little girl?"

My eyes filled with tears. There was suddenly a great gulf between us that neither Spanish nor English could cross.

I mumbled that it was not only possible but also that it was the actual experience of numerous women, including myself. Suddenly, I was exhausted. I did not feel capable of sharing the intricate details of how the rapes were carried out. I could not find the words to tell them that my mother penetrated my rectum with her fingers and other objects. I could not articulate how she stimulated my genitals with her mouth and fingers, then punished me for my body's response. There are many ways to rape which do not require a penis. Shoving my pain back into its box, I refocused the conversation back to the traditional—and more understandable—forms of abuse by their husbands, fathers and lovers. As the women resumed their discussion, I drifted off.

As I traveled throughout El Salvador during this visit, these responses were repeated each time I raised the subject of sexual abuse by mothers in communities where women were dealing with incest and family violence. By the end of the trip, I had stopped broaching the topic. Talking about abuse and violence by women, especially when there is a sexual component, seemed to be taboo in El Salvador, as well as in England and my own country. The topic renders most people so perplexed, uncomfortable and sometimes angry that it effectively precludes frank discussion.

There is a widespread cross-cultural belief that sexual abuse by a mother is, at minimum, highly improbable. Mothers are idealized and viewed as nurturers and protectors of their young. Largely ignored is the reality that the patriarchal structure under which much of the world is organized incubates violence in the family and spews it out into society. The majority of violent criminals were abused as children. It is no small miracle that so many people who are abused do not grow up to become perpetrators. The tragedy is that we often internalize the pain and destroy ourselves.

Patriarchy insists on a rigid pecking order, with the person at the top of the ladder holding power over the one on the next rung below. Generations of women have had their heads stepped on and kicked, as men still hold the majority of social, personal and political power. Women who are unable to fight their way to the top sometimes begin to kick at the small heads below them. They become enforcers and teachers of the patriarchal "power over" system in which children are at the bottom of the heap and have virtually no political rights or effective legal means to protest mistreatment by adults.

My mother internalized this system. My father held economic and social power over the family. In turn, she was granted absolute power over her children. That society imbues mothers with perfect nurturing characteristics more appropriate to fiction than reality serves to obscure the hollow thumping sounds of heads being kicked as we all hang fiercely to our designated rung on the ladder of patriarchy.

When a woman says her father molested her, no one questions how such an act could take place. But when a woman says her mother sexually abused her, stunned silence is a common reaction. Almost inevitably, the question that follows is a variation of Marta's sincere "But how is this possible?"

*   *   *

I discovered that a whole network of survivor newsletters existed in which people were sharing their stories of abuse and healing with others with similar histories. Most of the publications were clearly oriented to incest by fathers and stepfathers perpetrated on daughters. Many seemed to completely ignore even the possibility that women could be abusers as advertisements for survivor retreats and conferences were billed as "all woman safe space." But there were small indicators, buried within volumes of material often published on shoestring budgets by people who had suffered the devastation of childhood abuse, that not all victims had been violated exclusively by fathers, brothers and uncles. Gleaning contacts from the rare article that mentioned even briefly female perpetrators, I began to send letters to various parts of the United States, searching for women who were abused by their mothers.

I found them, and their stories were heartbreaking. Many described sadistic and violent acts that were perpetrated by mothers, aunts, sisters and grandmothers. The cultural isolation most of us suffered was profound. A social worker in New England wrote that she had developed therapeutic groups for women abused by men for more than a decade. In the past few years, she had become aware of at least a dozen survivors of female sexual abuse in her geographic region. Yet all of her efforts to bring these women together to talk about their experiences failed. The terror they felt about being vulnerable with other women precluded their participation. She was frustrated with her failure and asked me for suggestions. At the time, I had none.

After more than eight years of my own healing, I would tell her now that she had not failed. It is not reasonable to expect that a woman raped by her mother would feel safe in a group of women. No one suggests that a woman who has been raped by a man work through her pain within a group of men. Mixed gender groups of survivors, led by a male-female therapist team, hold the most potential for safety and possibility of connection.

The National Catholic Reporter published an article by a woman who was sexually abused by a religious woman who was a close friend of her family. She wrote of the way in which society perceives the woman-child bond as sacred, which added to the near impossibility of disclosure of her abuse: "Because there is so little impetus to examine the deviance of women within our society and church, those children remain invisible, their suffering unmitigated and unseen. And the acts of deviance remain a tragedy unexplored."[1]

Many survivors wrote of a deep sense of shame about gender identity, expressing disgust with their female bodies. I was amazed that my abhorrence of possessing a female body was not uncommon among survivors of mother abuse. Like me, these survivors did not want to be like their mothers. To be female was to be imprisoned in a body that replicated the abuser's body.

---

1. McLeod, AnnMarie (1993) Nun child abuser hid behind veil of service; National Catholic Reporter, April 23, 1993

A woman from the West Coast wrote that she had put out a call for stories from women abused by mothers, intending to use the collected stories in an anthology. Despite the solid gains she had made during her ten years of therapy as she struggled to heal from abuse by her mother and sister, she could not emotionally handle the content of the survivors' stories that filled her mailbox each day.

"Every letter decimated me," she wrote. "I had to stop the work for the sake of my own healing."

The volume of responses she received lent weight to the conclusions of another survivor who was doing post-graduate work on female sexual abuse. Originally hypothesizing from the belief that what she experienced was very rare, she had become convinced through her years of research that women sexually and physically abuse children nearly as much as men do.

*   *   *

In an effort to educate people about the reality of abuse by mothers and the connections between violence enacted on personal and political levels, I accepted two speaking engagements during which I shared some of my own story of healing, beginning with my journey to El Salvador. Although it was in one sense very liberating to say in public what had been held as a secret for such a long time, it was also depleting and exhausting. After hearing my presentations, the dialogue was inevitably focused on the connections between war and rape. I was pleased with these discussions because I believe we cannot understand the violence we perpetrate on community and national levels until we explore the depths of family dysfunction and abuse.

Yet I was dismayed that the issue of female sexual abuse which I raised in my presentations was almost completely ignored. People seemed to want to view sexual abuse by mothers as an aberration rather than a serious social problem to be wrestled with in the same way as abuse by men.

When I tried to direct the discussion into reflection on mothers as abusers, I was stymied by the same uncomfortable silence that I encountered in the home of Marta in El Salvador. We have developed a language in which to speak about war and rape by men. We have no language in which to speak about the abuse of daughters by mothers.

Eventually, I stopped putting myself through the agony that ripped through my body at the incredulity most people exhibited when confronted with abuse by women. I came to dread the long silence and bewildered questions that followed my disclosures both public and private. Disheartened, I increasingly retreated into the silence and isolation of the internal caves formed in my childhood. I left the house only to go to work and to shop for necessities. I dropped all social contacts and community involvement. I structured my life to avoid direct emotional interaction with other women.

This was not difficult because I participated in activities in which such contact with women was unlikely. I avoided eye contact with females in public, hoping to prevent any kind of conversation from starting in the grocery check-out line or at the post office. In the waiting room at the counseling center, I was careful to look away any time a female therapist came into the room for a client. I viewed females with power and in positions of authority as especially dangerous. Even a casual greeting or smile caused my guts to twist and my throat to tighten.

The only place I had contact with women was at work. And since I considered business a category that did not require emotional investment, I was able to deal with women without undue distress. One factor in my favor was that men held the positions of power in my corporate world. I worked within this circle of men, and any woman I came in contact with was either a subordinate or a manager in some other area of the corporation who did not hold direct power over me. Virtually all of my outside business contacts were male, as it was an industry dominated by men. When I went to a national securities convention in Arizona, about ninety-five percent of the several hundred participants were male.

I had a few female business friends with whom I could easily go to lunch and discuss the latest in fashion, television shows and corporate politics. I kept my pain and fear locked away behind thick protective walls, simply dropping out of conversations when the discussions occasionally turned to issues in someone's personal life.

Although Jim and Gary insisted there was goodness and safety in the world, I no longer believed it. The organized backlash seemed to control the media. The feminist movement disregarded the violence of women. Survivors' groups and resources were geared to females who had been abused by men. Those who were abused by their mothers were often too damaged by their experience to feel affinity with other women; we lived in the shadows and our pain was not acknowledged by mainstream or recovery culture. The solidarity group that had listened and offered support in the early years of my journey could no longer accompany me. My friendship with Susan had ended in betrayal and abandonment. My father had banished me from his consciousness for speaking the truth. It seemed as if there was no community that could include my experience and accept my pain and anger as I struggled to heal.

I felt like a small wounded animal that needed to hide and lick its wounds. But even hibernation and withdrawal from the world could not protect me from the memories that were about to surface. And when they did, not even my own caves offered sanctuary.

*   *   *

I began to grasp that signals in my body were often precursors to memory. Yet each time I started to feel the helpless terror that heralded this cellular kind of memory, I would tell myself that I would not let it happen. I refused to acknowledge the deep muscle spasms in my buttocks that sometimes were so acute that I could not walk. I told myself fiercely that I did not feel the burning pain in my genitals that left me gasping. I tried to ignore the fact that I sometimes had to relieve myself every ten minutes as memories of my mother punishing me for orgasms she induced and then misnamed as urination flickered through my mind when I least expected them.

When my body began to warn me that yet another horror was emerging to be processed, my mind would begin its protective function of shutting down, much like a computer system. A thick fog seemed to cover everything, disconnecting me from everyone, including myself. I struggled mightily to not hurt myself. My immune system weakened, and I endured vaginal infections, sore throats, bladder problems and flu symptoms. I had raging headaches that would not respond to any amount of painkillers. I could not concentrate at work. I had nightmares and was afraid to fall asleep.

When I finally managed to doze for a few fitful hours, I would wake to find myself completely buried underneath my quilt. Curled in a small ball, my hands would be wrapped protectively around my genitals. I slept with limbs twisted like a human pretzel.

Each time memories of yet another sadistic ritual surfaced during this period, Jim would try to reassure me with his belief that surely the worst had to be over, that I had reached the bottom and there could not be much more to be unearthed. But on this count, he was wrong. I had just begun to remember the worst of the abuse. And no amount of reassurance could stem the flow of pain that pressed for release. For better or worse, I had made an irrevocable decision when I opened up the carefully sealed Pandora's box of my childhood. And what happened now was beyond my control. I could only hope to survive it.

*　　　　*　　　　*

From my journal...
I need to try to write about the memory that pushed its way to the surface on Wednesday. When it began to intrude on my consciousness, my first

impulse was to try to fight it, to make it go away. I know from experience now that this is not the way to heal, but with each memory that comes I have tremendous resistance to having the knowledge returned to me. I still feel waves of shame when memories like this surface. At least now the feeling is more one that seems to be prominent when a memory is being processed, and washes away as I talk/write/cry about what happened. I keep telling myself that the self-hatred I feel at this moment will not last. It is a product of the abuse. It is based in shame that belongs to my mother, not to me. She is the one who committed the crime. Yet I am the one who continues to pay for her sins. I carry her shame.

*　　　　　　　　*　　　　　　　　*

It is very difficult to write about sadistic abuse. Most people dance around the topic as well as specifics because to speak bluntly may so shock and horrify readers that they will cease to relate to what is being said. Yet bizarre acts of violence against a defenseless child are an abuser's best friend. The more outlandish the abuse, the less chance the child will have of being believed if she attempts to tell her story. When sexual abuse is couched in the context of punishment, the child is doubly silenced. What child does not feel shame about being so bad that she is punished by someone in authority? And in a society that condones and even encourages parents to discipline their children by corporal punishment, how is a child to know when a parent is crossing the line? In many parts of our culture, it is still considered acceptable for parents to teach children by inflicting pain on their bodies. And it is this socially sanctioned infliction of pain that lies at the core of the torture that was inflicted on me.

The following chapter provides a glimpse into a few of the sadistic rituals that were part and parcel of my upbringing as a child. At one time, I thought what happened to me was normal. Jim tells me repeatedly that it was not, and I pray that he is right. But as I listen to stories of other survivors of sadistic abuse, as I read accounts of atrocities committed upon prisoners in concentration camps, as I reflect on the experiences of Salvadorans who have been tortured, I know beyond a doubt that depraved acts are committed upon the vulnerable far more frequently than the world is willing to believe.

Behind the faces of the guards in the camps and prisons, behind the face of each parent who abuses a son or daughter, behind the face of the rapist or battering spouse lies the twisted visage of a child who once endured similar cruelties. It is what creates the capacity for torture. I am convinced that my mother was sexually and physically abused during her own childhood in bizarre and terrible ways. This kind of methodical application of pain and pleasure has to be taught, and I believe that she had to learn the kind of torture she inflicted on me.

I will not spare my readers the details of what I experienced. My intent is to speak into the gaping silence around sadistic and female-perpetrated abuse. But if you are a survivor yourself, please be in a safe place before you continue reading.

Gather objects that make you feel comforted and keep them close by as you read, reminding yourself you can put down the book at any time. Have a list of phone numbers you can call and activities that you can do if you become upset. A walk outside, a warm bath, a cup of hot tea, and writing in a journal can help to ground you and bring you back to the present if the past seems frighteningly near. If a flashback or memory is activated, remind yourself that you can take all the time you need to sort it out. When you enter the realm of traumatic memory, you are on ground that is both dangerous and sacred. It has the potential to heal but also the power to traumatize you again. Walk with care.

You of all people already know of the abuse that takes place behind the closed doors of many fine houses and within families that are considered pillars of their communities. It is the rest of the world that needs to hear and understand these stories of private holocausts. We have already lived them.

Rage

Rage flows
    pushes urgently on fragile boundaries
    without words or form
    chaos too large for the space allotted
    it threatens to burst through walls
                and shatter the world.

A child huddles naked
    her mother towers over her
    raging shadow
    hands invading, tearing, hurting
    she tastes her mother's rage
                but does not know her own.

Trapped, a small animal
    snared, freedom stolen
    seeking to survive
    she buries the rage
    before it shatters the world
                she absorbs the blows.

Face placid, eyes dry, body unresisting
    she displays the proper attitude
    of respect and submission
    for a child raped and beaten
    who is not permitted to know any rage
                but that which belongs to her mother.

And by the act of not knowing

she survives

her shattered world.

Chapter 10

Surviving in the Wasteland

From my journal...

Maybe the only way I could circumvent my mother's absolute control of me was to take the pain and turn it into pleasure. It helped me to survive as a child. But I can't abide it inside of me anymore. If I ever chose to end my life, it will be because this one thing, so imprinted on my body and mind that it seems irrevocably part of me, cannot be banished. I am willing to struggle for liberation. But there can be no compromise with this part of me who craves pain—I will not be free until it is gone or transformed.

*   *   *

The worst of the ritualized and sadistic abuse took place in the Little House, the tiny brick bungalow which would eventually be converted to a garage when we moved into the much larger and impressive Big House when I was ten.

The beauty of the pink roses climbing on the white iron railings, the flowering rose of sharon trees along the side yard, the hand-built swing set and the manicured lawn belied the horror that took place within the walls of Little House. The only sign that might have been evident that something was amiss to the careful observer would have been the large green blanket that sometimes covered the window facing the country road which hardly anybody but my father's family traveled. If any of them saw the blanket, they chalked it up to another eccentricity of the strange woman my father had married. None of them dared to ask what the blanket might be hiding.

But when I came home from school and started walking up the long sloped driveway, my heart sank when I saw the green blanket. My mother hung it there on the days she wanted absolute privacy when she punished me. My feet grew heavy and the classes at school I had just completed seemed light years away. Reality loomed on the other side of that blanket. I opened the door to a house that was unnaturally dark and quiet. When my eyes adjusted to the gloom, I would usually see my mother sitting on the overstuffed chair in the parlor.

My mother would frequently focus her attention first on the dirtiness she inevitably found in my panties. She often inspected my underwear and used some imagined stain or spot to justify the punishment I came to expect nearly every day. On good days, she merely spanked me with her hand. She never allowed me to keep my clothes on when she hit me so even these "easy" punishments were painful and humiliating.

She was very methodical in her abuse, often ordering me to hold my body in certain positions and becoming enraged if I showed the least sign of resistance. One action that angered her greatly was if I tightened my muscles in anticipation of the pain I knew was coming. Usually it was inadvertent that I tightened my muscles as it is very difficult to keep your body completely relaxed when you know that you are about to be hurt. Yet this is precisely what she demanded of me.

She would lay me across her lap and fondle my bare skin, telling me how much it would hurt when she was through with me. There were certain words and phrases she repeated as though she followed a script. I was expected to respond in the proper form, using her proscribed language for sexual parts of my body. The words were a combination of baby talk and gibberish. To this day, I cannot bear to say or even write down the words that she used. The shame associated with them is too intense.

During this pre-punishment time, I would become so tense that sometimes I would commit the crime of stiffening my body. For this, she had several remedies. One was to suddenly smash both of her open hands downward with great force, shouting at me to open up my legs. The other was to slip her finger, covered with petroleum jelly, deep into my rectum and hold it there until I once again lay limply across her lap. I have no memory of my mother ever inserting her finger into my vagina. My rectum was the place of entry she preferred.

*   *   *

Amnesty International defines torture as a relationship involving "the systematic and deliberate infliction of acute pain in any form by one person on another, or on a third person, in order to accomplish the purpose of the former against the will of the latter." The term "systematic" distinguishes torture from other forms of abuse that may be repeated over time. That there is deliberate infliction of pain differentiates it further from abuse in which the degree of pain of the victim is a terrible byproduct of the violation but not the primary purpose of the perpetrator.

The word "torture" is not generally used by most incest survivors in describing their histories. However, ritual abuse survivors whose experiences frequently include the intentional infliction of pain under bizarre conditions describe what happened to them as systematic torture, often beginning when they were very young and continuing to be methodically inflicted in escalating patterns to bend them to the will of their abusers, in a manner not unlike brainwashing described by political prisoners. I feel a great sense of affinity with these survivors.

Forensic psychiatrist Park Elliott Dietz, best known for his evaluation of Jeffrey Dahmer, worked with a FBI violent crimes specialist and a medical social work professor to develop a profile of sexual sadists. Their research was based on interviews and published material on convicted sexual sadists who tortured their victims. It was not uncommon for these perpetrators to force their victims to repeat debasing words and phrases to deepen their sense of control and add to the victim's humiliation. The sadists studied by Dietz and others indicated a preference for non-vaginal sexual assault with emphasis on degradation of their victims. [2]

The nature of the abuse I suffered is eerily similar to that described by victims of political torture, sexual sadists and organized ritual abuse. Yet I was not a political prisoner, nor was I abused within a cult or abducted by a stranger who turned out to be a sadistic predator.

There are some sexual sadists who prefer to "grow their own" victims. Little is known about this group or how to help their victims to heal. Clinicians who work with survivors of political torture and those who work with incest survivors generally have little contact across disciplines. Sadistic and privatized torture is a topic that, like female sexual abuse, cries out for more study and public discussion. Healing the torn fabric of our families and larger social structures requires that we bring the issues we most fear to touch into our midst where we can look at them clearly and name them. Banishing them to the closet only fosters the evolution and growth of evil.

*   *   *

One particular afternoon that the green blanket hung in the window, I reluctantly entered the dim parlor to find my mother sitting on the large chair just inside the door. Her voice was cold as she told me she needed to see if my panties were dirty. Still struggling to adjust my eyes

---

2. Dietz, P.E., Hazelwood, R., & Warren, J. (1990) "The sexually sadistic criminal and his offenses." Bulletin of the American Academy of Psychiatry and the Law, 18:2, 163-178.

to the darkness, I put down my pencil box and hurriedly pulled up my dress as I stood before her. I knew the routine. I clutched her shoulders to steady myself as she roughly jerked off my panties, hastily pulling my dress to my chest to avoid the lightning-quick slap that would come for letting my dress slip. Trembling, I waited for her verdict as she inspected my underwear, sniffing the area of the small white cotton crotch with exaggerated slowness. Finally, she threw the underpants to the floor as though it were diseased. Shaking her head in disgust, she spit on her finger and began rubbing my genitals, bending her head close to them as she worked.

She was expert at stimulation of my small private parts, and I felt the horrifying but unbearable warm feeling flood through my body as I simultaneously dreaded the beating that I knew was inevitable. My eyes had adjusted enough to see the metal bucket of wood switches just a few feet away. My mother knew that I hated to be punished with these small branches that she painstakingly peeled the bark from before placing them to soak in the bucket we used to carry water from the well to the kitchen. Claiming that the most painful punishments her mother had given her were those with wet switches, she maintained the tradition with me.

My mother had many ways of forcing me into making choices about the abuse I would experience. At times, she made me select which implement she would beat me with. One of the horrors of torture is that the most ordinary items can be used to inflict unspeakable agony. Common household utensils, such as spatulas and large wooden spoons, became instruments of pain in her hands. Some days, she made me select the part of my body to be hit by reaching behind myself and touching my own skin. She would then strike this one place repeatedly until she finally decided I could pick a new area. In this way, she often drew me into a hellish web of participating in my own punishments.

But on this afternoon, she gave me the choice of redeeming my dirtiness—and receiving a lesser punishment—with a musical performance.

The deal was simple. I was dirty, and had to be punished. This we both knew. The proof was in my panties, which were so disgusting my mother had thrown them on the floor. But I could receive the lighter punishment of being hit with her hand, rather than the dreaded switches, if I played the piano for her without making a mistake.

The piano bench was cold beneath my bare skin. I wore only my shoes and socks, which she always insisted I keep on. She stood behind me so I could not see her. But I felt her breath on my neck as I placed my trembling hands on the keys. The room was too dark to read any music so I would have to play from memory. The bucket of switches was set directly beside the piano in my line of vision, making the consequences of my failure to play perfectly starkly evident.

The first notes sounded tentative but clear in the silence of the room as I started to play. But my fingers felt numb and clumsy. Horrified, I realized I could not remember the notes. My hands struck a sour chord. Time seemed to stop. Suddenly, my mother's arms reached around my body from behind and her hands smashed mine down into the keys. A loud crashing note ended my performance. At that moment, intense fear caused me to lose control of my bladder, and urine ran down the piano bench into my socks and shoes.

Berating me for my stupidity and carelessness, she grabbed my arm roughly, pulling me off the bench and into the adjacent bedroom. She ordered me to lie face down on the bed. My pleas that I would be good, that I was sorry, fell on deaf ears. Before returning to the parlor to get the bucket of switches, she tied my hands to the iron bed rail with a piece of rope. When she came back into the room, I watched in helpless terror as she carefully selected a wet stick from the bucket. And then she began.

It is difficult to write about pain. My body remembers it, but I struggle with words to describe the burning agony. I was not allowed to cry or make any sound since noise seemed to disturb her trance-like state during these episodes. The consequence for crying was severe escalation of pain. If I lost control and sobbed, she would pull apart my buttocks and use her body weight to hold down one of my legs. Pulling my skin back tight on one side, she would wait for what seemed like an eternity before she struck. The memory of feeling air on my exposed rectum and genitals brings more terror than remembering the switch suddenly snaking down between my legs, slashing my most tender places. This would cause my genitals to become inflamed and swollen, bringing excruciating pain when I relieved myself for days afterward.

It was the only time I remember screaming during the abuse. She seemed to accept and allow the animal-like screeching that erupted from the center of my being when she directed her attention to the vulnerable places between my legs. Without fail, she would then shift her weight so she could attack the other side of my body. She was always meticulous about balancing the pain.

She taught me to control my body and my emotions as methodically as any teacher instructing a student in the multiplication tables. I learned to be silent and still. I learned to relax my muscles rather than allow them the tension connected to fear. I left my body when the pain became too much for me to absorb. I think she somehow knew this. She would not allow me to escape by fleeing into the caves within my mind for any length of time. To bring me back, she changed the pain in some way, forcing me into a new position or concentrating her blows on a different part of my body.

Another method was to lull me back into full consciousness with deceptive gentleness. Exhausted with pain and terror, my body would slowly relax as she gently stroked my back and head, crooning words that were incomprehensible to me. When she suddenly picked up the switch and renewed her assault, the suffering was even more unbearable because I had temporarily lost numbness as defense. I had to endure what seemed like endless agony until the pain once again pushed me over the edge and I floated somewhere above the small body that was no longer mine which was lying so still on my mother's bed.

There was a strange, intense intimacy that followed these torture sessions. My mother was like God. She caused me to suffer unbearable agony and then at her will, she took it away. I loved her for taking it away. I somehow disconnected from the fact that she had decided I was to suffer the trauma of sexual beatings. I did not hold her responsible. I believed she was doing what mothers inexplicably have to do. She would cover my bottom with kisses, her tongue reaching everywhere as she covered every inch of my skin with cool wetness. Carefully, she rubbed my wounded places with soothing lotion, promising she would make me feel better.

She never failed to stress that all mothers who loved their little girls punished them to make them clean. I believed her; children are easily manipulated and lied to in the name of love. Above all, I believed that it was not her fault she had to punish me so much. It was mine. I was the one who got my panties dirty. I made mistakes playing the piano. I even urinated on my socks and shoes. I just hoped she would not tell my father as she sometimes threatened she would. I didn't want him to know how bad I was. And shoes cost a lot of money.

*   *   *

As a child, I had little recourse other than to accept whatever treatment my mother deemed justified. Yet I did engage in some forms of resistance. One was to leave my body when the pain became too overwhelming, a means of escape which she sometimes thwarted by changing her technique of abuse. Another kind of resistance that was more difficult for her to circumvent was the ultimate creative act of a child who was offered unendurable pain at the hands of a mother she loved and needed. This child took pain and turned it into pleasure.

Once that transformation was possible, there was less need to escape my body and possibly be forced back into it by a torturer who watched for such subtle rebellion. When a child learns to crave pain, punishment turns into a perverse form of contentment. But then again, perhaps that was my mother's goal all along. I can only recount her actions. I do not know her motives.

*   *   *

From my journal...
Whenever a memory surfaces, I am made aware of how terrifying the abuse actually was. As I feel the pain, I sometimes think that even now I cannot stand it. I am frantic at times, torn between wanting to deny/forget/split off...and knowing that I have to pass through this in order to heal. Sometimes I'm afraid I'll be so affected by the pain and terror I will lose my mind. There is a terrible place of dark chaos where my voice is taken from me and I am mute and helpless.

*   *   *

As I walked in the land of my childhood, remembering the sadistic abuse that routinely took place in the Little House, I experienced periods of times when I lost my ability to speak. My throat became so constricted with fear that attempts at speaking resulted in broken, hoarse sounds. This especially impacted me at work, where talking on the telephone was a major part of my day and necessary to my tasks. I blamed sore throats and laryngitis countless times when faced with a situation in which I simply could not speak during work hours. I pleaded with Jim to help me find a way to cope with the intense fear that stole my voice, but all of our efforts to remedy this failed. The terror would have to run its course. I just hoped my body was strong enough to bear it.

*   *   *

One night my cousin Nancy called. I had shared limited memories with her during the past few years and occasionally called her with questions about our family history as fragments of abuse surfaced. She was able to validate some external events that corroborated my memories, providing a texture and detail to the extended family context that I lacked due to my inability to remember much of what was taking place around me during those years. When I was younger, Nancy was the only child I ever played with, never at my home but only outdoors or at her house. Thirty years later, she still struggles to describe the ominous aura that seemed to surround our house and her fear about even walking past the house. She says she instinctively knew that I was being hurt when she saw my vacant eyes and my spirit drained of life when I emerged after several days inside.

On this particular evening, she had a question of her own. She prefaced it by explaining that she had been afraid to ask this question because of possible repercussions to my emotional well-being. She now sensed I was stronger, despite the agony of recovery, and asked permission to pose her question. With a feeling of dread, I pulled the stuffed bear the Child loved into my arms, clutching it fiercely. Drawing a deep breath, I told her to go ahead.

She spoke slowly. "Did you really cut yourself on the potty chair so badly that you needed stitches when you were two years old?"

I closed my eyes. Images of blood and cold rags between my legs swept through my mind. I felt sick.

"I don't know." My voice sounded far away, and I felt a chill run through my body despite the blanket tucked around my shoulders. "I remember a burning kind of pain and sitting on the potty chair. There was lots of blood. I remember my mother stuffing cold wet rags between my legs and holding them there as my father drove us to the doctor's office. I remember her telling the doctor I cut myself on a crack in the potty chair as he stitched me up."

My words came out in a rush. This was an early memory I had always retained. In fact, it was so central to my interior organization that my husband tells me I recounted the "potty chair incident" for him shortly after we met. He was horrified and never could fathom how a child could cut her genitals in that way. But he kept his doubts to himself at the time, puzzling over this strange revelation from a girl he barely knew.

I continued to speak into the phone, but I felt an odd sense of disconnection from the conversation. "I have the sense I was put on the pot *because* I was bleeding. What I can't remember is *how* I was cut so badly." There was a long silence as we both considered the fearful possibilities.

Finally, I asked the question that I had never allowed myself to approach. "Do you think she could have attempted some form of female circumcision and panicked when I bled so much?"

Although this form of mutilation of girls' genitals is primarily practiced in Africa, Asia and the Middle East, there have been documented cases in the United States and Europe. The most common form of circumcision is excision, in which the clitoris and all or part of the labia minora are removed with a knife or razor-like instrument. Usually, the mutilations are performed on girls between the ages of seven and twelve by women in the context of great ceremony; in some regions, girls are circumcised when they are as young as two since they cannot struggle as fiercely as older girls do when they comprehend what is about to happen.

Despite the fact that no anesthesia is used during this extremely painful procedure, girls are admonished not to scream or cry. Those who cry are ridiculed for their weakness, and their mothers tell them what they are experiencing does not hurt. Although the cultural and religious reasons for slicing off the sexual organs of little girls vary, a theme running through defense of the practice is that the genitals are dirty and must be removed. It is also assumed that girls will be too easily stimulated if this part of their body is allowed to remain intact, leading to promiscuity and bringing shame to their families. It is estimated that more than ninety million women alive today have been genitally mutilated. An unknown number of girls die from infection or uncontrolled bleeding following circumcision; those who survive spend several weeks immobilized, often with their legs bound together to facilitate healing.

My cousin's voice was sad when she finally spoke, responding to my question about the possibility of an attempted circumcision. "I've considered it," she said. "And given your mother's occult background and what I remember of her, it gets my vote."

Nancy recalled that following this incident, she was not allowed to visit me since I was kept in virtual isolation in our house for several weeks. With six-year-old innocence and curiosity, she kept asking her parents how the potty chair could hurt me so badly. After all, she had sat on a similar chair many times and it never hurt her. With practiced adult denial, they evaded her questions and told her to stay away from my house.

I put down the phone with shaking hands. For all of my life, I had retained vivid but fragmented memory of this terrifying and painful incident. I had struggled for years trying to fathom how my genitals could possibly have been sliced on a potty chair, working out the logistics in my mind that would make such an accident possible. But no matter where I imagined a crack in the porcelain pot to be located, I could not figure out how I could sit in a position that would result in a deep cut to my genitals.

My mother's obsession with my female dirtiness may have led her to attempt to eliminate the roots of the problem by "bathing" me. This term is euphemistically used by women whose cultural traditions demand that girls must retain no outer genitalia that might possibly lead them to sexual pleasure. If this was her intent, my excessive bleeding must have thwarted her plans, sending her into a panic and compelling her to seek emergency medical treatment to repair the damage.

Nancy's revelation that I was kept in seclusion for weeks following the incident gave weight to the suspicion I always harbored but never voiced that it was not the potty chair that cut me. I pulled the blanket over my head and wept without tears or sound.

*　　　　　*　　　　　*

My understanding of female circumcision is that the mutilation, although bloody and ritualistic, is not generally considered an occult practice in the nations in which is incorporated into culture and tradition. How it may be used or even further perverted by those who are involved in occult rituals is not easily documented due to the secrecy maintained by practitioners.

However, the occult interest that my cousin spoke of was increasingly evident during the last few years of my mother's life. My escape from the house at age seventeen, pregnant and newly married, seemed to usher a new downward spiral for my mother from which she never recovered. Her own mother died less than a year after I left. Following the death of her mother, she would sit for hours in a dark room illuminated only by flickering candles with framed photographs of her mother arranged carefully on a table before her, the object of her contemplation and point of entry into a trance-like state. Her lips moved in wordless communication with someone she alone could see, and she was completely unresponsive to outside distractions. During these times, the strange interior world she inhabited was the only one real to her.

She read extensively about occult practices and was obsessed with the Ouija board. She spent hours playing with it, muttering excitedly to herself as answers to her questions were given by what she believed were her spirit guides from another realm. Suddenly claiming my father had engaged in an affair with another woman, she demanded a separation and ordered him out of the house. He went.

She began attending meetings late at night about which she would not utter a word. I was worried about my younger brother and sister being left alone until the wee hours of the morning. But when I pressed her for information about where she was going, she was vague and said only she was meeting with a few friends. During the last few years while her behavior at home grew ever more bizarre, she had joined the parent-teachers association and become a cub scout den mother for my brother's pack. But PTA and scout activities could not be what drew her out of the house after 10 p.m.

A neighbor who cleaned rooms at a local hotel told me she was frightened of the new group that had taken up permanent residence in one entire hotel wing. The hotel was in dire need of repair, and the owners were making a last-ditch effort to stay in business. Antonia said the group claimed to communicate with the dead, and people came to visit with them late at night, presumably for seances. Once, despite management's prohibition of the maids entering one part of the wing, she and another curious employee slipped into one of the forbidden rooms. She described a room completely draped in black, with an altar and pentagram its focal points.

I had heard other people talk about the self-described "spiritualists" that had taken up residence at the hotel. But what Antonia was describing sounded more like a setting for Satanic rituals. She made the sign of the cross on her chest as she told me how the maids ran from the room, frightened not only by its appearance but by the evil vibrations which seemed to radiate from it. As soon as she could get another job, she was quitting this one.

When I found pens and little notepads bearing the insignia of the hotel on my mother's kitchen table one day, I asked her about them. She said she liked to stop there and have a few drinks from time to time, then changed the subject.

She grew very paranoid, complaining that her telephone was tapped by the FBI and that her car was under surveillance. She walked the fields and woods at night, looking for UFOs. Sometimes, she would become totally disoriented and not be able to find her way back to the house for hours, finally returning disheveled with wild-looking eyes, babbling about things no one could make any sense of or totally silent and withdrawn.

My mother became extremely childlike and dependent, relying on me for advice about proceeding with the divorce from my father and care of my younger sister and brother. My life became a series of constant trips between the small mobile home I shared with my husband and the home of my childhood that I could not seem to escape.

She fought fiercely with my father over money, accusing him of trying to starve her and the children into allowing him back into the house by not providing her with enough cash to buy adequate food and pay utilities. I mostly just listened to whatever she said, never challenging her assertions about my father's extramarital affair, the demons she swore lurked within the house or her stories about being harassed and spied on by the government. Although I was now a young adult, my mother still held tremendous emotional power over me. Even her most bizarre behaviors and delusions seemed sane simply because she told me they were. Whenever she wanted me, I was there because I had no concept that I could refuse anything she demanded of me.

During this period of time, my mother also stored jars of my brother's fecal material and urine on her pantry shelves. Jack was about ten years old and had developed multiple stomach problems after our father moved out of the house. My mother said she was studying his condition herself, since she could not trust any doctors. My husband clearly remembers this bizarre collection, each bottle meticulously labeled. I do not, but I rely on his memory.

No one outside the family would have guessed that the woman who baked cookies for PTA bake sales and helped cub scouts with their craft projects bottled her young son's bowel movements, talked to her dead mother and had sadistically abused at least one of her children. My mother was capable of the kind of metamorphosis that still rocks my sense of safety in relation to most other people. I am ever watchful for the twitch of an eye, the tightening of small facial bones, the sudden tension in shoulders that heralds the coming of another into the body of the one you think you know. It usually takes years for me to trust that a person I am in a relationship with will not suddenly, inexplicably transform into a monster that hates me and wishes to hurt me. I am grateful that there are people gifted with the patience it takes to accompany me. It is not easy.

After her death in 1975, my father moved back into the Big House to take care of Jack and Diane. He burned cartons of books my mother had accumulated, refusing to talk about the specific nature of the volumes, other than to mutter darkly that such books were evil and an abomination.

Once she recounted an incident which had both frightened and fascinated her. As she sat reading in the living room late one night, she felt a sudden cold chill. A deep menacing growl emanated from the kitchen. Her small dog exhibited frantic behavior, convincing her that the sound she heard was real. She confided that she believed a demon had been close to her that night.

My mother had become so thin she appeared almost skeletal. She lost interest in eating. She was pale, she paced the floors for hours and smoked cigarette after cigarette. When she told me this story, her eyes blazed as though she had a fever, and her narrow face flushed. She seemed more ecstatic than fearful about her experience. A deep chill penetrated my body as I listened to her. I did not doubt my mother could summon even the demons if she wished. She was a force to be reckoned with, even in her rapidly deteriorating condition.

Among her personal effects, my sister discovered a small box that contained black candles and a detailed drawing, a picture of a hideous demon with a distorted face and piercing eyes. This final drawing may have reflected the madness into which she finally irrevocably descended when she succumbed to the interior demons which drove her and which almost destroyed me. I can only wonder how many generations before us suffered the horror of sadistic abuse by their mothers. I strongly suspect that my mother was but one link in a chain of family secrets and violence that stretches back through decades of pain. The sins of the mothers, as well as the fathers, are all too often visited upon their children.

*   *   *

There were certain occasions when my mother's perversions demanded an audience. To satisfy this need, she enlisted the aid of the large mirror that was attached to the bedroom dresser. She wrote the script and produced the play. I was both victim and spectator to the horrifying images of my own abuse that were reflected in the mirror.

For these rituals, my mother always dressed up. When she greeted me after school wearing her best dress, heels and jewelry, I knew it was going to be a mirror day. On those afternoons, the blanket also hung over the window.

Memories of torture in the mirror were recovered in wrenching flashbacks over a period of months and were accompanied by floods of overwhelming sexual stimulation as my body remembered responding to her manipulation. The sexual response was not pleasurable in an adult sense, and feelings of rage that rose from within my center were quickly sublimated into an almost uncontrollable desire to tear at my body in order to satisfy the need for pain that the stimulation demanded.

Because the mirror rituals were repeated many times, the returning memories juxtaposed multiple incidents together. Torture has a way of distorting time and space so that its victims are trapped in a wasteland where a minute is an eternity and every second of relief is but a prelude to more pain. When you are subjected to its chaos repeatedly, it is often not possible to clearly separate one incident from another.

The nature of ritual, however, is repetition. The core elements of the experience are seared on the soul. The memories of torture in the mirror span several years. I will recount a small portion of what they encompassed. There is much more of which I cannot yet speak.

*   *   *

I was ordered to remove my clothes and fold them neatly before bending over or lying across her lap, whichever was her preference on that afternoon. My mother was obsessed with creating patterns on my skin on mirror days, and used various household implements, such as a metal spatula with diamond cut-out design, to gain the desired effect. She enlisted my participation by forcing me to bring her whatever implement she wished to hurt me with and by making me agree to her choice of pattern and degree of color ranging from turning my skin pale pink to a dark mottled red. She talked about this as calmly as if we were choosing material for sewing a dress.

Making these kinds of choices was agony for me. It has greatly impacted my ability today to make even seemingly simple choices. Even the slightest hint of the need to make a decision of a personal nature, particularly about my body, can send me reeling back in time to the horror of making selections about my own torture.

When she was satisfied with her work, I was marched to the wooden stool that she had placed in front of the dresser mirror. Placing a small mirror in my hands for multiple angle viewing, she would turn me around as I stood elevated on the stool and demand that I inspect the colors and patterns she had embedded on my skin. Solemnly, she assured me that the marks I bore were given by all mothers to little girls if they loved them. If my skin were not marred, it would mean she did not love me. I grew to equate signs of abuse with love. I also believed that all mothers who loved their daughters punished them incessantly. At times, I still struggle to dispel this childhood belief. Lessons impressed by pain have a way of becoming deeply rooted in your psyche, and logic and intellectual understanding does not necessarily banish them.

In what seemed to be staged moves choreographed by an invisible director, my mother would bare her chest and guide my mouth to her breast. Barely able to breathe, I did exactly as I was told. Slowly, she spun me on the stool, moving with my body so that the mirror caught us at all angles. She stroked my back and head as she crushed me to her body. She seemed to believe she was offering me a great comfort by allowing me to do this. Yet if in my childish clumsiness I did not please her, she would grip my bottom and pinch me hard. I knew better than to cry.

When this segment of the performance was concluded, it was time for the interrogation to begin. Pacing before the mirror, she fired a series of questions at me which were essentially unanswerable to her satisfaction. Each demand for my response was accompanied by a warning not to lie to her. My mother had ways of determining if I lied.

Desperate and terrified, I always tried to tell the truth, struggling to find the words that would exonerate me. Inevitably, her fixed gaze on my face as she stood with arms folded across her chest would reduce me to incoherence.

She would order me to watch as she bent down and located the place on my body that would prove my guilt or innocence. She could tell if I was lying by touching what she called my "trouble spot" with her tongue. Her test was simple—if it "wiggled" and "peed," I had not been truthful with her.

When she finally buried her head between my legs and skillfully manipulated this mysterious part of my anatomy, my heart almost burst with fear even as my body responded to her. Inevitably, her face would emerge with eyes blazing and triumphant. Her fluency in child stimulation resulted in my conviction of the crime. I had been caught yet again in another lie, and my body had betrayed me.

Before she punished me further for the sin my body had revealed, she would diligently wash me with a mixture of bleach and cold water in a valiant attempt to cleanse my stubborn and persistent dirtiness. The bleach stung like fire as she scrubbed roughly between my legs with a rag, warning me with escalating anger of the punishment to come. But her words had little effect at this point. The child standing on the stool gazing into the mirror with empty eyes was no longer me. I was not sure who she was. Some other child who was obviously hurt had taken my place. I was light as air, and my feet were not even touching the stool. Nobody could hurt me.

By the time my mother finished the ritual bath and laid me face down across the stool to further prove her love for me by marking my flesh as she chastised me for lying, I was gone. The play went on without me.

Cross the Bridge

Small wounded child, sleeping
huddled to save the one small flame of resistance
from the wind of terror
that howls inside the dark cold rain
of your house

Precious child, full of promise
reflecting hope, absorbing light
what have they done to your gentle spirit
with their cruel twisted hands
and their lies?

Cross the bridge, child,
to your dreamland
take my hand
we'll fly through time
to a place where all life, holy,
rests and waits a birthing time

feel the sunshine
see the rainbow
hear the song swept on the wind
take my hand, child, hold on tightly
cross the bridge
and rest a while.

The Deepest Wound

When you're stronger, we'll go back there
braced again to face the cold
Once again, the spark protected
One more time, the journey made
from death to life, from fear to hope

Rest in me, child,
Feel my heartbeat
Ride my wings upon the wind
Rest awhile within the garden

and know that I will come again.

Chapter 11

Entering the Danger Zone: Addiction and Anger

The relentless emergence of memories of childhood torture continued to take a heavy toll on my body with chronic bronchial infections.

I barely slept each night, giving my body little time to recuperate and heal before facing another day in a stressful work environment where I could no longer separate from my emotions and pain. Economic demands required that I continue to work to help support my family. Like most abuse survivors, I did not have the luxury of choosing to leave my job so that I could concentrate on my healing. I would some-how have to do both.

Jim said that an integration process was taking place and that it was a positive sign that I could no longer shut out the fears and needs of the Child who was silenced for so many years for large chunks of my work day. But he worried about my deteriorating physical health and began to direct his attention to the medical care I was receiving. I was reluctant to talk about this aspect of my life. In reality, I did not trust or like the doctor I had been seeing for the last several years. I had an uneasy feeling about the massive doses of antibiotics, often two or three kinds at the same time, which he routinely prescribed. He appeared unconcerned that I was taking one or more kinds of antibi-otics for months at a stretch. When I complained that I felt no better after weeks of treatment, he simply asked me what kind of antibiotic I wanted to try next, without offering any advice or suggestions. Once, when I was preparing to leave for a trip to El Salvador and needed protection from contracting malaria, he wrote a prescription for quinine in a dose that was so far from correct that the pharmacist refused to fill the order as written.

But there was one component of this medical relationship that I very much wanted to keep intact. This particular physician was willing to refill my prescription for the tranquilizer I now required for sleep. I knew that not all doctors would accommodate my demands for a continual supply of a drug that is considered to be potentially addictive. Although the medication is generally recommended for short-term use, I had been relying on pills for dreamless sleep for almost six years. In order to protect my supply, I was willing to put up with medical treatment that I increasingly suspected was below standard for my chronic illnesses.

Jim was not. His insistence that I deal with my physical health set me on a path in which I would inevitably have to confront my addiction. This would lead to the painful discovery that the re-parenting process that was the essence of my therapy was not entirely comprised of nurture and comfort. As a result, the dormant anger that was deep within the fragmented child called Amy rose to the surface for the first time. And it was not directed at my mother.

*   *   *

The issue of finding a new doctor continued to surface in therapy sessions for several months. Jim respected my right to make choices about the direction I would take in order to heal. We had both learned that I needed to feel in control of the process in order to move forward. His commitment to allowing me to set the agenda meant I was usually able to brush aside medical concerns when he brought them up, turning the discussion in a different direction. I wished desperately he would drop the subject. But what happened one weekend frightened me badly enough to actually bring up the topic myself in my next session with Jim.

I had been given another new antibiotic medication as I struggled to survive the most recent bout of bronchial infection that struck my weakened immune system in late March. Despite my husband's protests that I was not well enough to leave the house, I insisted one afternoon that he take me to a movie that I very much wanted to see. I was tired of being in bed and feeling sick and bargained with him that we would use the trip to pick up my new prescription at the pharmacy.

We stopped to pick up the prescription on our way to the theater. When we settled in our seats, Steve went to get drinks and popcorn. Although I was trying to pretend I was well, I was in reality feeling weak and dizzy. I decided to take the antibiotic immediately rather than wait until we were at home.

Slipping a pill into my mouth, I sipped my drink to swallow it and leaned back in my seat in the darkened theater. Within a few minutes, my entire mouth became numb, and my throat began to close. I leaned forward in my seat, breaking out in a sweat as I struggled to pull air into my lungs. I was having a severe allergic reaction, but the conditioned response of the Child was to admit no pain.

I finally managed to respond to Steve's frantic inquiries by gasping that I was having a reaction to the antibiotic. He wanted to call for help; I adamantly refused. He begged me to go to the emergency room of the local hospital. I shook my head, unable now to speak. The terror of not being able to breathe had driven me completely into the domain of the Child. Asking for help is not an option for a little girl who had been methodically taught to be especially silent in the face of trauma to her body. Desperate for air, I motioned for Steve to hold my drink to my lips. I hoped that I might open my air passage by forcing soda down my throat. But to my horror the liquid spewed out of my nearly closed windpipe and ran down the front of my sweater.

I began to feel disconnected and unreal. My body felt light, and I wondered with detachment if I was leaving it behind for the last time. My predicament had become like the movie on a screen within the darkened theater, and I was a passive viewer. Part of me knew that I could die. And the Child who was in control at that moment believed that she had no choice other than to endure what was happening.

Fortunately, the allergic reaction had reached its peak. It abated, leaving me limp and drained. As we walked out of the theater, I felt very small. The world looked huge and ominous. There was no safe space anywhere. When I crawled into bed that night, I lay for a long time wondering why I was not dead. That I could have died as a result of the allergic reaction was a chilling reality I could not ignore. I was also shaken by my plunge into child space at a time when I needed all of my adult competence to cope with a potentially life-threatening situation.

I called my doctor the next morning and described what happened in the theater. When I mentioned that I had elected a generic medication at the pharmacy because he had not marked "brand required" on the form, he immediately started to berate me for my poor choice in using an inferior brand; the fact that he had not specified "no substitution" on the prescription seemed to be insignificant. Seizing on this technicality to exonerate himself, he insisted what happened was not his fault. He brusquely told me to go back to the pharmacist and get the "real" thing. When I protested that I was afraid to follow these directions because I feared I might have another allergic reaction, he told me to suit myself and hung up the phone.

With shaking fingers, I dialed the pharmacy. Unlike the doctor, the pharmacist listened attentively as I described what happened. I told him about my doctor's instructions to get a brand-name prescription of the same drug. In a calm but concerned voice, he told me that in his opinion that option was not safe for me. He said that what I described was a severe allergic reaction to the drug; the fact that it was generic had nothing to do with my inability to tolerate it. I hung up the phone and cried.

          *   *   *

When I arrived at the counseling center a few days later, I felt fragile and wounded. My fever was up again, and I was without antibiotics that I could safely take. I badly needed the comfort and nurture that I had come to associate with Jim's presence. Somehow, I felt like this alone could heal me. But this session turned out to be one of the least comfortable I had ever experienced. Instead of the nurturing I had come to expect, I was confronted by a determined parent-like person who would not allow medical concerns to be brushed aside any longer.

Jim listened in silence as I recounted the details about my reaction to the drug and the doctor's response. As I watched his face intently, I saw something there which was unfamiliar to me. It was anger. Although it was not directed at me, it was going to drive the course of the therapy session. And when it was finished, finding a new doctor was no longer an option to be considered. It was a requirement.

          *   *   *

I was terrified of Jim's anger, and I came to the next session fearful and withdrawn. My mother's anger had been horrifying to witness. I lived in dread of the emotion of anger—my own and that of other people. In order to trust Jim, I had to allow myself to believe that he could never be angry. The strong emotions he had expressed about my medical mistreatment were a jolt to my sense of security with him. The moment I saw anger change his face, my whole body immediately shifted into a numb state. Anger meant I was going to be hurt.

Survivors of severe and chronic abuse develop physiological reactions to fear and stress that are more likely to produce numbness rather than the surge of adrenaline commonly experienced by people suddenly faced with danger. Research indicates that exposure to long-term trauma may actually alter the body's biochemical response to a perceived threat. Instead of getting the necessary burst of strength and anger needed to confront danger, a survivor's body may in fact do just the opposite by producing internal chemicals with analgesic and even anesthetic effects. Children who are repeatedly abused by a trusted and all-powerful caretaker quickly learn that neither fight nor flight is possible.

Our bodies are conditioned to automatically begin to shut down and become numb at the first hint that we are going to be hurt. Our biological systems are gradually modified by repeated trauma to allow us to survive unbearable pain and shock. In the path of harm, we become like frightened rabbits caught in blinding headlights, unable to run, cry out or protest.

When Jim realized that his anger was perceived by the Child as actually life- threatening, he carefully worked to repair the damage. He explained that he was angry about the medical treatment that I was given, not at me. His anger was derived from his fear that if I had followed the doctor's advice and taken another form of a drug that I clearly was allergic to I might have died. I struggled to look at his face. When I did, I could not hold my eyes there for more than a few seconds out of dread that it would change.

It mattered to me enormously that two of Jim's four children were daughters. Although he spoke very little about his personal life, at times he shared bits and pieces of his experiences with his children while they were growing up. He let me know that he valued and loved his daughters as well as his sons. That a daughter could be valued was something that I could only dimly fathom in a kind of puzzled amazement. Nothing in my history with my birth parents taught me that daughters were of any value other than ornamental.

Some of the deepest and most profound healing interactions with Jim came from the role of parent, rather than the role of therapist. The Child instinctively knew from which place he was reacting. I do not believe I could have healed with someone who understood about raising children solely from theory and psychological texts.

Jim's response to my fear of his anger came from his parent role. This was fitting because it was this place within him that gave birth to the anger that had so frightened me the week before. Directly confronting my withdrawal, he asked me to look at him. After what seemed like an eternity, I risked raising my gaze to his face. Gently, he explained yet another time that he was not angry with me but that his anger came from being afraid that I could have been badly hurt. In a thoughtful voice in which he seemed to be explaining his reaction to himself as much as to me, he said it was like when your child runs out into traffic and almost gets killed: you want to make sure she has a strong impression of the danger that she has experienced. In that respect, he wanted me to hear his fear and anger.

Tears spilled out of my eyes and down my cheeks. For the first time, I had encountered the protective fierce anger that is a natural occurrence in people's childhood experiences with loving parents who do their best to keep their child safe from harm. I would struggle for a long time to understand this new kind of caring that set limits, that confronted, that at times expressed itself with an anger that was not intended to destroy but to encourage self-protective behavior and healing.

The icy numbness that had gripped my body gradually receded as the Child met Jim's eyes and let them hold hers, seeking assurance that she would not be hurt. In some mysterious way I could not yet comprehend, his anger was a form of love. I could not understand it on an intellectual level. But the Child sensed it. His face was once again safe for us to look at.

*   *   *

Our discussions shifted from whether or not I would seek competent medical treatment to the more productive level of deciding whom I might be able to trust to be my physician. Short of looking in the phone book and randomly selecting a name, I had not even the most remote idea of how to choose a new doctor. In addition to the variety of illnesses that continued to plague me, I began suffering fairly frequently from pelvic pain. It was difficult to know if I was experiencing body memories or a current physical problem.

Resigned to the fact that I had to deal with medical issues, I asked Jim to recommend a doctor who was sensitive to the concerns of abuse survivors. Unfortunately, the physicians he believed were the most knowledgeable and best trained in working with survivors were women. We both knew a female physician was an impossibility for me because intense emotions continued to be activated whenever I attempted to interact with female people on other than strictly business or superficial social levels. After careful consideration, he gave me the names of an internist and a gynecologist, both men he had known for years and held in high regard. Although neither had ever mentioned working specifically with abuse survivors, he said their approach to medicine was holistic, compassionate and caring.

I had not had a gynecological examination for six years, and I was terrified. I told Jim that I could not deal with everything at once without becoming unable to function. We finally agreed that the most pressing issue was my current bronchial infection and constant flu-like symptoms, and I would approach the internist first. As I held the slip of paper with the doctors' names in my trembling hands, I tried one more time to express how afraid I was about giving up my link with the physician who refilled the prescription for the sleeping medication. In a voice that let me know we were not going to negotiate, he said firmly that my fear of not being able to automatically obtain my tranquilizer was less than his fear of what could happen to me if I did not get proper medical care. And that if I have an addiction, the addiction would have to be confronted. The agenda was no longer entirely mine.

*   *   *

My first appointment with Dr. Reicht did not go well. Although he was competent, experienced and a partner in a practice with an excellent reputation in the community, he did not demonstrate the level of sensitivity to issues of touch and control that are so crucial to developing even a minimal level of trust with an abuse survivor. By the time I left his office, I was shaking in terror and vowing I would never go back again.

The visit began in a positive way. Dr. Reicht reviewed the results of the lab tests I had taken the week before and took a detailed medical history. We sat in a comfortable office, and I was able to remain in my adult role as I described my chronic respiratory problems, bladder infections and pelvic pain. I talked briefly about the process of healing and current therapy and the tremendous toll the re-experienced trauma was taking on my body.

When he asked if I slept well, my heart skipped a beat. Drawing a deep breath, I told him about the need for tranquilizers that had developed as I began to remember childhood abuse. Writing intently on the chart, Dr. Reicht questioned me about dosage and frequency of use. When I told him I had needed at least 30 milligrams to sleep every night for the last six years, he looked up at me and shook his head.

"This medication is not intended for long-term use," he said briskly. "And it's clearly becoming ineffective, since you're only sleeping a few hours a night, even with these high doses. You have an addiction, and I suspect that this may be impacting your immune system and contributing to some of your other problems."

My stomach seemed to drop to my feet.

"We have to get you off of these," he said, shutting the file. "It's the single most important thing we can do for your overall health right now. We'll treat the bladder infections and other ailments. But we won't make any real progress until we get your system cleaned out."

I opened my mouth, but no words came out. He did not seem to notice my speechlessness. "Let's take you over to the exam room. We'll talk about the addiction after the physical is completed."

I was shocked about his matter-of-fact approach to giving up one of the most important things in my life as I walked to the adjoining room. From what seemed like a great distance, I heard Dr. Reicht tell me to take off my clothes and put on a gown and that he would be back in a few minutes. "You can keep your undies on," he said in what was probably intended to be a reassuring statement as he closed the door. "This is just a general physical exam."

The feeling of terror and shock intensified. I was not prepared for this exam. My other doctor had never asked me to undress. He rarely touched me, other than to perfunctorily press on my stomach through my shirt when I complained of pelvic pain. And Dr. Reicht's use of a childlike word for underwear instantly triggered memories of my mother's baby talk when she was abusing me, compounding my fright. I went careening into history, back to the times when my mother ordered me to take off my clothes. I began to shake as I removed my dress.

By the time Dr. Reicht returned to the examining room, I was moving mechanically to the table. I expected to be hurt. I answered no questions and did not respond to his attempts at cheery conversation. He seemed not to notice my sudden silence or the shift that had taken place within me.

After the exam, we sat down at a small table and he outlined his plans for weaning me from the tranquilizer. I was still wearing the gown, and I felt vulnerable, small and powerless. None of his words made sense to me. He was talking about switching to an antidepressant because he believed my exhaustion and depleted energy were partially a result of depression. Meticulously explaining options, he sketched out an alternative approach utilizing a similar tranquilizer and gradually reducing the dosage. This was not his treatment of choice, he said, saying that he definitely preferred the antidepressant and launched into a lecture about its benefits, explaining that it would take the edge off of the extreme anxiety provoked by the emerging traumatic memories.

I stared at the floor. I was struggling so hard to break free of the numbness that was my protection against the abuse and to reclaim my emotions. Now this doctor that I barely knew wanted to prescribe a drug that would "take the edge off" my feelings. That "edge" was where healing took place.

As a result of my intense engagement in the process of remembering and reclaiming, I was starting to feel real emotions for the first time in my life. And although most of what I felt was painful, it was preferable to returning to a state of perpetual numbness. I was finally becoming human. And now Dr. Reicht wanted to send me back to the internal prison constructed in my childhood where all emotion was deadened and the only imperative was to survive.

Having finished the blitz of choices, he asked for my decision. Dragging myself up out of the bottomless pit into which I was inexorably sinking, I found my voice. I asked what he would do if I decided I wanted to continue with my medication at current levels. He paused reflectively.

"If you and Jim believe that you need to do some intense work for another few months and then you'll be ready to deal with the addiction, I would be willing to write you a prescription for a limited amount of time," he said slowly. He finally seemed to be seeing me and trying to make some sort of human connection. But it was too late for that. He had already begun to wear my mother's face.

He was powerful and controlling. He wanted to take away something that was essential for my survival. He made me take off my clothes and he touched me. He was forcing me to make choices between terrible options. He wanted to put some foreign substance inside of me that was going to take away my feelings. And then he smiled at me and expected me to talk to him.

In a voice that sounded strange and distant to my own ears, I asked if he would write a prescription for the tranquilizer just once more so I would have more time to make a decision.

He asked for my permission to speak directly to Jim about it. I would have agreed to anything to get my pills and get out of there. Scribbling on a pad, he handed me a prescription. Instead of the 90-day supply my previous doctor had always given me, this order was for only 20 days and was marked for "no refills."

I got dressed and left the office in a daze. As in the beginning days of therapy, I was almost incapable of driving. Nothing looked familiar or real. I was in the land of childhood. As I headed out onto the bypass, a cold and mirthless joy began to flow through me. Death seemed to beckon me with open arms. Laughter which was more lament than mirth rose up from a hollow place within me. Anyone hearing it would have doubted my sanity at that moment. It was all I could do to not aim my car at an oncoming truck or a tree. It would be less painful than what surely awaited me at the hands of Dr. Reicht.

*   *   *

I first ingested street drugs into my body following the rape when I was twelve. By the time I was thirteen, I was smoking marijuana every day. The numbness of the "stoned" feeling of being outside of myself was welcome and dovetailed with my own natural dissociative processes rather than being scary or disruptive. I began using a variety of chemicals, including mescaline and LSD, when I was fourteen. Although I attended a small, rural school that was scoffed at by more urban teens as a "farmer school," a plethora of drugs were readily available for purchase.

However, I rarely bothered to buy drugs from students at my school since my favorite drugs were freely given to me by older men with whom I spent most of my free time. Once, I attended an "invitation only" party at the home of one of the wealthiest families in a nearby town. The host was Chip, who was in his mid-twenties and drove an expensive sports car. Blonde and good looking, he had his choice of women, and was generous in sharing drugs with his friends. His parties were legendary. I was thrilled he asked me to come.

His parents' house, in a secluded area about two miles from town, was ablaze with lights when I arrived in a car crowded with girls lucky enough to have caught Chip's eye and gotten an invitation. Dozens of cars, many of them expensive models, lined the driveway. It was clear Chip was not concerned about drawing the attention of the police.

I walked through sliding glass doors into another world. The furnishings and art were of the sort I had only seen in movies. Bowls of brightly colored pills graced antique tables. It was a supermarket of street drugs, all free to the guests who were sprawled in chairs and on the floor. A group of men were in one corner smoking hashish, watching a couple having vigorous sex just a few feet away. The room was thick was marijuana smoke.

Within a short time, I was stoned. At the persistent encouragement of a few men, I agreed to do a strip tease dance. As I swayed to the music, languidly taking off my clothes, a movement on the second floor balcony that overlooked the massive living room caught my attention. Chip's father, a graying and well-respected local business owner, stood in his bathrobe surveying the scene below him. He looked at me with interest, enjoying my dance. After a few minutes of voyeurism, he called out to his son that there was plenty of ice cream in the freezer if anybody wanted some. He waved to the crowd below him, and then disappeared behind the massive oak door of his bedroom.

*   *   *

I thrived on the challenge of using heavy hallucinogens, telling myself that my mind was strong, a place of refuge. Unlike others whose minds could not endure the shifts in reality resulting from LSD, I embraced whatever chemicals were able to shift my reality from my daily life at home and the feelings buried within me.

As my mother loosened her control, I now had no limits on my behavior and virtually no structure in the family setting. I often left the house at night through my bedroom window to meet with friends and party. I stayed away from home for days at a time with only the flimsiest of excuses. I had sex with any man who wanted me, often in a drug-induced haze. My provocative dress incensed my father, whose idea of moral guidance was to call me a "slut" and a "whore," quote Scripture verses about licentiousness and refuse to speak to me for several weeks. But I was no longer the compliant and submissive child who learned to endure suffering without protest. A dull hate burned within me for people in positions of authority. The natural rebelliousness of adolescence was multiplied by years of abuse and neglect by the very people who society entrusted with my care. My mother raped and beat me. My father failed to protect me. Relatives closed their eyes. Doctors backed off under threat of lawsuits. The state, generally quick to intervene when child abuse is suspected in poor families, rarely sends its caseworkers to upper-class or middle-class homes. I had no reason to respect family, community or institutions.

I occasionally brought motorcycle gang members into the house just to see my parents' horrified faces at their tattooed arms, scars and greasy hair. One particularly scary-looking man in his forties, garbed in leather and chains, flicked ashes on the kitchen floor one night as he entered the house at my invitation. Leaning up against the counter, he possessively stroked my body and asked my mother to bring him a beer. I relished her expression of disgust laced with fear as she complied.

By fifteen, my drug of choice was amphetamines, popularly known as speed. It allowed me to feel assertive and witty and opened doors to connections with other people that I so desperately craved. It mitigated my natural shyness and swept aside my chronic distrust of humans in general. It allowed me to develop friends within the drug culture I now considered my "family." Spurred on by the dangerous energy shot into the body with amphetamines, I often did not sleep for two or three days at a time, and my appetite was greatly altered by regular use of this drug; after two years of its use, I weighed little more than 100 pounds though I was two inches shy of six feet. When I became pregnant at seventeen, the knowledge that I was carrying a beautiful and precious child within me gave me the courage to leave the drug culture that had been part of my life since I was thirteen. Without any professional help, I broke a two-year addiction to amphetamines. My conviction that I had to protect my unborn child was the force that propelled me through the agonizing psychological and physical withdrawal.

        *   *   *

I counted my pills incessantly. The supply that I had on hand plus the new prescription from Dr. Reicht became the focus of much of my attention. The anxiety provoked by the thought of giving up the tranquilizers meant that I often needed to double my dose to sleep, further hastening the day when I would be completely without them.

The chains of addiction are strong yet subtle. Accommodations are woven into the fabric of daily life until they are no longer visible to the one who is bound. Morning and night, as routinely as brushing my teeth, I opened the door to the cabinet where I stored my supply of the tranquilizer to make sure it was there. A feeling of security washed over me when I saw the large bottle tucked safely on the shelf. I was unable to leave the house without having a few of the pills in my purse. Although I did not take them during the day, I was terrified I might not be able to get home and be faced with a night without my drug.

It was not only the nightmares that I feared. The process of slowly relaxing before falling asleep was fraught with terror for me. The pills preempted the need for relaxation, which made me feel vulnerable.

When the tranquilizer hit my system, I fell hard and fast into dreamless sleep.

When my mother held me on her lap as a prelude to abuse, my need for closeness and comfort eventually won out over the fear that was always present when she touched me. Relaxing into the warmth of her body was a terrible trap. In a dreamlike state, I would feel her fingers rubbing under my clothes. My body's response to her stimulation was her justification for the brutal punishment that inevitably followed.

Decades later, my body jerked to stiff attention if I let down my guard enough to allow relaxation to flow through my muscles in a natural preparation for sleep. Shaking in terror, I would sit straight up in bed and turn on the lights. Nothing could convince me it was safe to relax. The intense fear effectively annihilated any lingering sleepiness. It was a vicious cycle, and chemicals were my only means of defense against the terrible vulnerability that triggered it.

*   *   *

I pleaded my case to Jim, asking for more time before I faced the addiction. The visit with Dr. Reicht had triggered raw and chaotic emotions. In the center was an Amy-based rage that was virtually untouchable. I had no experience with expressing anger appropriately. My skill instead was in completely burying it. To the Child, Dr. Reicht was just one more adult in a position of authority who wanted to use his power to hurt us.

To avoid dealing with what felt like a bomb about to explode within me, I initially decided to take a rational adult approach to convincing Jim that I was not ready to give up my pills. Terrified of what might emerge, I did not allow the Child to speak. I reminded him that Dr. Reicht said I could wait a few months if we both agreed a delay was warranted. But my poor physical health seemed to take precedence with him over my need for choices and control. Jim asked me if I thought I would be more ready in two or three months. When I admitted I would not, he said firmly that he saw no reason to wait. I looked at him speechlessly.

Suddenly, the anger carefully held in check seemed to rip loose. I gasped in horror as I heard Amy scream inside that she hated Jim and never wanted to see him again. Seconds later, the Child was sobbing hysterically and abjectly pleading that she not be abandoned. My body stiffened with the effort of containing this volatile and dangerous new emotional dynamic. Jim asked me what was wrong. I shook my head and bit the inside of my mouth hard to keep from speaking, furtively digging my nails into the soft inner flesh of my arms in a desperate attempt to have pain trump emotion. Although there was inner chaos, the only sound in the therapy room was silence.

*   *   *

For the first time, the tranquil space at the counseling center no longer offered me absolute sanctuary from the tempests of healing. I alternated between resentment about Jim's imposition of limits which would force me to confront the addiction and fear that he would abandon me if I allowed the rage to inadvertently push past my defenses. It was Jim's fault that I was in this predicament in which a doctor I hated suddenly held enormous power over my life. My tranquilizer not only helped me to sleep; it was a faithful companion who never left me. And now it was going to be taken away. Dr. Reicht only wanted to hurt me. And Jim was not going to protect me.

To the terrified Child, Dr. Reicht had become the powerful mother who violates and destroys, and I was unconsciously replaying an old script from childhood. Jim, focused on his concern for my physical well being, did not immediately notice the silent language of my fear or the signs of my distress. That I could have told Jim how frightened I was of Dr. Reicht and that his actions during my first encounter with him provoked extreme alarm did not occur to me in the midst of my escalating panic. In the tradition of my childhood, I retreated into numbness. The nascent anger that had begun to surface was once again buried.

The Sanction of Torture: A Nightmare

I am walking down a hallway in an institution with a group of women. We are students, and everyone is carefully taking notes as the woman in charge tells us we are here to learn what it means to be a mother. We stop at a room with a closed door. Through a small window, we see a woman who is watching a little girl get undressed. The leader explains that the role of a mother is to break the will and spirit of her child. We are forced to watch as the mother methodically beats and tortures her daughter.

The leader, who wears a white coat like a doctor and speaks with great authority, presses a button, and now we hear the sound of the child's screams. The mother is calm and smiling as she hurts the child. The leader tells us what to look for in the child's physical condition, how to analyze her screams, how to judge her submission to her mother's will.

The other female students are absorbed in the torture of the child. Scribbling notes, they nod their heads approvingly. They want to learn how to be mothers. I am feeling sick. The woman torturing her child has my mother's eyes.

The leader explains that the mother must periodically change the pain for it to be most effective. The torture must include periods of gentleness so that when the pain starts again, it is felt with more shock. The leader notes that this child is not yet broken; she continues to scream.

Finally, the child is silent even though the torture continues. She opens up her body to her mother's hands and does not cry or move. Her eyes are dead. The leader tells us to note the condition of the child…this is the goal for a good mother: a child who is completely broken.

We move down the hallway, stopping at other rooms where similar scenes are repeated. We pause to watch a child who is begging her mother to stop hurting her. The leader's face darkens. When a child pleads for mercy, even stronger measures are called for. The mother is right to use the most painful tortures on this daughter who will not be obediently silent. With a voice no more than a whisper, I say, "But isn't it enough? The child is so hurt—she can hardly even stand up. Why must there be more?"

There is a shocked silence in the group. The leader glares at me and says that as long as the child protests, she is not sufficiently broken. The little girl's cries echo through the hall. I let my tablet drop the floor and I cover my face. I can't look any more. The child is shrieking as though she has lost her mind. The mother, who is clearly sexually excited by the child, looks triumphant when the screams finally stop.

We approach the next room. There is tension in the group. I am filled with apprehension. The leader seems angry because I questioned the torture in the last room. She shoves my face up against the window. There is a mother in this room, but no child. Suddenly, I understand that I am to be tortured because of my trembling protest. She opens the door and pushes me into the room. I hear her telling the group of women to take careful notes. She explains that even an adult can be turned back into a child with the right torture methods and enough pain.

I am trapped with no means of defense. My torture is sanctioned by the power of mothers and institutions. The group of women now watches me through the window. The woman with my mother's eyes tells me to take off my clothes and I do. When she reaches out to touch me, I wake up.

Chapter 12

The Will of the Child

From my journal…

I am crying and shaking. I sat up in bed and can't bring myself to lay down again. I'm terrified I will fall asleep and be back in a nightmare. The heavier doses of tranquilizers used to protect me from these dreams. I will light a candle and hold my stuffed bear and wrap myself in a Salvadoran blanket. I must stay awake the rest of the night to be safe.

If I could pray, I would ask that sleep come quickly and with no dreams. But I can't pray anymore. I will not speak to a God who arrogantly commands children to honor their parents. Where is the commandment to honor and respect the children?

I wish I could live without sleep.

            *   *   *

I met briefly with Dr. Reicht to tell him of my decision to break the addiction by switching to another tranquilizer and gradually reducing the doses. He made one final argument for consideration of antidepressant medication, emphasizing again that it was his preferred method of treatment.

He reiterated his belief my constant exhaustion was due in large part to depression and that the antidepressant would not only facilitate therapy, it would restore my energy level. Trying to offer incentive, he cheerfully described how some of his patients reported that once their depression lifted, they were able to resume physical activity such as aerobics, further contributing to their overall recovery. He sounded like a coach trying to motivate a recalcitrant player. I resented it.

I remained adamant in my opposition to a drug that I believed would take away my hard-won emotions. And the very fact that an antidepressant was Dr. Reicht's recommended treatment mitigated against my acceptance of them. We were already set on a course in which I heard every word he said with suspicion and viewed each action as a potential threat. If I had been bleeding, I probably would not have accepted even a bandage from him. The hatred and distrust of authority developed during my childhood and refined during my adolescence was now directed at the man who I was to trust with my physical well-being.

But I did not tell him any of this. I simply said coldly that I had no interest in aerobics and had made my decision. He wrote a prescription for another tranquilizer with a slightly lower dose than I was currently taking. He said he hoped I would change my mind. I assured him I would not.

*   *   *

As the time approached when I would make the transition to a new medication, Jim persistently encouraged me to express the conflicting emotions that I desperately fought to keep under control. It was a shock to discover that he was not blind to my submerged anger after all. That he could see what I tried to hide was simultaneously terrifying and comforting. He said casually and often that probably no one could give up an addiction without having some anger surface. Withdrawal was an increasingly difficult defense to use with him.

Consequently, the Child became more strident in her demands to be heard. To my dismay, she surfaced one afternoon before I could stop her and in no uncertain terms told him about her intense dislike of Dr.

Reicht. Jim was perplexed at first by the vehemence of my apparent hatred for the physician to which he had guided me. But he quickly comprehended that he had become a symbol of my mother's control and misuse of power as my words tumbled out in torrents.

The Child described her terror at being made to undress, her horror at the intrusive touch and her conviction that he wanted to take away all of her feelings with a new kind of pill. She revealed her hurt and confusion about Jim's failure to protect her from someone who wanted to do her harm. Her sense of betrayal over his perceived abandonment was enormous.

I heard her speak as though she was a separate person. Even the voice did not sound like mine. I looked down and saw hands much smaller than my own, twitching of their own volition on my lap. They were twisting my skirt in agitation, wrinkling it and almost tearing the fabric. When I began therapy, I could not comprehend what Jim meant when he expressed indignation over my lack of protection as a child. Now, some very young part of me had actually come to expect him to protect me. Although this was a source of embarrassment to the adult, it was a vital part of healing for the Child.

Having spoken her mind, the Child quickly vanished. I was left to deal with the consequences. The room slowly came back into a normal focus. My hands were no longer tiny. My voice was my own. I began to apologize to Jim, telling him that the stress of the past few months was making me crazy. But he knew when he heard directly from the Child. And he always treated her revelations with the utmost respect and tenderness.

In a quiet and firm voice, he said he would not make me go to a doctor I hated. He apologized for his lack of intervention in the process. Although he had briefly spoken to Dr. Reicht before my first appointment, he realized now that he should have carefully planned an initial joint meeting for the three of us at which my fears and concerns about medical treatment could have been discussed. If he had done so, I might have been spared the re-traumatizing experience that my transition to a new doctor had obviously become. He asked for my forgiveness for the mistakes he had made.

He said he wanted the Child to hear clearly that he would not abandon her, no matter what. That she could be as angry with him as she needed to be, and he would not leave her or hurt her. He reassured her he would never permit any doctor to give her medication that would take away her feelings. He did not believe an anti-depressant would do this, but he respected the Child's fear that it might. Her emotions were precious to him, and he would not allow them to be crushed again.

He finished by saying that I could opt to choose a new doctor. He promised to help me in whatever way he could to do this. But regardless of my choice of physician, he fully expected me to move forward with the process of giving up the addiction and obtaining adequate medical care. My health was too important to ignore and compromise.

The session was over. Jim stood up and held out his hand. Trembling uncontrollably, I allowed him to pull me up from the floor cushion into his arms. He always hugged me briefly at the end of every session. At times, this hug was the most important part of the hour for me. But today, he held me closely for a few minutes. The tears that I had struggled so valiantly to suppress for the many long weeks I had felt abandoned and unprotected spilled down my cheeks and I wept.

My internal and external sense of security was restored. I still had to face the addiction, but I was no longer spinning into chaos with no one to accompany me. Jim knew I hated Dr. Reicht and it was all right. He was sorry that I was frightened by being touched by him. I could pick another doctor if I wanted. Above all, he was not going to hate me or abandon me. He would protect me.

By the time he gently released me, his shirt was wet with my tears. But that was all right too.

*   *   *

I was not prepared for the intensity of the physical withdrawal that I would endure when I stopped taking the medication after more than six years. Dr. Reicht said I might experience some discomfort as my body adjusted to the new tranquilizer. He did not tell me that I would wake up in the middle of the night drenched in sweat and shaking in terror nor did he mention that I might suffer from violent headaches, dizziness, extreme anxiety, chills and panic attacks.

I took my first dose of the new tranquilizer on a Friday night, reasoning that at least I would not have to get up and go to work the following morning. This was a good decision, because I got less then two hours of sleep. On Saturday night, I slept for exactly one hour. On Sunday, I did not sleep at all. By the time Monday morning dawned, I had accumulated no more than three hours of sleep in the past three days.

In a dangerously disoriented condition, I drove the twenty-mile route to work, arriving at the office almost completely unable to function but too confused to make the decision to deviate from my routine. Like many survivors, I derive a good deal of security from consistency and structure. It is difficult for me to make any changes, even when structures are harmful, stressful or abusive.

Predictability and stability are valued by traumatized people above all. Even if there is only the certainty of knowing what kind of abuse to expect, many victims prefer to continue to suffer rather than risk the uncertainty of what may happen if they refuse to accept this way of life any longer. This dynamic was clearly seen in the 1994 Salvadoran elections when the poor majority who had endured torture and oppression at the hands of the military government elected Armando Calderon Sol, a representative of the right-wing party who spawned the very death squads that carried out unspeakable atrocities.

It was the first presidential election after the implementation of the Peace Accords. Many political observers were stunned at the seemingly inexplicable victory of the right-wing party, but people who understood the long-term effects of trauma were not. Influencing the election were complex factors, such as massive propaganda campaigns in poor communities, death threats against opposition leaders, army intimidation at some polling places and disorganization within the alternative parties. However, a primary force which drove the traumatized Salvadoran poor to elect a representative of the political party formed by the man believed to have directed the assassination of their beloved Archbishop Oscar Romero was their terror of the unknown.

When all of your energy has been devoted to surviving trauma for years, it is extremely difficult to let go of the pain and approach the formidable task of rebuilding your shattered life. Many of us choose the pain that is familiar rather than the terror of the healing. To people who have not endured atrocities, our choices are almost incomprehensible.

Like the Salvadorans who elected a leader they feared because they knew and understood the politics of oppression, I clung to my addiction because I had become intimately familiar with its chains. When I found myself confronted with the possibility of freedom, I regressed to my basic survival mode, too frightened to imagine a new way of living. I became angry with those who struggled to liberate me. I embraced the old dark voices that echoed up from the small corner of my spirit to which they had been banished as the truth of my childhood emerged, seeking solace in their call to inflict pain on myself.

And in the midst of severe withdrawal, I held fast to my routine of forcing myself to function even if it meant putting myself in danger by pushing my weakened body beyond its capacity. I sat at my desk with my head in my hands. Lack of sleep had greatly diminished my capacity to think clearly or function competently. I knew I could never make it through a day of work. I doubted I could drive home.

With fingers shaking so hard I could barely use them, I dialed the number at the counseling center. It was only the second time in three years of therapy that I had allowed myself to reach out to Jim by phoning him between sessions. I had no idea of what I wanted to say to him. I just knew I needed to hear his voice. As it was very early, I expected to hear the answering machine when my call was picked up. To my surprise, Jim answered the phone himself.

His response to my distress was immediate. He said that three days was much too long to be virtually without sleep and that the withdrawal seemed too harsh. He let me know he wished I had called him over the weekend. Within a few hours, I was on the phone with Dr. Reicht who wrote an emergency prescription of my old tranquilizer at a lower dose that I could combine with the new medication.

I left work early, leaving a note for my boss that I was not feeling well. As I drove to the pharmacy, I felt as though the car and I were floating several feet above the highway. I could not feel my hands on the steering wheel, and was amazed that the car was more or less under control, evidenced by my eventual arrival at my house intact.

I spent the afternoon in a state of agitated exhaustion. I was too nervous to sleep and too tired to pace the floor or embark on a cleaning project to alleviate my anxiety.

Jim phoned me that evening to see how I was doing. Taking the phone into the kitchen stairwell, I curled up on a step and cradled the receiver to my ear. The voice that responded to his questions was young and frightened. What he said was of less importance to the Child then just hearing his voice. Gradually, his voice soothed her. He made me promise to call him the next morning.

I sat on the step with the receiver in my hand long after the connection had been severed, trying to absorb the amazement I felt about Jim and Dr. Reicht's rapid and compassionate response to my insomnia and withdrawal symptoms. I might have to give up the drug I had come to depend on, but I would not be allowed to suffer needlessly. I dragged my aching body up the stairs to my bedroom, took both pills and slept.

*   *   *

There was a tremendous struggle inside of me during the following months as I slowly relinquished the chemical bonds that gripped me as tightly as I held fast to them. In order to let go of the chemical, I had to cling to a human being with the same fierce intensity that I had devoted to the drug. For the first time, I would need to trust human companionship with all its fragility instead of the predictable chemical relationship that I could more easily control.

Jim encouraged me to visualize him as a source of security when I was feeling afraid or sad. When the nightmares came, I pictured him sitting by my bed and stroking my head. I heard his voice talking to me softly. Slowly, my tense body would relax for a few minutes as the comforting image gained power before it vanished in the face of the terror that the vulnerability of sleep evoked. I held to his imagined and real presence as though it was a raft and I was adrift on a treacherous sea.

At times I was completely frustrated and convinced I could not continue with treatment. I pushed at Jim's limits to see if he would let me slide back into dependency on a chemical. On these occasions, he would succinctly remark that it was a bit like weaning a baby from a bottle. You did it gently and gradually and tried not to cause her undue distress. You knew that sometimes she was going to get really upset with you for not giving her the bottle she so badly wanted. But you continued to wean her because you understood that it was in her best interest to learn to drink from a cup. He apologized once for the use of this analogy, thinking it might have offended me. But there was too much truth in it for me to reject it as anything but apt.

If I had attempted to give up my addiction before I had formed a secure relationship in which the needs and pain of the Child could be heard, I do not think I would have been successful. I grieve for the survivors who are forced into some preconceived therapeutic framework that mandates that addictions must be confronted in the early days of treatment. That kind of thinking would have been disastrous for me. I might have given up the drug under those circumstances. I might have modified my behavior. But the addiction would have lain dormant once again deep within me, waiting for the right circumstances to be resurrected. This might be called a form of recovery. It is not healing.

*   *   *

The option of choosing another doctor helped to ease the powerlessness I felt in relation to Dr. Reicht. It gave me the courage to become clear about my needs with him. I did not relish the task of beginning over again with another physician. And in a way I did not quite understand, I had come to think of Dr. Reicht as a "good enemy." Despite the fact that we were locked into adversarial roles, there were qualities in him I admired. Unlike my previous doctor, he was unquestionably medically competent. And he was apparently determined to convince me to invest in the process of improving my physical health as a part of healing from the abuse.

Although he had not handled our initial interactions well, he did seem genuinely interested in learning more about what would help me to feel a greater measure of trust for him. Working with abuse survivors is not an area of expertise that most doctors develop unless they allow their patients to teach them. The re-traumatizing nature of medical procedures combined with a lack of sensitivity by providers keeps many victims of childhood abuse from obtaining adequate medical care. To my great surprise, Dr. Reicht was willing to be taught.

A major stumbling block was his approach to lowering the doses of my medication. The fact that he would arbitrarily decide when I would make a transition to a new dose worked at cross purposes to my ability to give up the addiction. If Dr. Reicht wrote a prescription that would require me to make a reduction in a month, as the thirtieth day approached, I became completely immersed in the belief that he was trying to hurt and control me. This belief led to severe insomnia, panic attacks and nightmares. Deadlines imposed by him meant I inevitably had to increase my dose to maintain any level of stability.

It also seemed to be at odds with the work I was doing in therapy sessions. If I was dealing with the emergence of a traumatic memory the last thing I needed was to be compelled to lower my medication level. Given the fact that memories and emotions were not amenable to scheduling, I was often faced with making a dosage reduction at the worst possible time. My therapy and my medical treatment seemed to be juxtaposed in a jarring manner.

Powerful childhood emotions were activated by his ability to refuse my demands for something that I so desperately wanted despite its potential harm. The only person with authority and power I ever trusted in my entire life was Jim. I was not able to extend any of that trust to Dr. Reicht. He had not yet earned it.

*   *   *

As a child, compliance and submission were the only options available, and obedience developed as my automatic response to my mother's demands. Expressions of pain and fear were not allowed except in extreme moments of abuse. However, after the crucible of hospitalization, the rape by Rick and the cessation of sexual abuse in my twelfth year, I shed every vestige of compliance. But my newfound defiance did not protect me from harm. In reality, it was just a fragile veneer constructed by a terrified child whose only real method of defense was to abandon her body and flee to safety within the refuge of her mind.

I was an easy mark for the predators who intuitively recognize children who have never learned to protect themselves because no one taught them they have value. My mask of indifference and toughness was easily recognized as a sham by those people who prey on those who are vulnerable. When you have been repeatedly beaten and raped by a parent, it is hard to develop even a shred of self-esteem and protect yourself from further exploitation.

I entered my teen-age years with no comprehension that I had the right to deny anyone access to my body. But despite the fact that sex is theirs for the asking, there are men who prefer to take it by force, and rape in a group setting is considered a form of sport. When I was fifteen, I was thrust into the game. Like my mother, these men took what they wanted and seemed to enjoy my pain and humiliation.

It is only now, decades later, that I have begun to feel the impact of what happened at the private club known only as "Marty's." Although its patrons called it a "club," there was no sign on the door. It was not a legal business establishment but rather a converted apartment in the downtown business district paid for by its members. That hot August night I was an invited guest.

*   *   *

Marty's was privileged domain of a group of men, mostly in their twenties and thirties, who desired a very private place to indulge in their perversions and preferred their sexual partners in the early teen-age years. Its door was never darkened by an officer of the law. The men who owned Marty's were powerfully connected so that drugs, weapons and sex with children would be overlooked for the right price. When the door at the club shut behind you, the rules the rest of the world lived by were suspended. My friend Lisa and I were appropriately awed that we were included in the elite inner circle.

Like most girls who allow their bodies to be abused by men, Lisa and I came from dysfunctional homes. Although we did not talk about our experiences within our families, children who are neglected, emotionally abandoned, and abused have finely tuned radar. We recognized each other.

Lisa lived in a ramshackle house in the country with junk piled in the yard. The paint was peeling, and the porch had collapsed at one end. When my mother discovered where Lisa lived, she forbade me to be friends with her. We did not, my mother informed me, associate with "those kind of people." By this point in my life, however, my mother's orders meant nothing to me. Lisa became my best friend.

Spending as little time as possible with our families was a major mutual goal shared by the two of us as well as the few other girls with whom we socialized. All of us were desperately in need of affection, structure and guidance. Not having access to fill these needs, we compensated by demonstrating our value as sexual playthings to older men. We kept lists of how many men we'd had sex with and how many LSD trips we had taken and competed with each other to pull ahead with the longest of either list.

The girl with the longest list of sexual encounters was Cora. She was the only one who talked openly about her life in her family, which included ongoing molestation by her father. When she was fifteen, her mother banished her from the house because she was a "slut." Cora lived on the streets, washing her hair and bathing at gas station sinks. We brought her food and clothes until the day she disappeared, presumably with a man to another city.

All of us knew at least some of the men who frequented Marty's. We believed they treated us well, providing us with free drugs in exchange for sexual favors. Lisa and I had been favorites with them for a few years.

We were issued a command invitation to come to the club one Saturday night at a specified time. This kind of invitation was highly unusual since most of our experiences at Marty's had been in the context of an individual member using the facility as a secluded space for sexual activity with a child. Neither of us even thought of refusing this invitation. Despite the fact that they took advantage of our bodies at every opportunity, we considered the men of Marty's to be our friends.

At least they never hit us, we told ourselves, and they kept us supplied with the drugs we craved.

I instinctively knew something was wrong. A man stood outside the door as sentry. This was unusual, as only members had keys and there was normally no need for a guard. The man whisked us in, and we found ourselves in the middle of a circle of about twelve men. Most were leaning back against the walls, casually smoking marijuana joints or drinking wine and talking quietly. The murmur of their voices grew silent as Lisa and I stood awkwardly in the center. A tall man with dark hair tied back in a ponytail came to us holding pills in his hands. Like obedient baby birds, we opened our mouths at his command. He patted each of us on the head as we swallowed. He smiled. Then he sat down to wait with the others.

Within a short time, I understood that we had been given drugs that we had never taken before. I was very experienced in altered states, both natural and chemical, but the hallucinogenic drug streaming toward my brain was a powerful derivative that was not yet being sold on the local black market. Later, I learned we were a test case. The men wanted to learn the effects of the drug before they began selling it locally.

I crumpled to the floor like a sparrow whose bones had just been crushed by a giant fist. Someone turned on a black light and set a flashing strobe in motion. Rhythm and blues music began to throb from large speakers. The effects of the drugs distorting my central nervous system combined with the pulsating light increased the intensity of the trip from which I was not sure I could ever return. Walls melted and rippled. I saw the notes from the music dancing in the air, and I tasted their metallic sound. The room expanded into a stretched-out tunnel like a scene from a cartoon. My body felt extraordinarily heavy. Like Alice when she went through the looking glass, I was a sparrow down the rabbit hole.

This drug was not like other psychedelics I had used which affected my brain and sensory perceptions but had no major impact on my ability to walk, stand or sit. This drug not only produced strong hallucinations but also virtually disabled my body. No amount of commands from my brain to sit up could do more than lift my head a pitiful inch from the floor.

I tried to rise from the floor where I had crumpled, but my body felt tangled and I was unable to move. Someone carried me over to a mattress that had been placed along one wall. I tried to reach out to touch the wall, desperate for the feel of something solid. My hand flopped like a limp dishrag and connected with the wall more by accident than intent. My hand seemed to go right through the plaster as though I were no longer bound by normal rules of matter and physics. I was surprised to see that Lisa was already on the mattress nearby, and she was naked. Hands were pulling down my jeans, but I could not feel my legs. I heard Lisa making little whimpering sounds. I struggled to form words, but my tongue was too swollen.

Suddenly, I could not breathe. A great weight was crushing me. I looked up and did not recognize the face attached to the body on top of mine. I turned my head and saw Lisa buried beneath a huge form. The circle of men crowded around us, casually talking as they waited their turn.

Casting my eyes around the mostly familiar faces towering above me, I caught a glimpse of one figure that did not fit in. He was outside the circle, and for a moment his eyes locked into mine. He seemed to be sitting down just behind the other men, yet his head was a bit above theirs so I had a clear view. I wondered what he was sitting on. I felt a wave of compassion and love emanating from him. Like the Lady in White, he communicated without sound, urging me to have courage and survive.

Although my memory is blurred by the effects of the drug, I believe that the gang rape continued for hours. I remember at one point thinking it was over because no one had come to take the place of the man who had just ejected his sperm into my almost inert body. I was jolted into the realization that they were not finished when someone grabbed my feet and flipped me on my stomach. Hands gripped my waist, pulling me up and forcing me on my hands and knees. I looked for Lisa and could not see her any more. But I found once again the face of the man sitting quietly outside and above the circle. His eyes glistened, perhaps with tears. I had the strong sense he wanted to intervene but could not.

The pain of being entered from the rear was a shock to my body that temporarily ripped away the protective numbness that engulfed me. But any screams I might have been able to voice were muffled by the penis that was shoved into my mouth to silence me. Mercifully, the drug and my instinctive dissociation allowed me to escape the full brunt of what was happening.

I woke up the next afternoon lying naked on the dirty mattress. My body hurt so much I could hardly move. The club was deserted, and bottles and debris littered the floor. Dazed, I woke Lisa and we managed to find our clothes. A note scrawled on a large piece of paper was placed conspicuously on a nearby table. It was intended for us.

The men who raped us and then discarded us with the trash from their party had left written instructions to "clean the place up" before we left. Moving in slow motion and with a heavy silence between us, Lisa and I picked up bottles and cans, swept the floor and washed dishes. That it never even occurred to us to refuse this outrageous order was a testament to our early childhood training in obedient compliance to authority, no matter how evil or corrupt. When we were finished, we hitchhiked home.

*   *   *

I no longer prayed to the God of my parents, who demanded obedience and meted out punishment, nor attended church with them. I had no use for organized religion or for the church of my childhood where the seating was silently predicated upon social class. I wanted nothing to do with the all-powerful God these people worshipped. Yet I secretly held a place in my heart for the one they called Jesus. He loved children and criticized his friends when they tried to shoo the children away. He said his family was not his birth mother and siblings but those who worked with him, helping the poor and healing people.

The man who radiated love and compassion throughout that terrible night at Marty's, offering his comforting presence but not rescue, may have been a hallucination. But whenever I remember him, I call him Jesus.

Lisa and I never spoke to each other of what happened that night. Within a few months, our friendship was dissolved. We drifted away, each too filled with shame about what had taken place at Marty's to be reminded by the other's face. Even decades later, there are still nights when I see her face and hear her cries as she was raped by my side. That I could not protect or help her haunts me more than the reality of my own rape.

I have always been able to weep for Lisa.

*   *   *

The gradual reduction of medication meant that every remaining vestige of chemical numbness was dissolving. Even though I had taken the pills for sleeping, the massive doses and long-term use meant that the drugs were constantly in my system, even during waking hours. The pain of things always remembered but never felt, such as the night at Marty's, flared like newly opened wounds. Jim commented during this period that he was glad that I had the protection of chemical numbness during the early years of our work. Even now, with all the strength that I had gained through healing, my stability was threatened as my body and mind struggled to cope without any drugs to dull the pain or ease the nightmares.

The relationship with Dr. Reicht, although difficult, opened up emotional pathways to conflicts about authority. Although I still resented and resisted almost every suggestion he made, something within me struggled for resolution over the dilemma of whether to be compliant or rebellious. That there could be a third choice never occurred to me.

Jim listened patiently to my struggles, always reminding me that I had the option to choose another doctor. That I did not pursue the option was evidence of the fact that some needed component of healing was being actively worked on through this relationship. One afternoon, as I was again approaching another medication reduction and beginning to panic because I would not allow myself to comply with Dr. Reicht's instructions, Jim remarked that the Child had already proven that she could say "no." The crucial question now was could she also learn to say "yes" and actually agree with someone in a position of authority whose power was used for good purposes.

I looked at him in consternation as he explained that true autonomy means being free to say yes OR no. Speaking directly to the Child, he made it clear that her will was of great importance to him and that compliance was not a goal he would ever pursue. Gently and persistently, during the chaotic months of being weaned from my addiction, Jim offered the Child who had only known submission or rebellion a third choice. It took me many months to comprehend what he was talking about.

When I finally understood, I asked Jim to set up a meeting with Dr. Reicht for the three of us. I was ready to move beyond compliance or resistance. There were other possibilities for me now.

*   *   *

I decided that I needed three things from Dr. Reicht. First, I wanted him to know some of my story. It seemed unrealistic to develop a medical relationship with someone who knew I was abused but did not understand the level of trauma I carried. With Jim as intermediary, I sent him a detailed written history that covered areas of my abuse and the healing process that I wanted him to know about.

I also needed him to be extremely cautious with physical touch in the future. It was important that he understood how triggering and frightening his actions had been during my first encounter with him. I wanted his commitment to sensitivity in this area.

And lastly, I wanted Jim and I to have joint control over the timing of medication reductions. I was able to accept directives from Jim with much less resentment than even mild suggestions from Dr. Reicht. It was equally critical that I not be required to make a change when I was in the midst of actively processing memories of abuse. Transitions would be much less traumatic if I had a role in the decision as to when to make them. Choices and control were essential to my sense of security.

Dr. Reicht listened intently as I outlined the framework I needed in order to fully engage in the process of liberating myself from the chemical bonds that still held me. He had read the material that I wrote about my process of remembering and healing, and he expressed his admiration for my courage in confronting my traumatic history. He apologized for his insensitively to the issue of touch and asked for my help in teaching him what I needed to be safe. To my utter amazement, he readily agreed to give control of the timing process for medication reductions to Jim and me.

We shook hands as the meeting concluded. For the first time, I looked him squarely in the eye without fear his face would suddenly take on the countenance of my mother.

"Someday," he said with a smile but a hint of sadness in his voice. "I hope I can be more than just a guardian of the pills for you."

I nodded, my eyes unexpectedly filling with tears. After almost seven months of battle, he was beginning to earn my trust. I did not know it then, but the day would come when I called him friend, and he would become a trusted and cherished companion on my journey of healing.

*　　　　　*　　　　　*

I sat on the floor of the therapy room a few days later, struggling to absorb the strange new feeling of empowerment that flowed through me. I had finally found the path of the third choice, which was not submission or rebellion but something entirely different. I could be protected and yet challenged. I could be nurtured and yet confronted. I would not be abandoned or hurt when I was at my most vulnerable. I could decide who would accompany me on this journey, and I could set the terms. I could touch anger and live.

I mulled over this in amazement, trying to find words to describe the spacious place that had opened up inside of me. I knew I still had a long way to go in freeing myself of the addiction. But in the process of gaining my liberation, I was healing much more than a chemical dependency.

I looked up at Jim and saw him beaming broadly. Our eyes met and held.

"That Child *does* have ears, doesn't she?" he said softly.

Not trusting my voice, I nodded. This man, who had become the only real mother I have ever known, learned how to speak directly to the traumatized child. And because he spoke with his heart as well as his words, she had learned to listen.

The Child indeed had ears. And they were open.

Chapter 13

All Things Female

From my journal...

I have never had the sense that I truly live in a body. I float outside of it much of the time. I refuse to be trapped in anything female. My mother was female, and I will not be like her. Jim has been gently pushing me to reconnect with my physical self. He says an important part of healing will be learning to see women as potentially good. But this I cannot do. Women are dangerous and cannot be trusted. They hurt you, rape you, tear out your soul in ways men cannot.

My mother's shadow falls on all the flowers, and I am afraid to touch them. And my body is nothing more than a bridge to pain.

*   *   *

If certain elements were present, even benign encounters with women could send me careening back in time This was made devastatingly clear to me at a conference for abuse survivors I attended in a nearby city.

The annual event was sponsored by a women's counseling center and was the only public forum for survivors of childhood abuse in my geographic area. I knew that exclusively female space and any form of group interaction was out of the question for me. But after making several inquiries, I learned that the conference would be taking place on a college campus. It was open to men and women and several workshops would be conducted in a lecture format. Gathering my courage, I decided to attend.

Arriving early at the campus, I walked briskly toward the building where the conference was scheduled only to stop in my tracks when I reached the edge of the terrace. A woman with an artfully painted face and dressed in a sunflower costume was presenting flowers to each participant from a basket draped over her arm. She communicated with elaborate miming gestures to the people she approached, sometimes acting out brief skits. Fear shot through my body as I watched her drop down on one knee to offer a choice of flower from her basket to a woman who approached the door. My heart began to pound. What if I picked the wrong flower? What if I could not understand what she meant with her gestures? What if she touched me?

Shivering in the morning air that had been comfortable only moments before, I skirted way out around her and slipped in through a far door. I went to the still-empty auditorium and collapsed into a seat along one wall, trying to still my racing heart and to reassure the frightened child inside that we were safe. But as the seats filled, the mime came inside with her basket, looking for participants who had not received flowers. I slouched down in my seat and buried my face in a newspaper. Making the wrong choice or not understanding immediately what was required of me brought hideous punishments from my mother.

By the time the conference officially began, the auditorium was filled with survivors and advocates stroking, smelling and waving brilliantly colored flowers. I was not one of them.

As my fear of women rose to the surface, it suddenly seemed as though the world was comprised of mothers with children. From pages of magazines to television shows to a walk down the street, I encountered women with their daughters and sons. Each time I saw a mother with a little girl, I automatically wondered how the adult hurt the child. I had dreams about rescuing children with dead and vacant eyes from mothers who tortured them. One afternoon, in a desperate attempt to see women as caring people rather than potential sources of abuse, I carefully cut pictures out of a stack of magazines. I selected photos of smiling mothers holding daughters who looked like them or attractive women walking through fields of flowers holding the hands of their children. My intent was to combine the pictures into a collage that could be a tangible reminder that not all women were abusive. I wanted to show Jim that I was trying to be open to healing this part of my life, even though I was filled with ambivalence and dread at the prospect.

As the pictures piled up on the floor, I grew tense and anxious. A desperate longing mixed with terror began to build inside of me. I stared, mesmerized, at the glossy colored photo on the page of a magazine open on my lap. A little girl looked up with a trusting smile at her mother's face as she was cuddled in her arms. Suddenly, agony as sharp as the scissors that had sliced magazine pages cut through my heart. In the next instant, I was acutely experiencing the child-need for closeness with my mother, which was always a prelude to pain. This was a need that could never be allowed. I started to tremble as pressure mounted in my head. A sound like thunder filled my ears. The smiling mothers holding their children seemed to mock my suffering, reminding me of what I could never have.

Driven by a burning hatred I did not dare name, I grabbed the pile of carefully cut photos. My body seemed extremely uncoordinated and clumsy as I struggled to tear the pictures with hands that inexplicably felt small and awkward. I could not shred them fast enough to assuage the unbearable feeling of need mixed with danger. I stumbled to the bathroom where I filled the sink and dumped the pictures in the water. When they were completely saturated, I ripped up the soggy wads of paper before I threw them in the trash, shoving them deep into the middle of the can. With relief, I piled other garbage on top of them. The mothers were gone. There was no more need or danger. I was safe now.

That I had to destroy the children with the mothers was a sad irony not lost on me.

*   *   *

Remembering is only the beginning of healing. Several years of reclaiming my history and allowing myself to feel the pain that I could not bear to experience as a child brought me to a place where I was finally able to accept the support, nurture and structure I needed to heal.

Recovering from sadistic abuse in childhood requires much more than accessing and cauterizing the deep wounds inflicted on body and soul by the trauma. A major task of recovery also means addressing the gaping developmental holes that are the psychological legacy of growing up in an emotional wasteland. Like many other survivors, I compensated by developing a detached but strong intellectual capacity that allowed me to function in the adult world. Emotionally, I remained a child ruled by fear and mistrust, with all the violence, betrayals and sexual trauma of the past just a heartbeat away from the present.

To my great relief, the relentless emergence of memories eased for a time. My body gained strength as I slowly recovered my natural sleep rhythm. The nightmares abated, and I delighted in my new ability to relax into a vulnerable state that allowed sleep to come gently and without terror. With excitement, I would relate to Jim that I had taken a nap on the weekend or that I had slept for six or seven hours without waking. His face always lit up with a smile when I made progress, and he was lavish with his praise over my growing capacity to sleep on my own. Unlike the early days of therapy when compliments were viewed with suspicion and outright disbelief, the child part of me now eagerly absorbed praise. This was a subtle but important measure of healing.

I gained the strength to occasionally refuse to enter the time warp leading to the past when I was triggered by events in the present. This was precarious and sometimes resulted in merely postponing the agony of a piece of memory that demanded acknowledgment and release. Yet it also afforded me a sense of control, albeit fragile, that provided me with the boundaries within which I could begin to approach some of the deep emotional wounds that are the legacy of abuse.

The present was like a deep lake covered with ice over which I skated. At any time, I could be triggered by a smell or sound; by reading a book or seeing a movie; by hearing about the abuse of a child on the news. Suddenly, the solid ice beneath my feet grew thin. If I could not skate fast enough to get back to safety, the hard surface would dissolve and I would be plunged into frigid waters. The risk of not emerging, of not being able to swim back up through the hole in the ice, was real. I learned to recognize the warning signs when the surface of the present was starting to shatter beneath me.

When a thunderstorm is drawing near, the sky darkens and the air feels charged with energy. Just before the first boom of thunder, the wind dies down. Birds go silent and animals take shelter. When a trigger was winding its way through my emotional defenses, I sensed the same kind of electrically charged tension present in the silence just before a storm. I knew something powerful and potentially dangerous was on the way. During its journey, I would often develop a severe headache that would not respond to any medication I tried. Nightmares punctuated my sleep, and panic attacks interrupted my days. Sexual stimulation that was painful rather than pleasurable washed over me in unrelenting waves.

During these periods, I did not allow myself to journal too much. Writing often expedited the emergence of memory for me. To keep from opening the floodgates, I learned to jot down brief notes and images that I could choose to explore more fully when I was with Jim, or later when I felt more stable. I discovered that going for a brisk walk could help to ground me when I was becoming overwhelmed. I found that eating crunchy foods, such as an apple or hard pretzels, reoriented me toward the present. I learned how to resist memories in order to protect myself. My goal was to have a measure of choice over whether and when they emerged. Often, I failed. But each success was a sweet victory.

Jim encouraged me to develop this ability. The near-constant immersion in traumatic memory during the past few years had been a crucial part of healing, but it extracted a great physical and emotional toll. It also prevented me from fully entering the grief that was always held at bay and from processing the complex mix of emotions that accompanied remembering the devastation of the torture that had been my primary bond with my mother. It was only during abusive rituals and the aftermath that I was close to her. My association of women with pain was woven deep into the fabric of my being. My only means of defense against becoming like my mother was to develop an aversion to all things female, including myself.

Jim steadfastly maintained this was a tragedy and said that part of our work together might involve him serving as a bridge between me and other women. He held women in high regard and counted several among his best friends. He periodically reminded me that I had also suffered because of my father's passivity in the face of violence and that I had been raped and abused by men. But as therapy focused on reconnecting with my body and revising my view of women, my journals increasingly reflected hateful diatribes toward all things female, particularly mothers. Fueling my incipient rage was the reality that the few women I had tentatively trusted in the beginning of my healing process had betrayed or abandoned me. That my mistrust and expectation of being hurt had contributed to the loss of relationships did not yet occur to me. In my deepest places, I believed that no woman could ever be protective, nurturing or truthful. I was also convinced that something about me precluded any female person from accepting me.

When Jim talked about women as potential sources of friendship and support, I withdrew into silence. What he did not understand was that women hated me. And there was nothing I could do to change it.

                        *   *   *

My body was numb from my knees to my chest. Other than pain, I experienced no sensations in this part of my body. Jim suggested I begin to experiment with exercise and deep breathing to reduce stress and regain a sense of connection with my body. I was not sure I wanted to establish any sense of relationship with my physical self, and most of the time I was too fatigued to take even a simple walk when I got home from my job. My efforts at deep breathing exercises in which I would attempt to feel my breath moving through my mid-section failed. This part of my body was a dead zone, and nothing moved through it, not even my own breath.

Jim knew Maggie, a woman who was teaching a "Mindful Yoga" class at a local church. Unlike the yoga that I had studied a decade earlier that encouraged concentration on a universal force outside of oneself, this form of yoga focused on turning the attention to the body and emotions as a part of meditative practice. Gentle stretching exercises, breath work and discussion on holistic approaches to health were included in the sessions.

Reconnecting with my body in a class led by a female instructor held considerable risk for me. Jim and I discussed the potential benefits and pitfalls of participation in such a class. Buoyed by my success at overcoming the addiction and wanting to move forward in healing, I decided to try the class despite my ambivalence. Jim said I was one of the bravest people he knew. But I did not feel brave just then. I would have rather entered a war zone in El Salvador than be even slightly vulnerable with a woman. I approached the yoga class with more trepidation than my earlier accompaniment of Salvadoran refugees in conflictive areas where the impact of exploding 500-pound bombs shook the earth. Like many survivors of severe abuse, I knew all too well that there were things much worse than death. In my case, closeness to a woman was one of them.

*   *   *

I arrived early at the first yoga class and headed for the back of the nearly empty room to find a spot along the wall. A far corner seemed to be the most protected place where I would not be surrounded by other people. I rolled out my mat on the floor and sat down to wait, warily watching the door as people began to converge for the class. I breathed a sigh of relief as several men entered and, like me, rolled out their mats. Although I had been assured the class was mixed gender, the early arrivals were female and I was beginning to panic at the prospect of being in a group comprised solely of women.

I had spoken to Maggie, the instructor, several times on the phone but had not yet met her in person. The anonymity of the telephone gave me the distance I needed to be frank about my situation and to express the reservations I had about being able to participate. Maggie had not worked in a direct way with abuse survivors although she was fairly certain that people in various stages of healing from childhood wounds were frequently students in her classes. She had a keen interest in understanding more about the experiences of trauma survivors and believed that yoga could be an avenue of healing from sexual violence, provided it was practiced in a gentle and non-intrusive manner.

Encouraged by our conversations, I sent her a copy of an article that I had written for publication about the connections between incest and war. She responded with a letter in which she expressed deep respect for my healing process and said she would be honored to work with me. It was her hope that our relationship would be mutually beneficial. She made it clear that I should only participate on a level that seemed safe to me and that leaving the class in the middle of a session was always an option if I was uncomfortable.

I was suddenly aware of my name being spoken. A slim blonde woman dressed in a black leotard was standing in front of me. In my concentration on the door, I had not noticed her approach. Before I could scramble up from the floor, she gracefully dropped down to a kneeling position at the edge of my mat.

She smiled at me. "You must be Linda," she said softly. "I'm Maggie, and I'm so glad you came."

She reached out her hand to touch my shoulder and I instinctively flinched and drew back. Her hand froze in the empty air for a moment, and her eyes registered recognition of her mistake. "I'm sorry," she said ruefully. "I will be more careful."

I opened my mouth, but no words came out. I struggled to regain my composure. It was one thing to talk on the phone, but it was quite another to meet in person a woman with whom I had shared fairly vulnerable information about myself and from whom I would try to learn about reconnection with my body. Fear gripped my stomach despite her gentle manner as I tried to concentrate on what she was saying as she reiterated that I could feel free to leave at any time or to not participate in any exercise. But her words seemed to be unintelligible, and I had difficulty hearing them. I was already beginning the slide into the past, and it remained to be seen if my new but fragile coping abilities would allow me to refuse to be pulled into the time warp that led straight to my childhood.

Maggie began each class with a reflection on a specific topic. The theme for the first night was connection to ourselves and others. As she talked about body awareness, I felt tension begin to build within me and the presence of the frightened child part grew strong. The room was darkened, with a candle illuminating Maggie's notes providing the only light. I was barely listening to her words as I strained to see what I could of the room, with the forms of students shrouded shadows. Candlelight may have been peaceful for the other students, but it was unnerving to me to have my vision so obscured in a group of strangers.

Suddenly, I heard her say that her tradition for first night of class was to have participants make brief introductions and say a few words about why they chose to explore working with yoga. I was not prepared to be visible, and I felt an immediate and violent sense of betrayal and disconnection. Although I had made formal presentations to groups of several hundred people in connection with the work in El Salvador, the idea of speaking my name out loud in this setting filled me with terror. Like a turtle pulling into a shell, I retreated into myself as the other students introduced themselves and briefly stated why they wanted to practice yoga. Everyone in the room introduced themselves except me. Several people smiled at me expectantly after the last person had made their introduction, and I felt exposed and ashamed at my inability to speak. Mercifully, Maggie quickly closed the introductions and moved on.

By the time the class actually started, I felt not only fearful but completely alienated from the rest of the group. They could all say their names and still be safe. I could not. It was not a good beginning.

*   *   *

Despite my wish for invisibility, my desire to disassociate myself from my gender led me to construct an appearance that attracted not only second glances but outright stares in the conservative small-town environment in which I lived. I developed an obsession about wearing only black or very dark colors. It was a tangible way of honoring the grief of incest for which there is no social sanction. There are no cards or flowers or sympathetic gestures when you are healing from childhood trauma. Survivors bleed quietly as they go about the daily business of living. On the outside, they may look like other people. But on the inside, the raw edges of the violation are always there, and any new pain tears open the wound.

I was not overweight, but I dressed to hide my body, choosing long skirts or slacks and baggy sweaters. Any hint of femaleness had to be hidden; I used the mirror only to look at small parts of my face for grooming purposes. Public rest rooms with their mirrored walls reflecting images of women were a chamber of horrors for me. I secretly feared that my mother would materialize in the mirror and I would be once again a naked, battered child forced to watch my own abuse. I entered women's bathrooms with fear and trembling, feeling like prey vulnerable not only to ghosts from the past but to women in the present.

I had worn my hair fairly short for some time. But my steadily increasing need to disown any female part of myself compelled me to find ever-new ways of neutralizing my appearance. I had no desire to be a man. But I would *not* be female. To be a woman meant to either be a torturer of children or to be a victim of abuse. There was no middle ground in my quest to flee my long-dead mother.

*   *   *

One day, I went to the salon to have my hair cut in its routine short style. When I emerged an hour later, my hair was no more than half an inch all over my head, much like a military boot camp cut. In one respect, I had given in to the compelling desire to shed what I considered the last vestige of outward female identity. But I was also driven by an older need to take from myself before it was taken from me. To preemptively cause your own suffering removes the power to torture from the exclusive province of your perpetrator. Resistance can take many forms.

As I continued to have my hair clipped every three weeks, I began to remember with unease that I had methodically cut the hair off the heads of my dolls when I was a child. I also pulled off their clothes, spanked them and tried to penetrate their closed rectums with sticks. I mothered them as best as I could, holding them in my arms and rocking them after I had hurt them. I loved my dolls just like my mother loved me.

Later when cleaning my bedroom closet, I found a box buried beneath piles of worn-out shoes and clothes. I pulled open the lid, and a shorn and battered doll stared back at me. Reflexively, my hands flew to my own head in immediate recognition of her condition. I recalled with a sick feeling in my stomach the day I sealed the doll in the box and buried it beneath my shoes. It was shortly after I returned from my first trip to El Salvador.

*   *   *

Maggie sought me out as soon as I arrived at yoga class the next week. She told me she saw how terrified I looked during the introductions and apologized for not forewarning me that introductions would take place. She hoped I noticed that she quickly ended this part of the session when she realized I could not speak. "I want to be very protective of you here," she said softly, searching my face for some sign of response. She did not reach out to touch me this time, but carefully maintained a distance between us.

The same mix of longing and terror I felt when I cut out the pictures of mothers and children for the collage rose in my throat. I nodded to let her know that I heard. I did not trust my voice. I could not tell her when I left the class the week before I almost collapsed on the street with what seemed like an asthma attack. Although I do not suffer from asthma, whatever was happening in my body took away my capacity to breathe and left me wheezing and gasping for air, stumbling down the dark city sidewalk to my car as though I was drunk.

*   *   *

I had purchased the doll at an antique show that I was persuaded to attend by my sister. A soft-bodied infant with cornflower blue eyes and blond hair, the doll moved her arms after being wound by a small button in her back. She wore a pale yellow nylon taffeta dress with blue ribbons, and dainty white socks with lace ruffles covered her tiny feet. Dating to the 1950s, this doll closely resembled one that I had as a child. I never named my dolls as a child. To name is to have a measure of power. I did not imagine I possessed any. I also expected whatever I loved to be taken away abruptly. I did not want to get too close, even to my dolls.

When I brought the doll home, I locked myself in my bedroom and rocked it for a long time. Tenderly, I laid it in a wicker basket and stroked its head. I felt so afraid for the doll although I could not say why. The horror of war in El Salvador was beginning to activate my own internal war zones, and my purchase of the doll was just one of many things I could no longer explain about myself.

A few weeks later, I once again locked myself in the bedroom with the doll. Compelled by a force I could not name which filled me with dread, I carried a basin of water, bleach, a wooden spoon and scissors. In a trance, I cut off the doll's hair, stripped it of clothes and struck the small body repeatedly with the heavy spoon. When I finished, I washed it carefully in water mixed with bleach. I had to make it clean. Before I laid the doll in the box, I held it close to me and told her how much I loved her. As I slid the box into the deepest recesses of the closet, I was almost overwhelmed with exhaustion. Within a few days, I had forgotten I ever purchased a doll.

Seven years later, I opened the lid to the box. And when I did, memory of the day my mother cut off my hair in a rage came flooding back to me.

        *   *   *

Participation in the yoga classes released more layers of memory. Straining to hold my body in certain positions caused acute awareness of the forbidden zones of my midsection. Hearing a woman's voice tell me to manipulate my body in a particular way as Maggie did when she instructed the class in the intricacies of various postures became a direct route back to the worst of the ritual abuse I suffered at the hands of my mother. Although Maggie continued to reassure me that I never had to attempt any position that made me even slightly uncomfortable, I inevitably lost the capacity to exercise my option to stop in class. It was as though I was once again a child and I heard each instruction she gave as an absolute imperative. It was unthinkable not to obey.

Feelings of exposure and complete vulnerability were evoked by positions such as "dead bug," where I lay on my back with legs spread wide and knees bent. Gripping my ankles and bringing them together toward my chest as I moved into the posture, the muscles in my genital area were forced open. I felt frightened and defenseless. The darkness of the room hid my distress from Maggie and the other students as I lay frozen on the floor, tears sliding down my cheeks to form small puddles on my mat. The Child's terror at inadvertently moving or not holding her body in the correct position compelled me to maintain postures perfectly even when they caused great physical and emotional pain.

I became completely numb whenever Maggie instructed us to bend over and hold our ankles. This was a position my mother often ordered me to assume after she abused me. As I stood motionless and bent before her, she sat on a chair and would methodically inspect the damage she had caused, soothing the welts on my buttocks with lotion and gently stroking my genitals. More than one night during yoga class, I saw my mother's face suddenly appear between my legs and I catapulted back to the times when the blanket hung on the front window of the Little House

*   *   *

My mother often hurt me when she brushed my hair. Even though my eyes watered and my head jerked back, she ordered me to stand very still as she pulled my hair into tightly banded pigtails. I loved my pigtails and did not complain, trying hard to stand motionless when she fixed my hair. But on this particular day, I must have squirmed or cried out in response to the painful brushing, provoking her to a violent rage. Lifting my dress, she pulled me across her knee and furiously pummeled my bottom, screaming an unintelligible mixture of curses and admonishments about being still. Her anger still not spent when she finished, she threw me down hard on the kitchen chair and shouted that she would teach me a lesson I would not forget.

Stomping to a drawer in the kitchen cabinet, she rattled through clutter while muttering to herself, until she found a pair of scissors. Returning with the scissors, she jerked my head back violently as she grabbed my hair. "Now let's see if you're so pretty," she hissed in a voice made hoarse with rage. Within seconds, both of my pigtails were lying in my hand.

I was taken to a beauty shop in a town some distance away the same day. The hairdresser did her best to create some sort of style out of the mess she was presented with. There was not much that could be done with what was left. I had a "boy" cut long before it was popular for girls. I never again had pigtails.

*　　　　*　　　　*

I carefully placed the doll back into the box, furiously brushing away my tears. Compared to the rapes and other beatings I had endured, I told myself that having my hair cut off was nothing, that it was stupid to be so upset.

I did not bury the doll in the closet again. But I kept the lid closed on the white box that now sat in a corner of my bedroom. The doll reflected too much of my own painful history for me to face her every day. But periodically, I risked lifting the lid and gently stroked her face. I had no desire to hurt her anymore; I only wished I could undo what I had done when the buried memory of my own torture compelled me to nearly destroy the doll. But some things cannot be repaired.

*   *   *

The inchoate rage was ever closer to the surface. Yet each time I attempted to access it, the anger was diverted into almost uncontrollable urges toward self harm. It also manifested in intense bouts of diarrhea, lower back pain and extreme exhaustion. Jim began expressing reservations about continuing with yoga classes, but I clung to the hope that I could somehow persevere. And despite the terror that Maggie's words invoked during class, the Child was filled with a longing to know more about what she was like.

I simultaneously wanted attention from her yet went almost stiff with terror each time she came near me as she walked through the room. It was her habit to carefully observe her student's postures, lightly touching their bodies to correct a position as she whispered encouraging words. My eyes and body must have spoken what my voice could not, because she gave me wide berth as she moved through the group, never coming near me while I was holding a yoga position.

She called me occasionally at home to find out how I was doing and to ask what I needed from her in class. She let me know about schedule changes personally, rather than put me on a telephone chain list with the other students. She affirmed my decision to leave class early each week before the ending meditation began because it was beyond my ability to tolerate lying still in the darkness in the midst of a group for any length of time.

But her very gentleness and attention intensified the need for female closeness that was so fraught with treachery for me. My mother was most dangerous when she treated me gently. Her gentleness was inevitably a ruse to persuade me to let down my guard. She seemed to take perverse delight in enticing me to trust her and relax my body, rendering me completely vulnerable to the pain when she suddenly attacked. Each time a part of me reached out in even a minuscule gesture of trust toward Maggie, a stronger part insisted she hated me and only wished to hurt me.

Jim encouraged me to express the anger in words to relieve my body of the terrible strain of rendering it mute. But there are no words to describe the helpless rage that accompanies torture when it is mixed with the desperate desire to be loved by the one who is inflicting the pain. He suggested I try to draw a picture to express the emotions that were battering my body from the inside in an endless quest for release that was seemingly unobtainable.

Without much optimism, I sat down that night with a large sheet of paper and crayons. What emerged from a place deep within me was a picture of a naked woman sitting on the floor of a brick-walled prison in a pool of her own blood. Stairs leading to sheer vertical walls flank her, offering a cruel illusion of escape. Symbols of unspeakable rage fly through the air above her head. Close to the ceiling, a small window opening to the outside from which a tree and the sun are visible mocks her pain. Nooses hung on both sides of this gateway to freedom, a stark reminder that the closer one gets to liberation the more dangerous the task becomes.

Awed by what had almost magically appeared on the paper, I picked up a second sheet. For the next six weeks, I would fill page after page with images of imprisonment, torture and the chaos of rage that was not possible to express with words. Jim and I often sat in silence before what was depicted on the pages spread out on the floor of the therapy room. At times, graphic illustrations of the abuse appeared on the newsprint sheets. My mother grinned from the pictures as she held enema bags, sticks and ropes. Other sketches reflected the fragmentation of body and mind left in the wake of overwhelming pain and terror. But when I finally laid down my crayons and ceased drawing, Jim seemed to more fully comprehend why I could not express the rage with words. Language cannot do justice to the violation and degradation of torture.

Rage like this is a destructive force. It is buried for good reason, and can only be approached on its own terms. For the time being, it was not safe for me to open this particular door. I would have to continue to allow my body to speak in ways that words could not.

*   *   *

Several months passed before I told Jim about the day my mother cut off my hair. I felt shame flood through me, and I kept my eyes on the floor as I began to speak about the day when my mother placed my pigtails in my hands in a fit of anger. I apologized several times for even mentioning such a trivial event. It did not seem important enough to be talking about in therapy. Compared to the other things I had endured, having my hair cut was insignificant. And the brutal beating that preceded it was simply one of countless such punishments.

But when I finally raised my eyes to Jim's face, I saw that it was flushed with anger. His hands gripped the arms of his chair, and his posture seemed uncharacteristically tense. He did not think it was nothing for a mother to cut off her daughter's hair. He said her action of cutting my hair was an act of cruelty. He said it *mattered.*

Another piece of pain denied for decades broke through my defenses, and I started to tremble. My hands flew furtively up to the back of my neck in a gesture from childhood rooted in my inability to accept that my hair was really gone. I did not want Jim, or anyone, to see me. Doubled over on the floor, I cried the tears of an eight-year-old girl who never experienced her body as her own. Every small secret place could be violated. The most vulnerable spots would be targeted for hurt. Everything precious would be taken.

Nothing belonged to this child. Not even her hair.

FEAR

Fear strikes a chord deep within my body
twines itself through my chest
threatens to kill the small part of me who survived your assaults

    when I remember your hands on my body
    searing pain, blows, objects in small places
    your smiling face
    enjoying my pain

childhood lived outside my own flesh
because it was too dangerous to dwell
in skin so easily torn and violated
by one called mother

    no access denied
    you could enter at will
    entwine pleasure and pain
    and forbid my tears
    as if they were an affront to your power
    to inflict suffering and then
take it away
with your mouth and your tongue

I was never your daughter
I was an object used for your
own twisted purposes
in your own private hell

The Deepest Wound

when I think that I once grew inside your womb
remember that your blood flows through my veins
I am ill with living

if I could tear you out of me without destroying
the child who survived against all odds
I surely would
but I cannot.

For now this child clings to the very body you forced her to leave
      when you stole her voice and her passion
      her trust and her right to a safe place
      and implanted fear.

Crying now, without restraint
      she breaks your command to suffer without sound
      and dares to whisper her protest
      that she has a right to be here, in her body
and you do not.

And after all of these years
of silence and shame
of hating my own flesh…

      I hear her.

Chapter 14

The Company of Men

The trauma hidden in my body was reactivated by participation in the yoga class. Memories, exhaustion and physical pain, which had been thankfully relieved with my recent medical treatment and the ongoing therapy sessions, began to return.

Each week, I arrived at yoga class determined that my mother would not win, vowing to stay present in my adult self. And each week, I fled the class before it was dismissed, bursting through the church door into the street in a feverish state of terror. Will power alone could not save me from falling into the past.

It was a fierce struggle to keep myself from sliding back into dependence on tranquilizers as nightmares once again threatened my ability to sleep. One night I fell into a fitful doze and encountered a dream with an entirely new twist. Instead of seeing myself as victim, I was the aggressor. But the transition from prey to hunter did not provide a sense of triumph or relief.

               *   *   *

From my journal...

I am stumbling in the darkness, lost and alone in a desolate wilderness. Suddenly, a figure shrouded in fog approaches. He is intimately familiar yet I do not know his name. I cannot see his face. He places his arm around my shoulder, and I am comforted and filled with a purpose I do not understand.

He places a knife in my hand, and we walk down a path that has appeared in the swirling mists.

I recognize my surroundings now. We are approaching my parents' house. I turn the knob on the back door, but the door is locked. Defeated, I turn away, but my companion will not allow this. He motions me to a window, and we slice open the seal with the knife, gaining entry to the still house. Together we walk down the hall to my parents' bedroom.

We open the door quietly. My father and mother are sleeping on the bed, their faces clearly visible in the moonlight. I try to close my eyes, but the one who accompanies me forces me to look at their nakedness. Suddenly, I am filled with rage as cold as death, and I move toward the bed.

There is a blank spot in my dream. I do not know what happened next. But I am standing in a pool of warm blood with the knife in my hand. My mysterious companion is by my side, his arm a protective shield around my shoulders. I am horrified at what has happened here, but he is not. I wake up, and I am crying and calling for the silent friend who guides my feet to the house of my childhood. I do not cry for my parents.

⋆   ⋆   ⋆

The dream was etched vividly on my memory, and I could not shake its vestiges the next morning. I felt agitated and disoriented as I showered and prepared for work. As I hurriedly washed the dishes that had accumulated in the sink, I dropped a glass that shattered as it hit the edge of the counter. Ignoring the potential danger, I brushed the largest jagged shards to the floor and plunged my hands back down into the soapy water. Within seconds, I sliced my thumb on a submerged butcher knife.

The blood spurted like a geyser as I stood watching. I felt a distinct sense of peace and satisfaction—it was only right that I should bleed. Splatters of blood covered the counter, floor and kitchen cabinet before an internal alarm finally broke through the paralysis, gripping me and propelling me into action. I made a tourniquet out of cloth and wrapped my thumb. Shaking, I wiped the blood away as best as I could and cleaned up the broken glass.

I went to work with the bloody cloth wrapped around my hand, which I tried to hide but to no avail. At noon and only at the insistence of concerned colleagues, I agreed to get medical attention. When the doctor carefully removed the saturated homemade tourniquet, the blood once again shot out in a stream. I had been bleeding for more than six hours.

Jim was not nearly as troubled by the contents of the dream as I was. He said it represented taking power into my own hands and acting out my anger. He questioned me about the male figure accompanying me, trying to discern what he may have symbolized. But I was at a loss to explain who he was. I only knew I was not afraid of him, and that he was not a stranger to me. He felt like the protective older brother I had longed for in my childhood.

Jim was concerned, however, about my "accident" in the kitchen the next morning as well as the post-traumatic stress symptoms that were surfacing in the yoga classes. Unlike the process of giving up my addiction that I had to be coaxed and persuaded to continue, I had grimly sunk my teeth into the yoga practice and was determined that I would not be defeated. I wanted to reclaim my body. It had belonged to my mother long enough. And despite my fear of being approached or touched by Maggie, there was a deep and aching longing for female connection in the Child that was briefly satisfied each week when we encountered her welcoming smile. Unfortunately, terror inevitably replaced need and plunged me back into the horror of a past in which femaleness and torture were inextricably linked.

Drawing a deep breath, I began to earnestly explain that I believed the only way for me to handle the body memories that were activated by the combination of Maggie's voice and the yoga postures was to occasionally hurt myself. I did not want to hide this information from

Jim but rather hoped to figure out a way of self harm that he did not find completely objectionable. And it seemed perfectly logical to me that the price of closeness to a woman would be physical pain.

But we did not travel very far in this direction. Gently but firmly, Jim said that it was time to pull back from yoga classes. To my tearful protests that I did not want to fail, he countered that I had done well and had not failed at all. Participation in the yoga classes had taught us some valuable lessons even though it had not been the vehicle for reconnection with my body in the good way we had hoped.

It was now apparent that my terror of women and my anger were intricately fused. Our task would be to separate them and approach each one in ways that were not re-traumatizing to me.

It was also clear that reconnecting with my body was the key to unearthing my long-buried rage. It was a part of my healing journey that was not safe to combine with female interaction.

For now, I would continue to heal in the company of men.

*   *   *

It is dangerous to open and clean old wounds without making provisions to cover the exposed places with healing balm. Periodically, I purchased a discounted plane ticket to Chicago to visit Gary whose caring presence was a most healing balm. He always pointed out the ways in which I had grown since he last saw me, helping me to validate progress even during periods when it seemed I was taking two steps back for each step forward. He spent long hours rocking the Child who continued to need safe touch as much as she required air to breathe. Although Jim and I had finally reached a compromise which allowed for limited safe touch during therapy, we were both acutely aware that it fell woefully short of meeting the Child's needs.

My relationship with Gary had no such restraints. His arms provided me with the soothing salve that allowed the wounds to heal in ways that were not possible with words alone. He was wonderfully free with my body, his lean frame holding me close to his heart. Repeatedly, he affirmed that my body was good and that there was no reason for me to feel shame.

I felt perfectly safe in the apartment he shared with his partner Joe. Their love for each other within a committed relationship created an oasis of trust and hope in a society that was often hostile to their very existence. In their home, I felt a sense of peace and belonging that I had never experienced in the house of my childhood. Although the church or state did not recognize their union, I felt sure the union was recognized by God. It was definitely recognized by the traumatized Child, who drank in the experience of watching two people interact in healthy, loving ways.

Meals were a time of intimate sharing and good conversation. The small kitchen table was always set attractively with brightly colored plates, even for a simple supper of pasta and salad. Fresh flowers usually graced the dining room table on weekends, which was situated in a windowed alcove with a view of Lake Michigan at the end of the block. Talk ranged from the ordinary trials and triumphs of the workday to politics, local gossip and upcoming travel plans. Each demonstrated sincere concern about how the other felt regarding what was going on in their lives, the larger gay community and the world. Disagreements were openly aired and usually resolved with compromise. Hugs and physical affection were freely asked for and given.

We went for evening picnics on the lake, spreading wine, cheese and deli treats on a beautifully woven Guatemalan blanket and watching sailboats while we talked about our hopes, dreams and struggles. We spent rainy afternoons at bookstores and in coffee shops. I felt welcomed and accepted by their friends. I was struck by the emotional honesty and depth of relationships I discovered in the vibrant gay community in which they lived.

In an environment where there was no shame in expressing emotions or asking to be held—and in which the enjoyment of life was evident—parts of me that were still frozen in constricted grief and fear melted to become soft and pliable. Like a flower pushing up through the earth seeking sun, I grew and blossomed each time I visited Gary.

I had never witnessed this kind of healthy relationship with my parents, whose means of interaction seemed to veer from weeks of stony silence to violent screaming matches during which my mother would be prone to throw anything in her reach. She once smashed nearly every dish in the kitchen, emptying the cabinets as she hurled plates and glasses at my father, who cowered in a corner until he could run for the door.

Gary's style of accompaniment often included a challenging analysis of my experiences and reflection on my process of healing. At times, his persistent questions evoked panic when my shame prohibited me from revealing some aspect of the abuse that still entrapped me. But Gary refused to allow shame to silence me. He had witnessed the powerful effect that giving testimony had for survivors of political torture in El Salvador. While reminding me that the power of the torturers would be broken by voicing our stories, he would hold me for hours, rocking me gently and patiently until I broke through the wall of shame to tell him the secrets that I had only whispered in broken pieces inside the confines of the therapy room.

The floods of tears that followed such naked disclosures were affirmed by Gary as a sign of life and hope. With him, it was possible to see rainbows in the aftermath of the storms that are an inherent part of deep healing. I learned to fall asleep in his arms.

The gradual loss of friends and erosion of community that I experienced as I moved deeper into my pain was a source of unremitting sorrow for Gary, who expressed grave concern about my lack of support. As a gay person who refused to hide his identity, he understood the necessity of constructing a supportive environment to sustain hope and courage in a society that largely condemned or denied his reality. He chose to live in a neighborhood in a major city with a visible gay population, which provided a kind of buffer zone against mainstream culture and gave him access to many social and institutional resources. He cultivated and maintained a wide circle of friends that gave encouragement and solidarity. This environment sustained him during the times when homophobic sentiment ran high and the airwaves were filled with political or religious zealots dedicated to eradicating those they considered "deviants" in the culture.

Like Gary, I lived in a culture either hostile or indifferent to my reality. But unlike him, I was not able to live in a community that would buffer me from the attacks of those whose ideology of "family values" requires silence about the prevalence of sexual and physical abuse in many traditional families. Survivors, for all their visibility in recent years, are not yet a potent social or political force. The nature of our wounds often keeps us from building the trust that is needed to create and sustain long-term projects for cultural or political change.

Although Gary was quick to assure me that he was there when I needed him and that the relationship with my therapist was a blessing, he believed it was essential that I develop other safe and nurturing friendships to sustain me through the long term. Although I agreed in theory, I did not know how to translate this vision into reality. My inability to tolerate any modicum of closeness to women severely limited my choices for support.

I had considered brief residential treatment in order to deal with some of the most traumatic memories and to experience sharing my story within a group of survivors in a safe and supportive environment. Although Jim and I searched diligently for a program that would meet my needs, we met with no success. The treatment centers we contacted segregated men and women in their sexual trauma programs. Most were staffed predominantly by female therapists. Some had authoritarian systems in which patients earned privileges and small amounts of freedom by demonstrating compliance with the program. These structures were reminiscent to the abusive structure in which I grew up. Neither Jim nor I viewed such an environment as conducive to healing.

Hours of discussion always ended with our sad but mutual conclusion that there was no discernible way for me to develop the kind of safety net that should be in place for people who live on the edge of a culture which does not value their existence.

*　　　　　　*　　　　　　*

It took me many months to regain the equilibrium I had lost due to the complex emotions that were triggered in the yoga class. Badly shaken by my venture into an exploration of my body that only confirmed my worst fears, I once again clung to Jim like a panicked child.

I refused to answer my telephone at home, and it took all my energy to push myself to function at work. I was involved in a serious traffic incident. Although I was not injured, I was forced to deal with courts, lawyers and the helplessness and confusion that is a result of being thrown into an unfamiliar judicial system that seems to dehumanize and disregard the suffering of those caught in its grip. Through the hot days of summer, I left the house only to shop for necessities on weekends. Although I loved the water, I felt too vulnerable and exposed in a bathing suit to visit the pool. I lost track of time and place easily, dissociating at the slightest provocation as the stress of the legal process exacerbated my heightened sense of fragility.

One hot afternoon, I entered the basement with a basket of laundry. Suddenly, it felt as though I hit an invisible wall. A hideous chemical smell simultaneously familiar and yet unrecognizable assaulted my senses, leaving me weak and dizzy. Terror washed over me, and I froze like a frightened rabbit. Backing out of the laundry room, I slammed the door as I turned and fled into the back yard, dropping the basket of clothes on the sidewalk.

I collapsed beside the huge tree that had given me comfort so many times before, pressing my back into the rough bark and silently begging for its protection. Gradually, the world seemed to come back into focus. My body ached as though I had been beaten, and I became aware of a burning pain in my rectum. As I began to walk slowly back to the house, I felt as though I could not bear the sensations of my legs rubbing together as I moved and awkwardly tried to hold my legs apart as I walked.

Entering the kitchen, I headed for the refrigerator to get a drink of water. As I stood gulping, my eyes wandered to the clock. I was suddenly unable to swallow—I thought I had been outside for just a few minutes, but the clock showed I had left the kitchen with the load of wash almost an hour ago. Feeling sick, I stumbled toward the bathroom. Sitting on the toilet, I put my head in my hands. What had happened to the time? Had I been under the tree for so long? What was that smell in the basement? And why did I keep feeling the horrible sensation of my mother's finger twisting into my rectum? I willed myself to stop thinking. I wanted to curl up and sleep. I needed to get upstairs to my bedroom. I reached for the toilet tissue.

What happened next I cannot explain in medical terms. But it irrevocably convinced me of the reality of the body, as well as the mind, holding memory of trauma.

I did not have my menstrual period. I do not have hemorrhoids. Yet I suddenly held in my hand a wad of toilet tissue that was saturated with bright red blood. I sat staring at the tissue, unable to believe what I was seeing. I reached to the sink, turning on the faucet to splash cold water on my face. The events of the afternoon left me mistrustful of reality. Maybe I was having a nightmare. I pulled another piece of paper, reaching back to gingerly touch my rectum. When I drew it away from my body, blood was abundantly evident. I sat for a long time, holding a tangible sign of my body's communication of what it had endured.

I have never, as an adult, bled from my rectum before or since that day. And when I later sent my husband down to the basement to investigate the awful smell, he came back upstairs puzzled. He did not notice anything unusual. The faint odor of bleach was always in the wash room, and he speculated that it must have been what I smelled.

For the Child whose mind and body carried memory of being washed with a mixture of bleach and water during rituals in which her rectum was frequently penetrated with her mother's finger, it was enough. The instruments of torture can be as ordinary as a wooden spoon, a mirror, a jump rope or a bottle of bleach. In the right context and with sufficient stress, these objects hold the power to catapult those who suffered their misuse back into the domain of their torturer, even decades later.

The smell of bleach on that hot summer day acted as a potent trigger for my senses as well as my body. The horror of being confronted with a memory painted in blood demanded my acknowledgment of how essential it was to incorporate my body into the process of recovery. The yoga classes had not been as helpful as I wished, and I was at a loss to find a safe way to work with my body.

In the safety of the therapy room, I began to experiment again with deep breathing and relaxation techniques. Lying on the rug, I closed my eyes and held to Jim's voice as he spoke of a loving, golden light flowing through me. Listening to its familiar and calm cadence mitigated much of the fear that usually arose when I became aware of my body. There were periods of panic when he named certain parts of my body as he described the flow of the gentle liquid light. I did not mind hearing about my feet or knees, but I did not want to even acknowledge I had buttocks or breasts. Despite the unease that naming these forbidden zones caused, I sometimes experienced what felt like profound, internal shifts as I relaxed and for a few brief but wonderful moments found my body a good place to live.

We did not pursue further relationships with women and did not work on accessing my anger. Occasionally, however, Jim told me stories about women he knew who were nurturing and kind, women who loved children and who protected them. I listened to these stories with a mixture of wonder and pain. I had never known relationships with women like those he described. It was hard for me to fathom that they existed.

Gradually I became calm, and my internal sense of security was restored. I had moments of laughter during sessions despite the rivers of tears that poured from my eyes. My emotions were becoming fluid rather than frozen. The memories abated. I began to take an interest in what was going on around me. By the first snowfall, I was ready to once again approach reconnecting with my body outside the therapy room.

And Jim introduced me to David.

          *   *   *

David retired from his career as a high school teacher to pursue his dream of becoming a full-time bodyworker. A gentle and sensitive man, he had established himself as a massage therapist and Tai Chi instructor who was also a practitioner of the Trager method, a type of bodywork that involves a series of gentle, rocking movements. He told me that he wanted to avoid re-traumatizing me in the bodywork sessions that would be the vehicle of my next attempt to move my body out of numbness into life. Together we began researching information about working with survivors of severe abuse.

We could find very little written material on this topic. The few resources available seemed to promote massage therapy, often with deep muscle work, with survivors to access memories of trauma held in the body. The pain and vulnerability invoked by the touch could serve as a catalyst for the emergence of traumatic memory.

Although such a route might be helpful for some survivors at certain stages of their recovery, triggering memories was not my goal. I had already remembered a great deal of my past, and Jim pointed out frequently that there was no value in endlessly re-experiencing the trauma. Healing is about much more than remembering. My challenge would be to allow myself to be touched in nurturing and safe ways in order to reconnect with the body I was forced to flee as a matter of survival as a child.

David had not worked with other abuse survivors in an intentional way, but he had done considerable reading and reflection on healing strategies since our introductory meeting at Jim's office. By the time I arrived for my first session at his home office, he was able to articulate a way in which he thought we might work together. Talking quietly, he appeared to choose his words carefully as he laid out his plan.

Current research theorizes that repeated trauma creates altered neurological pathways that become entrenched patterns of response as time passes. A slight stress experienced by a survivor may be perceived internally as an overwhelming threat, triggering a response appropriate to a traumatic event rather than the minor event experienced in the present. David speculated that if patterns can be laid down by long-term abuse, creating cellular memories of trauma, it might be possible to build alternative trails by consistent gentle touch and movement. His proposal was that we try to create new pathways in my body through nurturing means so that I would eventually have the option to bypass the trauma response. In essence, we would work at building a new road skirting around my body's minefields of ingrained triggers. While he was realistic about the high probability of setting off occasional explosions as we inadvertently stepped into a trauma pathway, his intent was to avoid this occurrence to the extent possible.

When he finished talking, the room was silent as he waited for my reaction. I was somewhat dazed as I attempted to take in the one essential fact about David that his proposal revealed. It would take me a long time to understand the full impact: David did not want to hurt me. He would take no pleasure in my pain. He would touch my body in a way that respected the fears of the Child. He understood how deeply the torture of the mother had implanted distorted lessons in the Child's body, teaching that pain is pleasure and pleasure is pain. David wanted me to know pleasure for its own sake.

I looked at him for a long time. David had been a teacher for years, but he had never faced a challenge quite like this in the classroom. I saw his anxious anticipation of my response, and his vulnerability as he waited for me to speak. This was new territory for him and not without risk. I slowly nodded. I was willing to try.

*   *   *

I arrived at David's house each week dressed in long-sleeved shirt, sweatpants, thick socks and shoes. For months, my shoes were the only object of apparel that I was willing to remove during the bodywork sessions. Even clad from head to toe in protective clothing, I felt exposed and vulnerable. Laying on a massage table and allowing another person to touch my body, I quickly regressed to a childlike state. David respected this and worked as best he could through the layers of material I needed as a protective barrier.

It soon became apparent that I could not tolerate the gentle, rocking movements of the Trager method that was David's area of expertise. Even the slightest rhythmic movement of my legs that reverberated into my hips caused dissociative flight and numbness. It felt as if my still new and fragile boundaries completely dissolved with this kind of motion. Working mostly by instinct, David modified his approach so that body movement was very limited. Most of the sessions focused on light and gentle massage in the areas of my body that we deemed safe. For many months, these areas consisted of my head and my feet.

Searching for ways to minimize my tendency to mentally leave my body when I felt frightened, David began talking to me throughout the course of each session. Sometimes he described and named the muscles, ligaments and tendons he was gently massaging. Other times he reminded me that I was safe. What he could not do, we quickly discovered, was ask me to make a choice about anything relating to my body once I was on the table.

Operating from the logical assumption that an abuse survivor would feel more in control of the process if she had choices and could offer feedback about the touch she was receiving, one evening David began to gently inquire about my preferences. Was the pressure on my foot too light? Did I want him to work into my lower calf? Should he put a pillow under my knees to ease my back?

I began to tremble, and I felt my body grow numb. I opened my mouth but no sounds came out. The fear and horror of being forced to choose where and how I would be hurt next as an integral part of the bizarre rituals in the Little House flooded through me. David later told me that he immediately felt the change in my body engendered by the sudden terror. Although he did not know why, he understood that his questions had sent me careening down a trauma pathway. He gently tucked a blanket around me to keep me warm, as I was shivering uncontrollably and had become so cold my teeth were chattering. He stroked my forehead, murmuring assurances of safely. He did not pressure me to talk. When I returned from the domain of my mother, David was there to welcome me back.

Gradually, the areas of safety expanded. Any decisions to be made were discussed prior to approaching the massage table. I was willing to take off my socks. I allowed my lower legs to be touched. I began to experience sessions where pleasant sensations were more dominant than pain. This was very difficult for me to accept. In my mother's house, gentleness was often a prelude to abuse. And the pleasure her manipulations inevitably resulted in brought me severe punishment.

Pleasure could betray me. Gentleness disarmed me. I feared these gentle times more than the pain itself, which could be controlled at times by numbness and flight. I understood pain. Sometimes, it was all I could do to keep from begging David to hurt me. What stopped me was that I knew it would be useless. He would not hurt me.

As though he was teaching a small child, David patiently reassured me time and again that he did not want to cause me pain and that I had the right to know nurturing, pleasurable touch. He was clearly shaken by the violent reactions and flashbacks I sometimes experienced and went to great lengths to create a climate of safety and trust.

He began each session by helping me to visualize the same golden light that protected and soothed me on the floor of the therapy room when listening to Jim's voice. Prior to playing music on a compact disc during a session, David encouraged me to listen to it at home to be certain the music was not upsetting to me. During sessions, I was extremely vulnerable to the slightest trigger. An unexpected piano solo could suddenly transport me into the past when my mother poisoned any love I might have developed for classical or religious music with her abuse. The sounds of nature were the music I preferred; compact discs with sounds of waterfalls, wind ruffling leaves in trees, bird songs and ocean waves comforted me. My bodywork sessions were accompanied with the sounds of the outdoors that I love, and where I felt safest as a child.

After seven months of weekly sessions, I risked wearing a sleeveless shirt. After nine months, I was able to come to sessions wearing knee-length shorts. My body was slowly releasing the shame that rightfully belonged to my mother. At times, I could allow it to know pleasure without paying the price in pain.

On the occasions I was triggered despite our precautions, David made sure I was grounded and functioning at an adult level before I attempted the long drive home. He made hot tea and gave me a blanket to wrap myself in while I sat in his kitchen, trying to shake the vestiges of terror that had been activated as my body responded to even the most gentle touch by regurgitating some aspect of long ago torture. Unlike the aftermath of the yoga classes when I was left alone to deal with the overwhelming emotions that had been evoked, the one-to-one relationship with David allowed me to immediately discuss at least some of the experiences that emerged. This opportunity to process usually halted the downward spiral into more painful memories that was frequently precipitated when I fled the yoga class each week, bursting out the door to the dark sidewalk like a terrified child.

*   *   *

This new phase of my healing would eventually not only re-establish ties with my body but also would provide me with another precious oasis in the wilderness in which I traveled. David would come to be a trusted companion, expanding the safety net of my support system. And when we stepped on any land mines buried deep within my body along the way, the impact of the explosions was almost as hard on David as it was on me.

He would learn that even the most gentle touch could set off a powerful earthquake in which the adult he knew disappeared through a deep fissure in the shifting terrain of time. He was left with a traumatized child, huddled under a blanket, who would not respond to his entreaties to come back into the present. She did not believe his assurances that she was not in the Little House. He would come to understand that hands once tied with rope could suddenly react to his touch as though he were the torturer who bound them long ago.

For the first time in his experience, he would encounter a body that would abruptly deaden and go limp, rather than stiffen with tension, when there was fear or stress. He reported that his hands sometimes sensed an empty shell on the massage table, devoid of human spark and essence. And in the deep connection with a client's spirit and energy that he brought to his work, he would encounter the force and malevolence of the mother who still lived in the body of the daughter of whom she would not relinquish control.

David suffered with me. And as he did, he was compelled to search the depths of his own soul and question his beliefs about the nature of good and evil, uncovering some of his own deep wounds in the process. In the way of true accompaniment, as we journeyed together, we taught and healed each other.

The Land of Milk and Honey.........

Then the Lord said: "I have seen the affliction of my people who are in Egypt, and have heard their cry because of their taskmasters; I know their sufferings, and I have come down to deliver them out of the hand of the Egyptians, and to bring them up out of that land to a good and broad land, a land flowing with milk and honey...."

Exodus 3: 7,8

Out of Egypt.........

And the people of Israel cried out to the Lord; and they said to Moses, "Is it because there are no graves in Egypt that you have taken us away to die in the wilderness? What have you done to us, in bringing us out of Egypt?"

Exodus 14: 11

Chapter 15

The Edge of Healing

From my journal...
    Five years ago when I began therapy, I was overwhelmed. My mind and body were beginning to remember, giving me more information than I could safely handle. Every waking hour seemed filled with shattered images from my childhood. Nightmares stole my sleep. Death was a constant and comforting companion, and suicide often seemed my best option. I needed desperately to trust Jim yet I was terrified at the raw need for nurture and safety he evoked from the child. I've come a long way from that.

*   *   *

    Almost 30 years after the night when I began screaming and could not stop, I held in my hands the many pages of chart notes, physician summaries and test results about my hospitalization in 1967.
    In my fifth year of healing, I had decided to obtain records from the hospitalization that began on Valentine's Day and ended just before my twelfth birthday in mid-March. The letters the chief of psychiatry wrote to our family doctor, school principal and my parents which I had previously obtained contained as much detail as I could bear to know for a long time. But as I slowly gained strength and stability, my curiosity about the actual records overcame my dread about reading medical documentation related to the abuse I had endured.

Part of me longed to believe that the abuse never happened. That I was raised by parents who loved and protected me. But the abuse had carved its indelible mark upon my life, making it impossible to take comfort in any doubt about what had happened for any length of time. Remembering and facing the truth about my own history was allowing me to grow and develop in ways I never would have believed possible. The evidence was in the healing. The hospital records, like my cousin's corroboration of my mother's behavior, provided confirmation from an external source.

There was almost as much about my mother written into the records by doctors who handled my case as there was about my condition. I suspect that if my mother was hospitalized today, she might be diagnosed as what is popularly known as Multiple Personality Disorder and what has been renamed more recently as Dissociative Identity Disorder. Her whole countenance — including her eyes, voice and language—radically changed during the rituals in which she blended lessons in pain and pleasure with her insatiable desire to cleanse my intrinsic female dirtiness. Other times, a mother of towering rage would emerge. During these episodes, her face would contort and grow mottled with her anger. Saliva sprayed from her mouth as she screamed, threw, broke and battered anything she could get her hands on—including me. And then there were days when she sat and rocked herself, humming tunelessly as she stared into a dimension of the world that only she could see. In between those mothers was one who baked cakes, cleaned the house, sketched wild horses in notebooks and lovingly tended the multitudes of flowers she planted in the yard each spring. Generally, only those who lived with her knew her lightning-like ability to transform into a person entirely different from the person she had been a moment before.

But during my hospitalization, her lack of access to me combined with the possibility that I would disclose the secret rituals at home plunged her into a frantic bid for control. It stripped the mask that she usually presented to the outside world. It was precisely this shattering of pretense that allowed the doctors who treated me to glimpse the reality in which I lived. Within hours of my emergency admission, the neurologist called for a psychiatric consultation. Even though there was not yet widespread clinical recognition of the prevalence of child abuse and incest was believed to be a rare phenomenon, the doctors suspected that my headaches, fainting spells, screams and "visions" of a woman in a white dress were more related to the bizarre actions of my mother than a head injury that she insisted had damaged my brain.

My father's two ironclad rules were challenged the night he reluctantly carried me from the house to take me to the family doctor. His values concerning the privacy of the family were expressed in his oft-repeated admonitions: "*What goes on in this house stays in this house*" and "*Our family is nobody's business.*" Mutterings about communists who plotted to turn children against their parents were interspersed with favorite Old Testament quotes, generally of the fire and brimstone variety. McCarthyism and a fundamentalist approach to religion provided the justification and rationale for a siege-like mentality in relation to the outside world and authoritarian rule within a home where parents had absolute power over children and were accountable to no one. My father did not consider it his job to question my mother's treatment of me.

My mother's abuse and my father's rigid belief in absolute family privacy was supported by a culture which generally allows children to be treated as the exclusive property of their parents. Our house became an island of madness and torture, protected by middle-class respectability and privilege. I wish I could believe my experience was an anomaly, an isolated situation that is not common. But clinging to what is not true can offer little comfort. The greatest danger children face is not from strangers but from within their homes; news reports of children beaten, raped, tortured and sometimes killed by parents abound. Many islands like the one where I lived exist today.

I do not believe my father has forgiven me for my violation of the unwritten contract of absolute silence and privacy that governed our lives. My refusal to abide these rules was demonstrated by the screams I could no longer keep inside when I was on the cusp of my twelfth year. That I waited until my father got home from work to begin screaming was testimony to the hope I continued to hold that if he only knew how bad things really were, he would save me. But this was not the case. There would be no rescue by my father.

*   *   *

Several months into my bodywork sessions with David, I began to remember fragments of the day my mother bound my hands, laid me over a kitchen chair and scalded me with steam from an iron. I fought harder against remembering this incident than any other. The intrusive memories and flashbacks had gradually abated during the past year, and I wanted to keep it that way. I wanted to live in the present day without the fear of being constantly dragged into the horror of my childhood.

When the image of myself as a child of eight—dressed in my best clothes, standing before my mother who was seated on a kitchen chair—floated into my mind, I did everything in my power to banish it. The image was encased in a vaporous moving mist around its rim. The chair was inexplicably placed where it did not belong, nearly blocking the doorway between the kitchen and parlor. The light in the kitchen wasn't like it should have been. It seemed hazy, as though it was filtered through rain and fog. I only wore that dress on Sundays, and she did not hurt me on Sunday because that was the day my father was home. I refused to accept the memory as real.

But in the end, there was no force that I could muster to send the memory of that terrible afternoon into the darkness of unknowing. During a period of three months, the body sensations connected to the image became overwhelming. Jim tried to shelter me from plunging into its depths by encouraging my inclination to avoid it if possible. We already knew a lot about how I was tortured, and every re-lived memory exacted its own terrible toll on my physical and emotional well being. We agreed that exploring new areas of my traumatic past was not a current goal and decided not to pursue what lay behind the image.

Yet the healing process has its own agenda and does not always abide by the ones we try to set. The bodywork was a catalyst for remembering an incident that was so terrifying that writing about it even now evokes great fear. I stop when I need to and take care of myself before I am sucked into the hungry mouth of the past, which will not cease to feed on pain until the strength is gained to extricate the self from its grasp. It is little wonder I could not bear to remember one day to the next what happened to me when I was a child alone with my mother. Survival requires forgetting. Healing requires remembering. For those who have suffered the violation of torture as children, it is a cruel double jeopardy.

*   *   *

The hospital records were validating. They were also very difficult to read as yet another layer of my childhood history was revealed. The charts confirmed my long-standing suspicion that my mother occasionally used drugs to insure my compliance and forgetfulness and that at times she kept me home from school for her own purposes. She admitted to the doctors she gave me "nerve relaxants" and that I had not been to school for "about a week" before I was taken to the hospital. To justify the daily enemas I endured, she maintained that I was constipated "a lot."

Most children are frightened and homesick when they are hospitalized. But my removal from the house of my parents had the opposite effect. Notes on the chart reflect that I improved rapidly once I was secure in the relative safety of the hospital. My headaches stopped; I was not dizzy; I did not faint. I had no need to scream. My body slowly adjusted to eliminating its own waste. I began therapy with Dr. Weiss, the hospital's chief psychiatrist. I started talking about the "pictures" I saw in my mind in an attempt to articulate the unspeakable horrors I had endured.

The effect of my hospitalization on my mother was dramatic and negative. My fledgling therapy with Dr. Weiss apparently triggered a full-scale panic. She badgered the doctors, insisting I was brain-damaged and demanding tests that supported her contention. She became frantic as test after test revealed no neurological damage from the concussion I suffered a year before.

In addition to her daily barrage of phone calls, my mother sent what the records describe as "floods of letters which were extremely inappropriate" to the doctors and nurses who treated me on the ward. A terse summary by Dr. Weiss described typical encounters with my mother as including demands, among other things, that I was to be given a new hairstyle every day and that the doctors should tell me I was pretty. Tears spilled down my cheeks as I read my mother's long-ago words that were documented and preserved in quotation marks in the records. I remembered the painful way she brushed my hair and her rage on the day she cut it off, triumphant in her belief that I was no longer pretty. Was she recalling this incident in some part of her fragmented mind as she penned these letters?

My mother was also unable to contain her obsession about my inside dirtiness. In her letters, she implored the doctors to examine me for worms. Frightened by my visions of the "Lady in White" who appeared when the pain of the torture was too much to bear, she told anyone who would listen that I saw "visions" because my grandmother—her mother Frances—was clairvoyant. In her panic about her loss of control over my body, what she never intended the outside world to know was being laid on the table as evidence before the horrified eyes of the hospital staff.

*　　　　　*　　　　　*

I felt as though I was walking on eggshells during each bodywork session, trying not to do anything that would expand the terrible photo-like image which haunted me into a memory of what lay around its edges. Body sensations unlike anything I had experienced before were associated with the afternoon I stood before my mother wearing a dress always reserved for Sunday school. What felt like a hot liquid fire moved down the right side of my body from my head to the top of my thighs, sometimes creating an agony so unbearable I could not keep from crying out. My hands often became numb, tingling as though they had fallen asleep. Twice my right eye became so swollen after experiencing the phantom burning pain that I lost vision for a few days. The doctor was unable to find any sign of infection or offer a medical reason for the swelling.

Experimenting to find areas of my body that could accept safe touch, David and I agreed to incorporate massage of my arms and hands into a particular session. To reduce the risk of being triggered, I moved into a sitting position on the edge of the table, reasoning that I would feel more control if I were upright rather than prone. We could not know that touching this part of my body would accelerate the release of the very memory I was trying to avoid.

David began to massage my upper right arm, talking to me while he worked so that I would stay grounded and aware of my surroundings. Yet almost immediately, my whole body seemed to move to full-scale alert, which intensified as he moved from my elbow to my wrist. An unspeakable dread came over me, and words fled. I could not tell David to stop. I could only watch in silent horror as his blue shirt faded into my mother's dress and a piece of rope snapped and danced in her hands. By the time David grasped my right wrist, I could no longer see him or feel his hands. Instead, there was only my mother, and she was jerking my right hand toward her so she could secure it with the rope. A terrific, almost electric, jolt snapped through my body, and I lost any sense of connection with reality. I was alone with my mother, and no one could help me.

I can only rely on what David tells me to describe what happened because the next several minutes are blank in my memory. I came to an awareness of the present huddled in a pretzel-like position on the bodywork table. Both of my hands were tangled between and beneath my legs, attempting to protect my genitals and hide my hands. I had pulled the blanket over my head like a terrified child, and my teeth were chattering so hard that I feared I would break them. David, badly shaken, was trying to call me back from the place I fled when he touched my right hand. My sudden, violent reaction as I jerked my hand away from his grasp and scrambled for cover under the blanket had frightened him. Neither one of us had been prepared for it.

*   *   *

In the immediate aftermath of the powerful memories triggered during bodywork, I was as devastated and helpless as I had been in the early years of therapy. The key difference was that the repercussions were less severe and disruptive to my life. The recovery period during which I felt only a fragile connection to the present while my body re-experienced the physical consequences of the abuse as though it had just taken place was reduced to a few days. It was a vast improvement over the four- to six-week period I often needed when I was beginning to work with traumatic memories.

I was also now able to talk about memories with Jim without being completely plunged into the travail of the past. I know how to take care of myself in the difficult period after the emergence of a new memory, paying special attention to getting lots of rest, moderate exercise and plenty of fluids. I learned to eat small amounts of food I especially enjoyed to combat my self-punishment pattern of refusing meals to hurt myself for my natural remembering and feeling. As I became less fearful and ashamed of having emotional needs, I was more capable of reaching out to telephone Jim or Gary when I needed help.

Re-living trauma as memories emerge never becomes easy, no matter how good the coping skills. One of the goals of healing is to have control over when and if you will answer the door of your present in response to a sudden and persistent knock from the past. There are times when the past holds pieces that you need to know in order for life to move forward unimpeded by the chains of trauma. But there are also times when it is best to refuse to answer the door because doing so involves a greater risk of harm than potential for healing. The key to the door must ultimately come to rest in the hand of the survivor.

The memory that was being urgently communicated by my body during sessions with David during a period of months was important for me to remember. It provided an essential piece of the puzzle that I began to assemble five years before. Although only partially completed, the newly forming puzzle was providing me with great insight into my life patterns, behaviors and choices. But after I remembered why the image of myself as a child of eight with the kitchen chair placed in the doorway evoked such horror, I worked hard to get a firmer grip on that key. I wanted to gain the ability to refuse to open the door in the future if I decided it was not in my self-interest and would not enhance my ability to embrace life.

Healing does not require us to sacrifice our lives to remembering trauma. We need only to complete enough of the puzzle so that we may live with joy in the present and look forward to a future not dominated by the past.

*   *   *

After several weeks of interaction with my mother, including numerous telephone calls, letters and meetings, Dr. Weiss wrote on my chart:

"I believe patient's mother is manic/schizophrenic paranoid." One week later, the neurologist concurred, basing his opinion on his frequent and increasingly bizarre encounters with the woman with whom I had lived for my entire twelve years.

My father's great reluctance to meet privately with the team of doctors who were treating me was noted several times in the records. Despite his promise to Dr. Weiss not to speak of the meeting or the facts discussed, he divulged the doctor's concerns to my mother within hours after his return home.

My mother's fury at the doctor's challenge of her control could not be contained. After a respite of a few weeks, I was returned to the care of a woman that a team of doctors believed to be a paranoid schizophrenic.

A doctor today might use the power of the courts to protect an abused child from being returned to a seriously mentally ill and dangerous mother. But on the week of my twelfth birthday, there was no one to intervene and protect me. The medical establishment, the school, the church and my father turned away from a child who finally could do nothing but scream at the unrelenting violations of body and spirit that were a staple of her existence. I was returned to a house where the privacy of family was valued above the life of a little girl.

*   *   *

At times the quiescent anger rose to the surface. Most often, it would be misdirected at Jim as my need for his nurture and protection mixed with the growing dread provoked by the surfacing memory of being bound and tortured in the kitchen. That he felt like a parent was enough to trigger chaotic emotions when I was slipping into the terror that the Little House held for me. I wanted him to save me from the horror that awaited me there. Yet I could not name what I felt as rage.

The Child screamed that she hated Jim when she bumped up against a raw piece of the pain, and he could not protect her from the subsequent anguish. I could not tell if the words were actually escaping my lips, and I held my fist tightly against my teeth, biting hard on my knuckles in the hope of preventing catastrophe. I was terrified her howls would erupt and destroy a relationship that I cherished and needed.

One day, I gathered my courage and risked asking Jim what would happen if I temporarily lost control and the Child told him she hated him. Despite our years of work together, I still feared abandonment if I inadvertently broke some unwritten rule. It seemed there had to be a rule against telling your therapist you hated him in a fit of anger. My heart felt as though it would burst from my chest as soon as the question was out of my mouth, and I focused my gaze on Jim's shoes.

The room was still with silence. I felt sick, thinking I should not have voiced this awful possibility. I had grown to love and trust Jim as the only real parent I had ever known. The Child's expectation that he would protect her from harm—and her rage which threatened to erupt as an outburst of hatred when he could not shield her from the pain of remembering—was actually a sign of healing. But this was not evident to me as I huddled miserably on the rug, ashamed at the tidal wave of emotions which threatened to bypass my defenses and hurt this gentle person who accompanied me so steadfastly as I struggled for life and wholeness.

But when I finally raised my head and looked at Jim's face, I saw compassion and patience rather than condemnation and judgment. He began to speak.

"I raised four children," he said slowly. "And at one time or another, every one of them probably said they hated me for something. That did not change the love I felt for them."

He paused. Time seemed to be suspended.

"And if at some point you told me you hated me, I would view it in the same way. I would hear it as your anger. It would not affect in the least measure how I feel about you."

Tears began to slide down my cheeks. The cold kernel of fear inside of me was rapidly dissolving into a place of spacious warmth and freedom. Unlike my birth parents, Jim not only allowed but also welcomed my anger, no matter what dreadful form it might first take.

And then, he spoke quietly and firmly to the heart of the fear I could not voice. "I will not abandon you, no matter how angry you get with me."

Our eyes locked together, and he smiled. In a moment, I found myself smiling back through my tears. With Jim, it was increasingly possible to laugh and cry simultaneously. My emotions, buried for so many years under the weight of secrets and silence, could no longer remain stifled. They rose to the surface with the resurrection of the Child, flowing freely and often unpredictably. Winter was finally giving way to spring. I was healing.

*   *   *

It was perhaps inevitable that I remembered the afternoon my mother dressed me in my best nylon taffeta dress and proceeded to embark on a strange cleansing ritual unlike any other. My sense is that it took place on or near my eighth birthday. I do not pretend to understand its significance or fathom its meaning; I can only recount what I remember.

The pale peach taffeta dress was one of the few reserved for Sunday school. The fact that my mother dressed me this way on this particular mid-week day serves to emphasize that it was somehow an event of importance to her. The chair was placed in the doorway between the parlor and kitchen because of the necessity of plugging the iron into a socket close to where she intended to use it. The iron stood spurting steam on a towel-covered table while I stood before the chair on which my mother sat.

As she wound the piece of rope around my hands, she talked of how mommies who loved their little girls put special marks on them and made sure they were clean inside. I do not recall much more of what she said. The terror that overtakes me as I remember being placed face down over the kitchen chair, my bound hands extended above my head, rendered the rest of her words meaningless as I slipped into the familiar and protective land of numbness.

I do remember complete shock when she ripped the back of my dress to expose my body. My mother held clothes in high regard and was always careful not to damage them during the abuse, often folding them neatly after she ordered me to disrobe. I associated Sunday school dresses with safety since I was not subjected to her rituals on Sundays when my father was home. It seemed like a terrible betrayal to be hurt when I was wearing the peach dress that I loved and in which I thought I was safe.

I remember the iron coming towards my face and my mother's hand on my back, pressing me into the chair. My head was twisted to the right, and as the steam flooded over me, it burned my eye and billowed into my nose and mouth. My vision was distorted by internal fear and external steam, and it seemed as though the iron was still in my face even as I felt the steam move slowly down my back. My left side was against the back of the chair, so the portion of my body most exposed was on the right. I remember my mother talking, almost singing, as she guided the hot steam to my buttocks, holding the heavy iron steady just above my flesh as it reached its destination. I remember a pain that was so huge that I blessedly lost consciousness.

I do not pretend to understand my mother's perversions, her insanity, or the meaning of the ritual. It is more than enough that I remember. And that I survived to tell.

*   *   *

In the past 25 years, public awareness of the prevalence of physical child abuse has grown. As incest survivors began speaking out in the 1980s, sexual abuse in the family was finally recognized as a far more serious problem than previously acknowledged.

Child abuse prevention, education and protective services exist today in structures that were not developed in the mid-1960s when doctors returned me to a mother they knew was abusive. Under-funded institutional services designed to protect children are often tangled with bureaucracy and sometimes inept, but they still manage to provide a fragile safety net that did not exist when I came hurling through the doors of the "system."

It is frightening to contemplate that social forces are organizing to roll back the progress of the past decades under the guise of "parental rights" legislation. The agenda advanced by backlash supporters includes provisions to make it more difficult for agencies to investigate allegations of abuse by allowing parents to sue if the abuse cannot be substantiated.

This kind of legislation will insure that many children will continue to suffer with no hope of rescue. Abuse can be very difficult to substantiate, especially since many of the worst forms of torture leave no visible scars. Most children, bound by chains of love, dependency and shame, will not easily admit abuse by a parent. And there are far too many family members like my father who resist any form of outside intervention, preferring to take the side of the perpetrator instead of protecting the child.

My mother would be pleased with the burgeoning public support for so-called parental rights. It is the spirit of violators both alive and dead that help to fuel this backlash movement and others which are designed to strip even a modicum of protection from the most vulnerable and accrue more power to those already in a position to abuse it.

When I encounter published propaganda thinly disguised as scientific research that mocks and denies the memories of adult incest survivors and when I read proposed legislation that will further silence the cries of tortured children, I know that my mother's spirit is alive and well.

It is not a thought that comforts me.

*   *   *

I have written into the edge of my healing. It has been more than a decade since I set foot in El Salvador in 1987. My journey is far from finished, although I have come a long way. I chose to speak from the middle of the wilderness because I believe that the pain and hope are strongest when survival is not assured. There is no guarantee that my journey will lead me into a land of milk and honey like the ancient Israelites sought when they fled the oppression of Egypt and began a walk through the wilderness. Like the former slaves cried out against Moses when the journey of liberation became too hard, at times I cry out at those who walk with me, convinced I was better off in the land of numbness.

The wounds of incest span generations. They are passed from father to son, mother to daughter, grandmother to grandchild and other familial combinations. They are wounds that are inflicted in secret by the perpetrator and carefully hidden by the victim. They pave the way for continuation of the cycle of abuse. It is only with great courage, the right circumstances, access to needed resources and the will to break free of the chains of shame and secrecy that healing is possible.

It is an indictment against our political system, culture and social institutions that there are many survivors with courage and a strong desire to heal who are unable to extract themselves from the nightmares of the past because they lack access to the necessary external resources. Managed care has greatly diminished the availability of long-term treatment. To expect victims of years of violence to recover in six to ten therapy sessions with a psychotherapist selected by an insurance company is to disparage the depth of their wounds. Such unrealistic expectations set survivors up for failure, adding yet another layer of shame to the muck of self-hatred many have been mired within since childhood. It took me more than a year of weekly sessions to even begin to trust Jim. And without trust, there is no healing from childhood abuse.

Many survivors find little understanding or support within their churches. Most pastors are not trained to sensitively deal with survivors of childhood abuse, even though one in four women is sexually abused before the age of eighteen. I have never heard a sermon about incest. Churches reflect the denial of the prevalence of the problem within the wider culture. They have not been sanctuary and places of healing for most survivors.

I was fortunate to have encountered El Salvador, with all its tragedy and beauty, at the right moment in my life. The Salvadoran people taught me the importance of knowing my own history and of maintaining hope in the face of despair. They taught me the value of resistance to unjust authority rather than submission and compliance. With tenacity and courage, they risked publicly speaking the truth about atrocities committed by the powerful, even when by doing so they incurred the wrath of the death squads.

Without the example of the poor *campesinos* as my teachers, I would not have survived the emergence of the traumatic memories that began when my internal war zones recognized the external war zones in El Salvador. I would not have been ready to accept Jim's framework of tears, protest and anger as the one that would support my healing. Without the scholarship fund at the counseling center that reduced the cost of my treatment, I would not have been able to afford therapy. My insurance coverage was good in that it at least permitted me to select my own therapist. But it paid only one-quarter of the cost of a year of weekly one-hour sessions.

It is essential that more community counseling centers be established to provide low-cost and long-term treatment for victims of incest. Therapists must be especially trained to work with survivors of severe physical and sexual abuse. They also need a network of supportive professionals to help them deal with the vicarious traumatization that happens when days are spent listening to anguished women and men describe atrocities by family members that rival those inflicted by prison guards in Nazi Germany during the Holocaust.

Communication between counselors working with victims of political torture and those treating survivors of sadistic domestic abuse should be encouraged in order to facilitate the exchange of professional expertise and find ways to expand treatment modalities for both groups. For example, survivors of sadistic and ritualized abuse within families or cults could benefit from the type of safe-house system developed for survivors of political torture, which allows for long-term treatment in a small group home setting. The homes are usually in residential neighborhoods, and are staffed by therapists, physicians and volunteers. The programs encourage reconnection with others and the greater community. My only long-term option was expensive hospitalization in a clinical setting with a structure that replicated an authoritarian family system which, by its inflexible nature, could not be modified to meet my needs.

I cannot say that I am fully healed. I still fear women and avoid close friendships with them. I can manage to have a business lunch or dinner with female associates because the conversation is primarily focused on external events and does not include the intimate kind of sharing about lives and relationships I expect with my male friends. Although I am slowly learning to live in my body, I have no acceptance of it as female; it is intolerable to be like my mother in any way. Female bodies, including my own, repulse and frighten me. I am still afraid to see myself in mirrors.

I am unable to endure the interaction of most groups and remain socially isolated. I belong to no clubs and do not participate in any community activities. I no longer attend worship services, having discovered that the church is not a safe and supportive environment in which the stories of incest survivors can be spoken aloud and honored. I cannot participate in a full sexual relationship, although I like to be held and kissed. As the reality of what I have experienced penetrates my defenses, I am more prone to depression. I grieve my losses—of my childhood and of years of my adult life.

I am just beginning to access the deep rage that lies beneath the surface, flowing like poison within my veins. Until recently, it was far too dangerous to even consider releasing anger because the prohibitions against expressing any protest at being beaten and raped as a child were deeply implanted into my very soul. I have paid a high price for holding the anger within me, the coin of my physical and emotional health. The cost has been in relationships that could not bear the strain of unresolved child-based rage.

Yet I can say with assurance that I am healing. The nightmares, flashbacks and intrusive memory fragments come with less frequency, usually when I feel external stress. Sleep has become a natural, restorative process rather than a state that is feared. Although I still suffer from occasional periods of insomnia, it is no longer a chronic condition. I have not returned to addiction even during times when I have been overwhelmed and lost my capacity to relax into the gentleness of the night and rest.

Bladder, urinary and vaginal infections, which constantly ravaged my body, gradually have become less frequent. I am less prone to respiratory problems and flu. Although I still dissociate under stress, I am gaining some measure of control over this once-automatic response. I can honor dissociation, once critical to my survival, as a trusted friend while slowly letting it go because it hampers my ability to live in the present.

The language of "recovery and reclaiming" is often used to describe healing from abuse. For those of us who were sadistically tortured in our childhood, healing is more about creating new structures than about reclaiming old ones. To speak about "re-claiming" my sexuality, for example, would be misleading. I never had my own sexuality; for as long as I can remember, pain and pleasure were methodically woven together by my mother's tortures, and my sexual responses were manipulated to satisfy her needs. I have not yet developed my own sexuality.

Adult survivors of rape often speak of the shattering effect of the trauma on their lives, reflecting that their history subsequently seems to be forever divided into a "before" and "after" configuration. Their healing focuses on reclaiming who they were before the rape violated not only their bodies but also their sense of safety and trust in the world.

There is no return to a "before" time for a survivor of severe and prolonged early childhood abuse. I cannot point to a time in my childhood when I felt loved, nurtured, valued and protected which was suddenly disrupted by abuse. When these experiences were offered to me in adulthood, I had no real capacity to accept or absorb them. These emotions have been experienced for the first time as I have allowed the traumatized Child frozen in time to be heard, held, nurtured and protected. Healing is as much about allowing the child who never had a chance to grow up in a nurturing environment to experience and develop in a healing environment as it is remembering the horrors that caused her to flee her body. It is a long and difficult process, filled with danger and treachery as well as joy and hope. There are no shortcuts on the road to wholeness.

Much of the popular literature about recovery from abuse emphasizes the role of forgiveness as an integral part of healing. Survivors are often encouraged to develop or reclaim a spiritual tradition in which forgiveness is viewed as a necessary component of the therapeutic process. I believe this emphasis on forgiveness of the abuser places an unfair and unrealistic expectation on those whose lives have been near-ly destroyed by the atrocities inflicted on them as children.

Like many other survivors, I no longer find a place within the insti-tutional church. Yet religion has been present in my life, shaping my experiences. The religion of my parents served to oppress the vulnera-ble and legitimate the violence of those in authority. The ideology of submission and obedience reinforced that whatever God—or parents—did was always "for our own good." The pastor in my childhood ignored obvious signs of distress in our family, defending my parents against doctors' accusations of abuse. When I was grown, another pastor coun-seled me to "act out" violent fantasies with my husband, drawing me deeper into already dangerous waters.

The church of my young adulthood was shocked when I answered the Salvadoran call to walk "the way of the cross" they professed to believe. The church in El Salvador was strong and courageous in advo-cating justice for the poor, but pastors counseled women to stay with abusive husbands. Rape as an act of war was denounced. Rape within a family was not even acknowledged to exist.

And yet it was a call from a bishop that led me to El Salvador, which in turn made my own healing possible. And it was a pastoral counselor who, when I was ready to heal, accompanied and loved me to whole-ness.

The God who moves in my life today is not usually found within the physical and theological structures of the institutional church. This God is found with *el Pueblo*—with the people who suffer and who struggle for justice. This God is found on the margins, walking with those whom society deems to have little value. The poor. The abused. Gays and lesbians. The vulnerable elderly. And especially, the children. I walk with them.

I do not forgive my mother, nor do I feel any ethical obligation to forgive her. I leave that action to God, who knew her before whatever terrible circumstances she was born into, twisted her mind and spirit toward evil and made her a torturer of children. My tears, forbidden by her even as she inflicted unspeakable pain on my body, now fall freely.

But I do not weep for my mother. The tears I shed are for me.

*　　　　*　　　　*

Feminist writings on healing often discourage or disparage dependency as a part of the therapeutic process. Allowing the child parts of myself to develop an intense and almost fierce dependency on Jim was one of the most critical aspects of healing for me. Wisely, he allowed this dependency, understanding that a child is not free to grow until she feels secure and protected. He also emphasized the "grown-up" value of inter-dependence over absolute autonomy. In a culture in which rugged individualism often prevents the development of real community, to chose inter-dependence over individual autonomy is to walk a healing path that is not heavily traveled or well understood.

It has been essential for me to learn that someone with greater power than me would not automatically abuse this power and hurt me. There is an inherent imbalance of power within the therapeutic relationship. It was extremely difficult for me to accept this imbalance in the beginning stages of healing. Yet I am grateful that Jim did not yield to the temptation to change the nature of the relationship to one of complete equality. If he had, I would have remained convinced that power and authority is always bad and will be used for evil. I would not have been able to see my potential power and claim it as good. My childhood concept of power as inevitably leading to great harm would have remained.

I learned that accompaniment is not a concept that could be exported from the war zones in El Salvador and used as a framework for healing without modification. Like any good and valuable model, it must be tailored to fit the circumstances in which it is to be used. In El Salvador, the people of a community collectively, through much reflection, prayer and discussion, made decisions about their direction. Sometimes I did not agree with their conclusions, but I accompanied them on the path they chose, trusting they had made the best decision for themselves.

Jim could not accompany me in quite the same way I accompanied the Salvadoran people because at times, he was dealing with a terrified child whose choices would have put her in grave danger. In those circumstances, he needed to assert his authority and power to prevent further destruction. However, he was very careful not to impose his direction and will on me other than during those critical moments when it was clear the Child was in control. I chose my path and my way of healing, and he walked with me. He encouraged the development of an internal nurturing adult who would protect and honor the Child without ceding control to her when crucial decisions concerning issues of health and well-being had to be made. He delights in my growing autonomy.

Like the Salvadorans, who endured a decade of war only to discover that peace was not an automatic consequence of the absence of gunfire, I have learned that remembering childhood trauma and re-experiencing the pain does not bring healing in and of itself. My healing has brought me from numbness into pain. I trust in the faith of those who accompany me when my own faith is not strong enough. I hold on to their assurances that I will pass through this agony into the fullness of life, giving birth to myself while they serve as midwives.

When despair threatens to engulf me, I remember that I am alive. That there are many others who will never enter the wilderness of healing because they have been silenced forever. That I survived, against all odds. That I do not walk alone. That I am loved.

And so, with fear and trembling, I speak. I am not brave. I have no map. I still often walk in the shadow of my mother, the darkness illuminated by only a small candle.

But there are other small lights, flickering in the distance. It is my hope that someday those who are healing will shed a collective light on the violence and evil we have endured without sacrificing our humanity.

Survivors of war, political torture, rape, concentration camps and childhood abuse have much to teach the world.

Until the world listens, understands and takes action to make changes, the seeds of violence and destruction that are planted and nurtured in our families, churches, schools and institutions will continue to erupt into crime on our streets and wars at our borders. Suicide, addiction, mental illness and despair take root in their wake. Those who survive and who dare to struggle for wholeness bear witness to the human capacity for good as well as evil. The cycle of abuse that has spanned generations is broken as we slowly heal our shattered bodies and spirits. Our legacy is our testimony of survival and our ability to love. It is the inheritance we leave to our children.

Touch our wounds. Hear our stories. Accompany us.

And learn.

Therapist Afterward

Linda and I first met on the telephone. She called seeking a therapist, and she had heard that I had traveled to Nicaragua. I had, in fact, made one trip to that war torn country as part of a Habitat for Humanity exploration, and I could not imagine how that trip could qualify me to be a therapist to a woman I had never met. It was only later, after we began our conversations that I came to understand the powerful connection in Linda's experience between those who had survived torture at the hands of their own government in El Salvador and her own personal story of abuse at the hands of her mother and betrayal on the part of her father and extended family. For Linda it was important that the therapist to whom she tell her story should at least have some appreciation of the conditions of people who lived in the midst of oppression. So to my surprise, my trip to Nicaragua became the starting point for building a remarkable relationship of mutual accompaniment.

The author Antoine de Saint Exupery in his book, *The Little Prince*, describes a meeting between the little prince and a fox. The little prince invites the fox to play with him, but the fox replies, "I cannot play with you....I am not tamed." The little prince asks, "What does it mean—'tame'?" The fox explains, "It is an act too often neglected....It means to establish ties."[3] When the little prince inquires what he must do to tame the fox, the fox gives him these instructions: "You must be very patient. First you will sit down at a little distance from me—like that—in the grass. I shall look at you out of the corner of my eye, and you will say nothing. Words are the source of misunderstanding. But you will sit a little closer to me, every day..." [4] The scene of the little prince "taming" the fox provides a wonderful description of how my relationship with Linda developed and how, I assume, most therapists must learn to relate to survivors of abuse. Words do, indeed, become a source of misunderstanding. What becomes paramount is establishing ties by building trust and by creating a "non-anxious presence."[5] In our early sessions, I felt constantly tested by the little Child in Linda, a Child who had learned to survive by being hyper- vigilant and cautious. I was aware that our bond of trust was fragile and could be easily broken. However, each session gave a new opportunity to "sit a little closer." The greatest challenge was learning to be very patient.

I would be dishonest if I did not say that I struggled continuously with my own feelings of inadequacy at the beginning of the therapy. Although I had worked with survivors of the many forms of abuse in my twenty years of practice, I had never been with anyone who had experienced ritualistic abuse at the hands of her mother. The thought that a mother, the archetype of nurture, should be the source of such pain and evil I found repulsive. I knew I needed to address my own reaction to Linda's story and to find a place beyond my own repulsion and fear if I wanted to be a part of her healing process. Fortunately, as part of my therapy training, particularly in transactional analysis and

---

3. Antoine de Saint Exupery, The Little Prince (New York: Harcourt, Brace & World, Inc, 1943), 80.

4. Ibid., 84

5. The phrase comes from family therapist, Edwin Friedman

gestalt therapy, I gained a deep appreciation for the power of the inner Child within all of us that can learn to survive under the most hostile conditions, although not without wounds. My orientation as a pastoral counselor gave me confidence that there is a healing force at work within and among us that transcends human intelligence and imagination. Linda's extraordinary capacity for survival, the resilience of her spirit, expressed partly in her ability to articulate verbally and in writing, was a gift she brought to me as her therapist. Through her narrative, she offers this gift to many others who have either suffered abuse or who provide support to those who have suffered at the hands of others.

As she gained strength through her healing, Linda began to speak publicly about her abuse. Despite the risks survivors face of social disapproval, derision or disbelief, she expressed a strong desire to give others who have been severely damaged by childhood abuse hope that healing is possible by telling her own story. She sometimes reminds me she has known Salvadoran peasants who risked torture and death by speaking openly about the atrocities suffered by their families and communities at the hands of the authorities. I have witnessed Linda publicly tell her story before diverse audiences of lay people and professionals, survivors of abuse and those who were skeptical. I have never been with any speaker who has been more powerful in her presence and in the sharing of her experience. It is a potency that comes from her own experience as well as from her exposure to the resistance and resilience of the poor in El Salvador. Accompanying Linda on her healing journey has helped me to appreciate that therapy is about being set free from forces, internal and external, that keep us from experiencing the full abundance of life.

The typical image of therapy is based on a medical model of a healer who makes the diagnosis and prescribes the appropriate treatment. But in fact, the process of therapy is much more mutual, although the mutuality is not always apparent. It is true the therapist is responsible for creating a holding environment that is safe and trustworthy, a safe, hospitable place where previously forbidden feelings and thoughts can be expressed, where early decisions, often made before conscious thought, can be revealed. Therapy is about assisting the client into finding new pathways into healing, unlocking painful memories and giving up or redefining old survival strategies, such as dissociation. It is finding creative ways to help a client take back control of his or her life, while at the same time taking responsibility for his or her life. It is about learning to listen with the "third ear" to what is not expressed or is only indirectly expressed as well as to what is being verbally revealed. As writer, systems theorist, and theoretical physicist Fritjof Capra has stated, "The therapy process is no longer seen as a treatment of disease but as an adventure in self-exploration."[6] And in this adventure of self-exploration the therapist is not the dominant actor but is a facilitator of a process in which the client is the main protagonist and bears responsibility and maintains control.[7] Linda was anything but a passive recipient in this process. She kept an on-going journal of our conversations and of her insights and reflections on our sessions. She would often share journal entries as a way centering our conversations on the path the therapy was progressing. She would use her extraordinary intelligence to research books and articles on issues of trauma and abuse. She would mentor me with information and her personal reflections on issues of oppression.

In my work with Linda, I discovered how important it is to give constant permission to those who have experienced physical, sexual and emotional abuse to break the taboo of silence that has been imposed on them. For a child who is punished for the slightest resistance, silence becomes a way of life. The Child in Linda had long since given up the right to experience hurt and anger. She had learned long ago to relinquish these basic emotions in the interest of survival. She also surrendered the option of protesting her abuse or of claiming her right to be treated with

---

6. Fritjof Capra, The Turning Point (New York: Bantam Books, 1983), 387
7. Ibid.

dignity or retain ownership of her body. Like the little prince and the fox, the adult part of Linda and I had to draw closer, a little at a time, to the scared, distrustful and well defended Child, all the time telling her that it was OK to come forth when she was ready.

Fritjof Capra writes, "...the new experiential psychotherapy requires that, to achieve the best therapeutic result, both therapist and client suspend as much as possible their conceptual framework, anticipations and expectation during the experiential process. Both should be open and adventurous, ready to follow the flow of experience with a deep trust that the organism will find its own way to heal itself and evolve."[8] There was no doubt that many of the basic assumptions I had learned would be stretched and redefined in my work with Linda. I listened carefully to her direction. But where does that deep trust come from? Linda and I shared a common belief in a healing force that was part of our journey together from the beginning. Walking with Linda and hearing her story and experiencing her healing process give me a renewed faith in the resilient love of God. It has also challenged many of my assumptions about what comprises a healing relationship.

Entering Linda's "Child space" was a precarious experience. We could never be sure what would come forth. We did not know when a new, painful memory would be unleashed that could disrupt Linda's life for days at a time. The most difficult times were those when she felt let-down or disappointed with me for having to cancel an appointment, failing to call her at an appointed time or not following up on a commitment. The little kid in her would experience such occasions as catastrophic times of abandonment. I discovered the uncompromising importance of maintaining commitments if one is to work with survivors of oppression and abuse. Linda and I knew we had reached a new level of trust when we were able to discuss these painful times, adult to

8. Ibid.

adult, and resume our relationship knowing it could persist and even grow through such times of disappointment.

It became clear as the therapy progressed that I was being called upon to be "mother" to Linda's "Child." Since the perpetrator was a female and Linda's Child was very frightened and suspicious of females, it did not surprise me that, as a male therapist, I became a candidate for that role. The role, however, was daunting since the Child carried tremendous expectations that this new "mother" would provide all that the female mother failed to give. But how could I as a male supply the nurture that a mother typically supplies? I had to search deep in myself for images of mothering that I could draw on in relating to this hurting and needy Child. The mothering images I found came from two sources: my mother and my paternal grandmother. Both women were strong, independent and extremely nurturing, even protective, towards their children. Although my mother died when I was seventeen years old, images of her strong and protective support have always been a part of me. My grandmother survived incredible odds to migrate to this country and managed to raise nine children even after her husband died leaving her very poor. There was something powerful in these relationships that has imprinted itself into my mind and soul. I am grateful that these woman provided the images of nurture and strength that I could draw on and express in my relationship to Linda's Child.

The subject of safe touch, which Linda addresses in her narrative, represented a particularly challenging issue in the therapy. I have come to appreciate the tremendous significance of touch as a part of the healing process with many survivors. In the case of the incest survivor the issue of sexuality is particularly sensitive. I would not push Linda more than her inner Child could handle. However, there are times when health considerations require a survivor to confront extreme fears, such as those related to exposure of the genital area in a necessary medical procedure. This became a major concern with Linda when she required a gynecological examination. We were very fortunate to find male physicians (for Linda they had to be male) who understood and were sensitive to the fear a routine exam presented for an incest survivor.

There was another, more personal way in which touch became an issue in our therapy. As part of my new role as the Child's substitute "mother," I felt great pressure to provide the safe touch she had never received. My own discomfort in transcending that boundary presented a major issue of trust in our work. We clearly needed to find a way to meet the Child's essential need for the reassurance that could only come from safe touch, while respecting the boundaries I thought were important to sustain the relationship. This presented the greatest threat to our ability to continue to move together toward the healing the Child so desperately needed. Over an extended period of time, we were able to re-negotiate boundaries so that I could provide some limited safe touch but it was not sufficient to meet the needs of the Child for whom lack of physical contact continued to reinforce her long-held conviction that she was "dirty" and not worthy of being touched in safe and non-sexual ways. In the end, Gary, a friend of Linda's who had worked among the oppressed of El Salvador, provided the critical need for being held and nurtured through safe physical contact. In addition, David, a massage therapist, was tremendously instrumental in facilitating the work necessary to support Linda in reconnecting with her body.

As the connection with Gary and David illustrates, Linda's healing journey involved a community of people all of whom were brought together by respect and love for this courageous person. Jim Poling, who wrote the foreword for this narrative, has been a faithful interpreter of Linda's experience. He has been a welcomed co-traveler on this journey. In any true relationship, we are changed. Accompanying Linda on her healing journey so far has impacted my life in a most significant way. I have learned to trust in that healing force that constantly works for our wholeness, and I have learned to respect the resilience of the human spirit to overcome the most hostile expressions of evil.

J.H.
August, 2001

About the Author

Linda Crockett is a poet, social justice activist and community educator dedicated to the healing of the wounds of abuse. A founding member of a church social action group in Pennsylvania, she frequently traveled to El Salvador during the 1980s to lead church delegations and accompany refugees struggling to survive in war zones. For information on inviting her to speak at conferences or to facilitate workshops, the author may be reached by e-mail at LindaCrockett@dejazzd.com or by mail at *P.O. Box 184, Adamstown, PA 19501.*

Editor's Notes

It has been an honor and privilege to support Linda Crockett in telling her story. I have greatly appreciated her trust in my feedback as editorial consultant.

Most readers, no doubt, will identify Linda's courage in disclosing her painful and remarkable story of abuse at the hands of her mother and neglect by her father and others entrusted with her care.

Her story is indeed powerful, but what I have found most touching and courageous is the raw honesty that she shows when she allows us to meet the vulnerable self that lives in her deepest interior. This vulnerable self is the part that feels so scared, so bereft of any ability to function in the "real" adult world, and that has been carried inside a woman who is seen as competent, intelligent and articulate. Equally powerful is Linda's dedication in integrating that part of herself with the outward strengths.

As a psychotherapist, supervisor and trainer specializing in working with trauma, addictions and creativity, I know there are many ways to heal and many ways to grow. Linda has shared her personal story with passion and dedication. Her story is in service of the survivors who will walk their own healing roads and helping professionals who can enlarge their own knowing of what it means to survive and heal from severe abuse.

—Karen Carnabucci, MSS, TEP, Racine, Wisconsin

0-595-19922-4

Printed in the United States
120318LV00001BB/196/A

9 780595 199228